The Consumer's Guide to
VINTAGE CLOTHING

The Consumer's Guide to VINTAGE CLOTHING

TERRY McCORMICK

Dembner Books • New York

Dembner Books
Published by Red Dembner Enterprises Corp.,
80 Eighth Avenue, New York, N.Y. 10011

Distributed by W. W. Norton & Company, Inc.,
500 Fifth Avenue, New York, N.Y. 10110

Library of Congress Cataloging in Publications Data

McCormick, Terry.
The consumer's guide to vintage clothing.

Bibliography: p.
Includes index.
1. Costume—United States—History—
19th century—Collectors and collecting—Catalogs.
2. Costume—United States—History—20th century—
Collectors and collecting—Catalogs. I. Vintage clothing.
GT610.M26 1987 646′.3′0973 87-14347
ISBN 0-934878-91-9

Illustrations on pages 216–218 by Barbara Levine.

Designed by Antler & Baldwin, Inc.

To Mark Weiss, who gives unstintingly of his support, if less generously of his closet space, and to Kate, Jan, and Abbie, because they've had to live with a mom who dresses funny.

ACKNOWLEDGMENTS

Lots of kind people helped with this project. Many of the readers of the *Vintage Clothing Newsletter* provided ideas and sources and a fine sharing bunch they are. I want especially to thank Horst Grimm, Nicholas Unger Furs, Marianna Mace, Ron Ede, Carol Plaia, Susie Prokop, Kaethe Kliot, Jacquie Greenwood, Linda Ver Meer, Sharon Bramlett, Bobby Ann Loper, Nadya Henry, Shirley Tait, Bobbi Athay, Marta Mathis, Lois Mueller, Karen Skoglund, Pahaka, Shirley O'Neall, Bill Lewis, Debbie Hannah, Hazel Hynds, Carole Daniel, Rita Sewell, Zola Northcraft, Barb Levine, Barb Kralj, and Peggy Tomlin for being generous with helpful information. Harriet Love, Ray Cantrell, and Zeke Waranch, who not only help make the selling of vintage clothing the class act it deserves to be, they are also open and cheerful about giving advice. Janie Sky, my best shopping buddy, has contributed in many ways. This book was possible because Karen Jacobson knows how to be a good friend, Therese Eiben knows how to edit, and Kay Staats took it for granted.

CONTENTS

PARDON ME, BUT YOU'VE GOT MY BOA STUCK UNDER YOUR SPECTATOR PUMPS OR AN INTRODUCTION

I remember finding an elaborately embroidered twenties white lace dress and a black velvet hat that had a paper label printed in French(!) at an antique store: $25 for the dress, $5 for the hat. I was torn between having a heart attack for sheer joy and fear that the dealer would grab them away and say he'd made a mistake. I hesitantly approached the checkout counter, eyeing a basket of Indian clubs nearby (Headline: "Crazed Woman Bonks Antique Dealer, Steals Old Dress") and was greeted with a big smile and an offer to knock $5 off the total. By the time I got to the car, I knew I was in no condition to drive but did anyway, secure in the knowledge that there is no official test for DUIV (Driving Under the Influence of Vintage).

Sometimes I wonder how a sensible person like me has gotten into such a state. Why I go shopping for new blue jeans with the best intentions in the world and return home with a vintage lace boudoir cap and a parasol instead. Then as I stand in front of the mirror admiring my new/old cap and twirling my parasol, with a breeze blowing through the holes in my britches, I know why. I love vintage clothes!

It all started, as I recall, when I was young and innocent, and realized that I adored silk underwear, fur coats, and uniquely styled clothing. After waiting in vain for a rich shipping magnate to come along and support me in the manner to which I planned to become accustomed, I had to look for other options. I found a vintage fur coat at an estate sale and decided that vintage clothing deserved some investigation. In those days there weren't any vintage clothing stores, so you had to scrounge through thrift stores and estate sales to find things. As I started bringing home silk underwear and stockings, beautiful leather shoes, and one-of-a-kind dresses, I decided that vintage clothing was the answer to my prayers. I've never looked back.

The world of vintage clothing has changed a lot since those days. More and more people are discovering vintage clothing and how it can add to their wardrobes. Not everyone gets so involved, some just buy a few good pieces to wear occasionally, and they take just as much pleasure in their clothes as someone who has a house full. Other people get as excited as I do and find themselves completely immersed in the fun of seeking out new treasures.

One of the biggest trends in vintage fashion in the last couple of years has been the increased demand for men's clothing. Until recently, men's vintage clothing was relegated to theater prop departments or Halloween racks in thrift stores. Then all of a sudden guys discovered how much a well-tailored pinstripe suit or a classy felt fedora could add to their looks. Now there are vintage clothing stores that specialize in men's clothing and they can hardly keep their racks full.

Of course the biggest changes in vintage clothing over the years have been the stores and the price factor. Vintage clothing, which used to nestle under tables at garage sales, has developed a following all its own. Stores that sell it are found everywhere, not only in large cities but also in towns and hamlets all over the United States. The advent of vintage clothing stores has brought vintage clothing to a wider variety of people. Folks who would never consider crawling through the attic after an old dress can find equally enchanting old dresses hanging on a rack—cleaned, pressed, and ready to wear. Of course the price is higher, but the convenience is worth that to some, and the enjoyment is not dimmed one bit.

My first vintage fur coat cost $4 and it was in perfect condition.

This story comes under the heading "Stories from the Good Old Days," because that will likely never come up again. I'm not going to try to kid you that I don't regret the days when I could fill a sack full of vintage clothing at a thrift store for $25, or even $5. As I've watched the price of that sack rise, I've shed many a tear for times past. Even so, I know that most vintage clothing is still a bargain, and that a good thing is a good thing. There are still serendipitous treasures out there for those who like to scrounge!

After all is said and done, and charm aside, vintage is just a classy word for old. Old clothes look better and last longer if they're cared for a little differently than new clothes. Shopping for vintage clothing is fun, but it's even better when you have some ideas about what to look for and what to avoid. Which brings me to the subject of this book. We're here to talk about the world of vintage clothing and how to maneuver successfully and happily through it. Maybe you've inherited your Aunt Minnie's best thirties dress and want to know how to clean it or find some way of wearing it. Or you've just bought your first few pieces of vintage and think you'd like to get some more, but you're unsure what to look for or what to do with your treasures once you've got them home. Maybe you've somehow (certainly you didn't plan such a thing) acquired a closet full of vintage clothes, with more spilling out of a box under the bed, and want some storage information. If you have some vintage clothing or a lot of vintage clothing or are just curious, I think you'll find something here to enjoy. And resources for buying clothing, supplies for keeping it up, reference books, and other helpful information are listed in the Appendix.

Most important of all—have fun with vintage clothing. Its delight and charm is what this is all about. Make a pot of tea and sit down for a good read. When you've finished, put on your best hat and go shopping.

CHAPTER ONE

LET'S GO SHOPPING
OR
PRACTICALITY IS NOT NECESSARILY THE BEST THING FOR YOUR SOUL

When I'm asked why I'm so into vintage clothing, I carry on about the quality of the clothes and how unique they are, the beauty of the handwork, and what a lift it gives my wardrobe. All of this is true. But I tend to leave out any mention of the thrill of the chase and the indecent high I get (skyrocketing blood pressure, increased pulse, inability to touch the ground with my feet) when I find something wonderful in an unexpected place, preferably cheap. Aside from its therapeutic value (vintage shopping ranks right up there with chicken soup as a cure for ills), for me vintage shopping has a mystique and charm that is unequaled by any other experience. While shopping trips vary in levels from disappointing to perfection, you never know until you're back in your driveway which level a vintage trip will reach. It's entirely serendipitous. Sometimes you go from one shop to another finding nothing, getting gloomier and gloomier, and then—wham!—up pops something so perfect that the Richter scale simply can't keep up with your heart rate. It's for these moments that we live. If the powers that be ever find out how much fun we're having, they'll either make it illegal, tax it, or decide it's carcinogenic!

Fun's fun, but nothing can knock a hole in a good time like having spent more money than you can afford on something you can't use or don't want, that doesn't fit, or is so damaged that (no matter what you thought in the heat of the moment) it's irreparable. It helps to know what to look for and to have some information to hold on to in the few lucid moments you have while on a vintage shopping trip.

Many times "what you know" equals "what you gets." Don't ever assume that the person who's selling vintage clothing knows more than, or even as much as, you do about the stock. While there are plenty of knowledgeable folks around who sell vintage clothing, many are not. I've seen a 1940 beaded dress in a shop with a label saying "1920" more than once. And I've even had a lovely elderly lady swear to me she'd worn a polyester double knit mini dress in the 1930's.

I don't think this is deliberate (usually) so much as simply not knowing. On the other hand, I once visited a shop where the owner told me at great length about her expertise in textiles and then tried to sell me a silk nightgown with a scorch mark, claiming that "it might come out." I knew, if she didn't, that a scorch is direct damage to the fabric, not a stain, and is not removable without cutting out the mark. So until you are positive that the information you're getting is coming from an unimpeachable source, better to arm yourself with your own guidelines and proceed according to them.

Your first step is to have a wonderful time in the name of research. Track down vintage clothing stores, thrift shops, and other likely sources of vintage items in your area. Look through the garage and estate sale ads in your local paper. Check for used or vintage clothing sources in the yellow pages of your phone book. Check the phone book and newspapers from other communities within easy driving distance as well. Sometimes treasure troves await a mere hour's drive away! Then go shopping. See what's available, and get a good general idea of high, low, and medium prices in the area.

Once you've gotten an overall picture of price range you have to work with, it's time to set your guidelines within that range. Each garment is individual, and so are we. One man's "spectacular" can be another's "I wouldn't be caught dead in it" not to mention "What do I do with it now?" Dare I mention one's pocketbook and the inherent limitations therein? While one might prefer to tiptoe past this sticky subject, and in practice it's often forgotten at critical junctures, some of us can afford mistakes more easily than others. In vintage clothing, as in so many areas of life, "Know thyself" is a worthy motto.

Keep in mind that most vintage clothing and thrift stores will not take returns. It isn't that the shops are trying to make things hard for you. They have to cope with the sorry reality that some folks will buy a vintage garment, wear it to a party, and then try to return it. These unpleasant types save a rental fee if they can get away with it. You and I don't do that, but we have to pay the price of no returns because of it. So be sure you've got what you want *before* making a purchase.

A bargain is something that you can afford, that you want, and that you can use. I include in this category things that you love, even if their only use is to give your heart a lift when you take them out to fondle. Sometimes a $10 dress is not a bargain, but a $50 jacket is. Vintage clothing is an individual thing, and that's why we love it.

CONDITION OF THE CLOTHES or IS YOUR HEART BIG ENOUGH TO LOVE A DRESS WITH NO UNDERARMS?

I hate to rain on anybody's parade, but this is the category that can cause more grief than any other. As I've said before (and will again), vintage means old, and these wonderful old garments have lived a long and sometimes hard life before they come into ours. If you're someone who feels that price is no object and purchases vintage only at shops that repair and clean garments before putting them on the floor, this is not a problem. For the rest of us a good hard look is required before deciding whether a garment is a bargain or a burden.

Make it a habit to examine every piece you buy carefully. I know, I know . . . it fits, looks good, and is what you've been looking for. Just humor me. Say you find a 1940's jacket that you like and it costs $15. Your pricing research tells you this is a bargain; however, it has a couple of holes. You know that you can take it to a reweaver who will fix it up so you'd never know it had been damaged. But it'll cost $25–$30 for the work, and that means your $15 jacket is now a $45 investment. Now how do you feel about it? Get used to adding the cost (either in time or money) of taking care of damage or wear problems.

Turn garments inside out and look at the seams and the fabric from that vantage point. It's too easy to overlook problems when you're busy being enchanted. Seams that are fraying away can come apart and leave you uncovered in a public moment. This can be repaired but does require extra fabric, at least 1–2 extra inches all around, and takes time and expertise. If the garment just fits with no leeway, you may find yourself with a dress that is too snug to wear comfortably after the repair.

Always hold garments up to the light. Some old pieces (and I include some things as late as forties, particularly rayon crepes) have lots of tiny pinpricks, which indicate some disintegration is taking place. You should be able to get some wear from it, however, if you handle it carefully and make sure it's cleaned by a knowledgeable cleaner.

Always check the underarms. Many otherwise good-condition garments may have problems here, particularly silk and rayon. In many cases the garments were put away looking clean, but had been worn a few times after the last cleaning. Over time traces of perspiration can interact chemically with the fabric, and the fabric may have either begun to fall apart or may be irreversibly stained. This is not something you would normally notice while trying on, unless you're looking for it. It is something that becomes noticeable when you're wearing the garment, unless you keep your arms close to your sides and this can be amazingly inconvenient in day to day life. Underarm repairs, if you'll pardon me, are the pits to do, even assuming that you can find matching fabric and have the skill to do it yourself. And it's an expensive repair for a seamstress for the same reasons. In this situation you are buying a problem, rather than a wearable garment, and should make decisions accordingly.

Missing buttons can also be a trouble area. For example, I found a very nice print rayon that closed down the front with loops and ball buttons. The buttons were fabric covered, with a rhinestone, and an important part of the look of the dress. Unfortunately, two were missing, and obviously the remaining buttons couldn't be matched. Although the dress was reasonably priced, the thought of finding thirteen tiny ball buttons that would look good on the dress put me off, and I left it for someone who was willing to take on the project. In some cases missing buttons can easily be replaced, but take a critical look and think hard if they are part of the design. It could be years before you find the right number of the right buttons, during which the garment will just be sitting on your mending pile waiting patiently not in use.

Take a good look at the hem, especially in dark garments. It's another easy-to-miss problem spot, but one that I've encountered enough to add a warning about. Many times the attempt to alter the hemline has been made at some point in a garment's lifetime, and it may have turned into a mess. I found a lovely 1920's chiffon velvet at what I considered a reasonable price and then realized that someone had hacked away at the hem, apparently with kitchen scissors. Chiffon velvet is wonderful to wear and wicked to work with, so I had to figure on a few hours of work before the dress would be wearable. All of a sudden the price seemed not so reasonable. I bought it anyway (being a sucker for velvet), but at least I had my eyes open while I did it.

Stains are a risky business at best. A stain is a chemical reaction between some substance and the fabric, and it takes another chemical reaction to remove it, if that's possible at all. In most cases it isn't. All stain removal references say loud and clear that time is of the essence if you're going to get a stain out. Needless to say this doesn't bode well for a stain that's been imbedded for fifty years.

Some people are somewhat successful in removing stains from cotton, linen, and wools, although you risk damaging the fabric in the process. Stains in rayon and silk should be regarded as permanent. Scorch marks and water spotting are not stains. They are permanent damage to the fabric. Check carefully for them and for faded areas, particularly on rayons and silks. You may be able to salvage the garment for wearing in some cases if it lends itself to such coverups as a lace collar (for stains around the upper bodice), embroidery, braid design, beading, or appliqué of some sort. You can also decide to live with it and wear it, stains and all, without apology. Dying is always a tempting thought, but stain and fading damage will take the dye differently than the main part of the garment, so you'll end up with something multi-colored anyway.

I've had generally better luck purchasing clothing that is soiled all over than I have with stains. While still a risk (since you can't really tell what you've got until it's clean), if the price is low enough, it may well be a good gamble. This is often true of cotton whites, always keeping in mind that vigorous cleaning will shorten the life of the garment. I once bought a grimy, gray, grungy-looking brocade jacket at a thrift store for a song. It was iffy, but the fabric was in good condition and the style nice. It returned from the dry cleaner glowing in lovely colors, with a wonderful blue background. These are the moments we live for! Once you've cleaned a few vintage garments, your guesses will be more accurate.

Loose beads always look like such a small problem. While it's possible to learn enough beading to make repairs, beading is a tedious, boring, and time consuming occupation. If you're not going to try it yourself, be aware that it's difficult to find someone who can do beadwork, and very costly. Try it once, and you'll know why. Finding replacements for missing beads can be a major pain as well. If you decide to buy a garment with dangling or loose beads, handle it carefully, and keep it in the sack until the minute it will be worked on. Beads are much harder to locate on the floor than contact lenses, believe me, and more difficult to replace. I know, personally, how hard it is to keep my head focused on practicalities when faced with a lovely beaded garment (no matter what era). However, trust me when I urge you to take a deep breath and a realistic look at beaded clothing with problems.

Here's a tip that most experienced vintage clothing people have learned the hard way. Given our druthers, we'll always choose a rayon beaded dress over a silk one. Rayon tends to be stronger and is less likely to fall apart under the weight of beads. While others wax enthusiastic over silk twenties beaded dresses, we search high and low for the rayon versions.

Learn to tell the difference between a tear and disintegrating fabric. A clue to this is that a single tear will usually be in one spot. Disintegration often is indicated by tears in several places. Always check at stress points, particularly shoulders, for signs that the fabric is coming apart. Once the fabric starts to go, it's time for a memorial service. I know a woman who wore a pretty silk 1920's beaded dress to a party and found the whole dress falling apart right on her body.

She grabbed a coat and got home without too much exposure, but this is a lesson worth paying attention to. Rips, tears, and holes that are situational damage are repairable, particularly in cotton, linen, and wool garments. Silk and rayon are much less easily fixed, and the mends tend to be both noticeable and distracting. I always feel more comfortable taking on a garment in need of repair if there is extra fabric in the seams or hems, or a belt that can be used for creative patching.

Keep an eye out for repairs done by previous owners. I've found otherwise fixable garments destroyed by people who didn't know what they were doing. For instance, if someone has used an iron-on product to repair velvet, and the velvet is flattened, that's permanent. On the other hand, darning on cotton garments is acceptable and traditional. It's only because we modern types are so used to tossing away anything that isn't perfect that we've lost the art of mending. Women and men in the early part of the twentieth century often had darns on their cotton garments, even on silk stockings.

With careful shopping even a vintage fur can be a wonderful bargain. Many old furs are in surprisingly good condition and only need minor repair or cleaning before taking you out in style. Regretfully, others have lived out their useful lives already, so it's good policy to look furs over carefully. It would be great if we could unpick the lining and get a good look at the inside of the pelt, but realistically we have to make do with learning what we can from the outside. A major clue is several rips in the pelt: This is usually a sign that the fur has about had it. I've purchased a couple of fur coats in this condition, largely because they were just a few dollars, and find I spend as much time repairing as wearing them. This is true love on my part not true common sense.

Also feel the fur to see if the pelt is dry and stiff, and if so avoid it. A stiff, dry pelt is at the end of its road and not worth purchasing. If you notice lots of loose hairs flying around, you can diagnose that the moths have been at it (moths attack the fur at its root). Unfortunately, this condition is as hard to repair as it is to live with, so you'll have to decide if you want to walk around in a cloud of loose fur. How elegant will you look sneezing with every step? While fondling the fur to check for pliability, notice whether the pelt feels lumpy or if you can feel stitching. These are clues that a previous owner has done some repair work. This isn't necessarily a bad thing in itself; many a fine fur has had several years added to its life by judicious repairing. However, I've found that few people know how to do proper fur repairs and almost invariably I have to redo the work before using the garment. But for the right coat at the right price it's no deterent. It might, however, sway you one way or the other if you're on the borderline.

A dirty fur can be cleaned and glazed and made to look wonderful—for a price. Call around to various furriers and learn the cost of cleaning and glazing, then add it to the price of the garment. Furs should be cleaned and glazed once a year for maximum longevity and beauty. The cost of maintaining a vintage fur can quickly outstrip the initial price, which is something you should be aware of and plan for.

I adore vintage shoes of all eras, excluding the killer pointies of the early sixties. I did my time once, and that was enough! Be prepared to be pleasantly surprised that sizes in vintage shoes tend to run a little larger than modern ones, and that there is often more room for the wide part of the foot. However, while we all fudge on size to some extent, with vintage shoes this is not the best policy. Walk around awhile, and be sure that you can navigate reasonably in them. It's possible to stretch the width somewhat (with leather stretcher, available at shoe repair shops), but there is no way to lengthen or shorten a pair of shoes. Check the leather carefully for signs of dryness or flakiness, particularly around straps. Picture yourself trying to get home with a broken ankle strap on your shoe. It puts glamour on a new, low plane! Heels and soles can be replaced easily by a shoe repair shop; add the cost to the price of the shoe, like any other repair expense. If the heel is too high for you, it's possible to have the height lowered about one half inch (more or less), without ruining the shoe.

Check purses inside and out, and along seams. Put something in the purse to make sure the straps are strong enough and double check the clasp. No matter how inexpensive that alligator bag appears to be, if the clasp won't stay shut while you're using it, it's worthless. Do check the bottom as well. I once bought a honey of a lizard purse, checked everything (I thought) twice, and then found one of the seams at the bottom was coming out. It turned out the shoe repair shop couldn't sew it up (the bag was lined), and I've since tried all kinds of super glues with only temporary effects.

CONDITION OF THE BUYER or THE "IT'LL FIT WHEN I LOSE TWENTY POUNDS AND LOOK GOOD WHEN I LEARN HOW TO SEW" SYNDROME

Get into the habit early on of trying everything on. At a flea market or such, it may not be possible. If that's the case, it'd best be gosh-darned cheap! It's too easy to find something that is irresistible, but either doesn't fit or makes you look like a bag lady in the last stages of going downhill.

I hate moments of practicality, preferring the illusion of the thing whenever possible. If I've been looking high and low for a forties print rayon dress with a side drape, I don't *want* to know that I look god-awful in this particular one. I don't want to know that the waist is too high or the bust is too tight, or that I resemble Ma Kettle in it. I'd rather hold it up in front of the mirror and decide it's just what I want. However, if I spend money on it, I won't have any left to buy the perfect forties print rayon dress with a side drape that will appear two days after I bought the one that doesn't quite make it.

Those of us who love vintage clothing have a tendency, even if we do try things on, to look just at the garment, not at ourselves wearing the garment. In this lies madness, or at least lack of appreciation for our own lovely selves. It is a terrible temptation if, for example, you love beaded twenties blouses and one turns up to ignore the color. I recently bought a muddy green blouse of that type (how could I resist, I ask you?) in which I look like a warmed over corpse. I wear it, of course, and even get compliments on it, but it's the garment they like, not me in the garment. A little of this goes a long way. Just because something is vintage doesn't mean the general rules of color, line, and so forth are suspended. You still look best in the things you look best in and will be happiest sticking to those colors and lines that flatter you.

Don't hesitate to ask for advice about how something looks from other shoppers, even if they are strangers. I've met some delightful people this way. Most folks (at least those who frequent vintage clothing stores) are only too happy to give opinions and get into the spirit of the thing. More than once I've found myself in a group of two or three strangers trying things on and critiquing for each other. Not only was it more fun, but I've been saved a mistake or two. Even better have been the clothes that someone else has spotted as perfect for me and which turned out to be much loved purchases. Vintage clothing shopping is a joy in itself, and a pleasure to share with other aficionados.

Just because a garment is old doesn't mean it's beautiful. It may just be old. Some vintage garments are simply awful, no matter how quaint. This is not a rule that collectors have to pay attention to, but those of us who plan to use the clothes need to keep a firm grip on it. Try to keep your blood pressure on hold when you find a "darling little cotton dress from the late 1880's" that happens to be drab, dull, and unwearable, no matter what your inner voice is whispering to you. People who are just getting into vintage clothing find themselves banging their shins on this one constantly. Take heart that this tendency will eventually thin out.

Realistically, all wearable vintage clothing type people end up bringing home a certain amount of unwearable stuff for a variety of reasons. From "The poor thing needs a good home to end its days" to "I'll never find another, and I may want one someday" to "I don't have one" to "With some creative alterations it'll look wonderful" or (most disastrous of all!) "It's so charming," the reasons for buying vintage clothing are endless and certainly make sense at the time. Goodness knows, I'm not one to point a finger. However, one of the best pieces of advice I'll give you is this: There'll be times when you feel yourself in a trance, grabbing things off hangers, pulling clothes out of boxes, and making a huge stack at the checkout counter. Ask the proprietor to hold everything for you for a half hour and go have a cup of coffee or soft drink (no alcohol or you're sunk). Take several deep breaths, try to review everything you're about to buy, and ask yourself, "How will I feel about this when I get home? Will I be glad I got it or groan and clutch my head? If I go home without it, will I call up and ask them to save it for me?" This small maneuver has saved me money and even heartache.

An especially good time to use this rule is when you find yourself in a shop that features prices out of range of your checkbook. I've been caught like this many a time. As I walk around with my tongue hanging out, trying to convince myself that it really isn't possible to sell the house and mortgage the car to buy a few pieces of clothing, I may see something that I can actually afford. Almost invariably it's ugly, doesn't fit, and is in bad shape. If I'm not set in advance to use my time-out rule, I'll often buy something I regret later. This can happen to all of us at one time or another, and it's well worth preventing if possible. Then there *is* money left to spend when something wonderful does come along.

Speaking as a devotee of the "It'll look great when I lose twenty pounds" school of shopping, I probably am a bad example of how to buy vintage clothing that fits. However, it's my duty to give good advice, and sometimes I even follow it. I must admit I'm much happier when I do.

People who expect their clothes to fit perfectly may find themselves in heavy weather with vintage clothing. It is rare indeed to find a garment that you love, can afford, and fits all at once. The usual place to hedge is the fit, and many vintage clothing lovers are used to making do with a belt and an "I dare you to notice this doesn't fit me" attitude. It's amazing how we get accustomed to this way of thinking. I remember trying on dresses with a few other women, respectively sizes 7, 9, and 11. We were often able to wear the same dress (not all together!) by the simple expedient of tightening or loosening the belt, as the waist demanded.

How much alteration can you really do and still have a wearable garment? A lot depends on its age, condition, and fabric. Look the garment over thoroughly, and if you see lots of small rips, figure that the fabric is too fragile to fuss with. Generally, few very old clothes will take much abuse in the way of cutting and sewing. Age should be a large factor in your decision making. I've seen some turn of the century wools recut and substantially altered with success, and wool suits from the forties and fifties can be retailored with fine results. Silks, even as recent as the forties, are risky propositions. Cottons vary a lot; sometimes they can be cut down with good results.

Usually there is very little leeway in terms of enlarging garments. Some clothing does have excess fabric in its seams (our foremothers often planned that garments would be altered or recut, and allowed for that). Unfortunately, it's been a long time since that dress was new, and often the outside of the fabric is a different shade than the inside. A seam line that's been in place for sixty years will show when you let it out, no matter what you do.

A good general rule is: if it's too small, don't buy it unless you're planning to lose enough weight to get into it. It's easier to alter your body than most vintage clothing. If this is your game plan, whether or not you really will lose the pounds necessary is between you and your conscience. I refuse to get in the middle of serious debates like this.

Before shopping, look over Chapter 7 on alterations to get an idea of what is possible. Take along some pins, a belt, shoulder pads, and maybe a lace collar. Then you can get an idea in the store of what the garment could look like, and whether or not it's possible to make it fit. If you plan to pay for alterations, the same rule applies as for mending. Add the cost of any work to the price of the item.

Sometimes even a garment that is large can be so difficult to alter that it isn't worth the bother. For example, dresses with short waists or too much room in the bust area are virtually impossible to renovate. Unless you can do something creative with a belt or lace collar, be wary. Men's suits usually have a fair amount of altering possibilities. But at the point that you are considering taking more than 4–5 inches off the waistband of the pants, you are looking at a serious recutting project, not something to take on lightly.

Men's and women's suit jackets can be taken in fairly simply in the back and side seams, and the sleeves made narrower without too much stress. Think long and hard, however, before getting yourself mired in a shoulder job. This is a job for an experienced tailor, if it is to look good.

How about the "I'll buy it and make a pattern out of it" school of thought? I don't know anyone who hasn't done that at one time or another. Unless the garment is very cheap (and I mean a few cents or very few dollars), you would probably be better off to make a rough sketch of it and rework a commercial pattern to that style. There are a number of companies that make patterns of vintage clothing for men and women, covering most eras. If you can sew well enough to make a pattern out of a finished garment, you can certainly alter a pattern to another style. Especially if the pattern fits and the garment you plan to work from doesn't.

Here's a good rule to engrave on your heart: *Leave it for someone else to enjoy*. If it doesn't work for you, even though you adore it, keep in mind that somewhere out there is someone whom the garment will fit, who will love it and give it a good home. You'll find yours in time, just be patient.

There are times when it is legitimate to ignore size completely. You may stand 5′ 2″, weigh 165 pounds, and be a champion mud wrestler on the outside, but Jean Harlow on the inside. If you should stumble on a size 7 peach silk bias-cut evening dress that makes your heart flutter, you may want to throw reason to the wind and buy it. At times like this practicality is not necessarily the best thing for your soul.

HIDDEN TREASURES: HOW TO LOOK, WHERE TO LOOK or DO COBWEB EARRINGS COMPLEMENT VELVET?

If it's important to keep an eye out for problems, it's equally (maybe more!) important to learn how to spot treasures. You probably know people who are able to find wonderful treasure anywhere. They're like the old diviners who could locate water in the ground by means of a forked stick. Successful treasure hunters don't really have special magic, they've just spent enough time looking, touching, and following up leads so that it appears as though they do. You can develop that magical touch yourself with enough experience.

Luck (defined as being in the right place, at the right time, with enough money in the bank) is important to vintage clothing lovers. I think of myself as pretty lucky when it comes to finding vintage clothing, but my friend Darlene could win the luck Olympics. It seems as though she can walk through a thrift store and every silk blouse, cashmere sweater, and beaded dress in her size in good condition jumps into her basket. However, Darlene's luck, my luck, and yours, too, have more behind them than the conjunction of the stars. Unless you know what you're looking at, you could get buried in an avalanche of vintage treasures and not even know it.

Spend as much time as you can studying authentic vintage clothing. Very quickly you'll begin to develop your eye for old cloth and styles. The patina of age becomes so apparent that you'll wonder how you ever got new and old confused. At this point, I can sit in the audience at the theater and distinguish the production's authentic vintage clothing from the reproduction clothing. Even in cases when genuine old patterns have been used to make the reproductions, the old fabric looks very different to me. This skill is invaluable when I'm scrounging around in thrift stores or rummage sales. I can spot a potential jewel across a crowded room, pick up my lance, and charge through the multitudes, knowing I'm aiming at something that's at least interesting.

A highly developed sense of touch is nearly as important as a well trained eye. Can you tell the difference between cashmere and other soft wools? Practice touching the various types of wool and you'll be surprised how different they feel. I've taken home more than one $1.99 cashmere sweater because I've learned to operate by touch, not thrift store labeling.

Familiarity with styles and characteristics of various eras is something you can learn and become very comfortable with. When you know that zippers were used in women's clothing after 1935, that padded shoulders were never worn in the twenties, and other details that distinguish vintage clothing from modern versions, you'll be well armed for ferreting out the best of the keen junk.

Determination is another big piece of vintage luck. Vintage clothing may be lurking anywhere. Unless you're willing to roll up your sleeves and dig, you'll miss out on many a find. Make it a point to look through the cartons under the tables at sales. Many people will put what they consider to be undesirable out-of-date clothing out of sight. Never pass by a barrel marked "rags" for the same reason. Rummage through boxes of shoes, even if the ones on top are obviously battered and dull. You don't know what's at the bottom until you get there. The person who emerges triumphant with a cobweb hanging from her ear and a smudge or three on her nose is often the one with the best luck.

Get in the habit of trying on everything that is even remotely interesting. For example, many 1940's hats don't look like much on a shelf but are fabulous on a head. I recently saw a flat, round, gray felt hat on top of a rack. When I put it on, it turned out to have a shaped band and took on a darling tilt. It's important to give them all a chance. This goes for dresses, suits, blouses, shoes . . . the whole gamut. Vintage clothing is usually such a different shape from modern that it can be difficult to predict what something looks like on the body. Pleasant surprises, as well as an occasional good chuckle, await the adventurous.

Vintage clothing can be found almost anywhere. Once you've gotten used to looking, you'll find that your eyes become attuned to possibilities and catch little hints as you drive down the freeway. (Of course, this is a little rough on a person's driving, but first things first.) I've found treasures at flea markets that otherwise had nothing but old engine parts and junky transistor radios, and in thrift stores that featured polyester double-knit pant suits. I've bumped into treasures in second hand stores that seemed to carry nothing but ugly lamps and various scarred plywood chests of drawers. I've tracked them down in a friend's basement and once even in a mobile home garage sale. I've even found them in vintage clothing stores! Never pass up anything remotely possible.

Wherever I go I look for vintage clothing. When I visit a new city, I look in the yellow pages under "Clothing Bought and Sold" and "Antiques," and check out the listings that look interesting. Some city directories now have a "Vintage Clothing" listing and others a "Used Clothing" section. A good plan of attack is to arm yourself with some quarters and a pay phone, and call first. This can weed out the unlikely places quickly, as well as prevent a trip to a shop that's gone out of business. My absolutely favorite vintage clothing source was found that way. Surprisingly enough, very few people who live in that city even know the place exists, but there it is, right in the telephone book!

This is a nice way to spend a vacation (contrary to the opinion of my family), because you can often find yourself exploring places that you'd never see otherwise. If you're familiar with prices in your own stomping grounds, you'll be better able to assess whether a bargain's a bargain someplace else.

My latest unusual source is vintage clothing by mail. I've found some absolutely wonderful clothes this way and strongly recommend it. However (why must there always be a however?), I've learned to proceed by some basic rules that help keep this method fun, rather than dicey.

It's important when buying by mail to purchase only from people who sell with a return policy. This means they give you a certain number of days (usually three to five) after the box arrives to examine the clothing and return any of it that you don't want. Some dealers will send photographs, but this is not enough to guarantee that the item is what you want, let alone that it will fit. The one and only time I decided to take a chance on "no return," I got stung. Some high topped boots arrived cracked and dry, and completely unusable. I was angry, but I was taking a chance when I did it, so didn't have any recourse. The dealer lost a customer, so neither of us came out ahead, but that was small consolation at the time. The customer's part in this is to be religious about observing the time frame when returning things.

When you send a check, take a Xerox copy and purchase a "proof of mailing" (twenty-five cents at the post office), so that you have proof that you've done your part. If you need to return some or all of the garments, make sure they're fully insured. You will have to pay shipping costs when you shop by mail. I've found, however, that I don't spend any more than I might for gas money on a serious shopping trip.

Now for the fun part. I must tell you, when the delivery man knocks on the door with a box full of vintage treasures, it's a replay of Christmas when I was a kid. I admit to some disappointments . . . dresses advertised as size 10, which turn out to be a size 3, for example. But in the main I'm hooked, and I'll never give it up!

In the beginning all this looking and learning will be conscious, but at some point you'll find yourself operating on instinct. You'll walk down the street in your lovely vintage treasures and someone will ask you, "How do you find all those wonderful clothes?" You'll find yourself saying, "I don't know, I guess I'm just lucky."

WHERE DO PRICES COME FROM or "PUT $50 ON IT, AND WE'LL SEE IF IT SELLS"

Now that we are well fortified with the information we need for setting our own price guidelines, I'm emboldened to take a plunge into the morass of how others set prices. Every once in a while you hear about an auction where some vintage clothes sold for thousands of dollars and everyone races around saying, "Oh, boy, these clothes are worth a fortune!" Well, my friends, there's one heck of a big difference between an original 1910 Worth (house of couture famous 1860's through 1920's) suit and Great Aunt Minnie's best 1940 bridge dress. There are certainly far more Aunt Minnies than Worths, and considerably more people in the market for Auntie's old dress too. Collectors are looking for specific garments and/or accessories and may be prepared to pay a lot of money when they find what they want. They are equally prepared for the enormous amount of time, money, and effort required to keep a serious textile collection in good condition. These dedicated souls are making purchases based on the antique or collectible value of the garments, and using those criteria in deciding what to pay.

With wearable vintage clothing it's a different ball game. Setting values depends on a number of variables. All the variables add up to whether the garment is usable, and if so, how usable. Signs of wear, tears, stains, and degree of dilapidation all should be taken into consideration when a price is set. While beauty is a more nebulous criterion, pretty clothing is more salable than ugly clothing, no matter how good the condition. As many women had atrocious taste fifty years ago as now, and many of their garments have survived in good shape. That doesn't mean anyone with an ounce of taste would want them, but there they are. Vintage clothing is just as subject to style changes and popularity shifts as any other type of clothing. One year slinky thirties dresses are in demand, the next lacey whites from the teens command more customers. The prices for garments in these categories increase and decrease as the demand changes. The size of an individual piece will have as much bearing on the price as any of the above criteria. A beautiful, mint-condition, fashionable vintage dress that's a size 3 is not going to appeal to as many customers as a size 9 or 12.

Location has a decided effect on the price. What part of the country, the size of the city, and local fashion awareness are all factors. I've even found prices that vary considerably from one part of a city to another. Five blocks can sometimes mean a 100 percent difference in price for the same type of garment.

A shop has to cover basic expenses, rent, utilities, salaries, taxes, insurance, the cost of unsold stock, advertising, and (with luck) make a profit of some sort for the owner. Shops that sell restored clothing have additional expenses of time and money as well. Most shops use a formula; a common one is to sell the garments for three to four times what they pay for them, plus cleaning and mending costs. Shops that take consignments normally keep 50 percent of the selling price. Before I get into "what the traffic will bear," let's run an innocent little 1940's evening dress (assuming it is in good condition, a wearable color, and a reasonable size) through the above system.

Put that dress in a shop in downtown Gotham City, where the rent is $3,000 a month, other expenses commensurate with that, two experienced sales people, expert beaders and lace makers to pay, plus a clientele that is used to paying high prices for clothing in general and has occasions for evening clothes, and you can see a $150 price tag with no problem. Put the same dress in West East Podunk (population 30,000 and growing), rent $350 a month, owner works in the store most of the time with a little minimum wage help, has a clientele who will only pay medium to low prices, and has little opportunity to "put on the Ritz." You've got a $50 price tag—and the dress may sit in the shop for a couple of months at that. The Gotham City shop can afford to pay as much as $50, wholesale, for the dress, while the Podunkian will pay $12–$15 wholesale, for the dress.

Having provided you with rational pricing guidelines for shops, I'll now add that good bargains and bad buys can be found almost anywhere. A fair number of vintage shoppers walk around under the charming, but often mistaken, impression that great clothes can always be had for low prices in small hamlets around the country. Sometimes that's the case, and if all shops used cost plus profit for pricing their merchandise, it would be a fair expectation. But in actual practice, some shopkeepers in out of the way locations may be using prices they've seen listed in a book or in a vintage clothing store in a large city, without paying much attention to differences in cost. A vintage clothing store in a large city might have a high enough volume to be able to use a lower mark-up; or be forced to use competitive pricing because there are more vintage clothing shops in the area. With vintage clothing stores it's safe to say, "You can't predict what the prices will be until you've gone inside and looked for yourself."

Antique stores, estates sales, thrift stores, garage sales, etc., have different overhead situations. For instance, many estate sales are run by professional firms that take a percentage of the total income, but otherwise the owner has no overhead. Thrift stores vary in their overhead: most have rent, utilities, and other standard expenses, but many are run by volunteer help, and the stock is all donated. Garage and rummage sales, by this formula, should have the lowest prices of any source. Antique stores that carry some vintage clothing usually don't depend on it for income, and often purchase what they have along with other antique items when they buy out entire estates.

There are trends in vintage clothing styles, just like there are in modern clothing, which affect prices as well. A good example is Edwardian whites (petticoats, camisoles, dresses), which were hot items in the vintage clothing world until recently. Prices soared, sometimes into the hundreds of dollars, for very good examples. Interest in these items has dropped, and the prices, while slower to follow, have also. As rhinestones go out and plastic jewelry from the thirties and forties comes in, expect price ups and downs. Trends in vintage clothing styles frequently follow the style shifts in modern clothing. When fashion magazines and new clothing stores show fifties-style evening wear, expect that vintage fifties clothing will be more in demand and priced accordingly.

Now, we could probably figure our way through all of the above, if it weren't for the factor I mentioned earlier: "What the traffic will bear." Some sellers of vintage clothing have their fingers on the market and can gauge this pretty accurately. Others simply refer to a book that lists prices (that have been set with no regard for the variables I've mentioned) and slap some figure on a tag, then wait to see what happens. This is why you can find yourself looking at an old, dilapidated, soiled cotton dress with big rips in it and then see a price that makes you gasp. It's also why you can find an attractive, wearable garment for a price you feel very comfortable paying.

When vintage clothing is lumped with antiques, rather than clothing, it can affect prices unrealistically. There is a substantial difference between an 1890 oak table and an 1890 silk dress, and if the seller doesn't know that, the buyer certainly should. There are people who collect vintage clothes with the object of conserving them, but the majority of vintage customers expect to use them. That means the dress has to fit that person, has to be usable to her, has to at least hold together while it's being worn, and the customer would probably like to wear the purchase more than once before it falls apart. Keep in mind that a piece of glassware or furniture can sit around a store for years without losing value, while a garment can quickly become shopworn and shabby.

Price setting in the vintage clothing world is definitely erratic, wildly unpredictable, and only occasionally makes sense. People who come from an antiques background have tried to set standardized prices for clothes, but the results have been unhelpful, to put it mildly. To set too low a price lessens the credibility of shops that must charge more in order to make a profit. Too high a price makes it hard for low and moderate priced shops to purchase stock, and they can be faced with someone trying to sell them vintage clothing at costs over their retail. The best way to maneuver through the shoals and pitfalls of all this is to be very aware of your own wants and pocketbook.

GOOD VINTAGE SHOPPING MANNERS or EVERYBODY HAS A GREAT AUNT MINNIE

Customers need sources for vintage clothing and vintage clothing sellers need customers, so one would think everyone would get along nicely. But (as I know from both my experience and mail I get from frustrated folks on both sides of the fence) this is not always the case. So I'm taking a deep breath and plunging into the middle with some suggestions for buyers and sellers that would make life more pleasant and profitable for all concerned.

A good customer encourages and supports a good seller. When I find a shop, a flea market merchant, or particularly good mail order source I like, I return frequently, tell people about them, and spend my money there. This is the ultimate in good manners, not to mention keeping fine folks in business. The best way to deal with a source that you're not happy about is to stay away and keep your hard earned dollars in your pocket.

A shopper with impeccable manners won't try on vintage clothes that are too small. It's painful, not to mention embarrassing, to have a horrible ripping sound come from your dressing room. If you're in doubt, ask for a tape measure and measure any part (of you or the garment) you're not sure of. No one objects if you keep your ego together by pretending you're a size 5 when you're really a 12, but this is one time to be realistic.

Even if you're prepared to be ruthlessly honest about your corporeal self, you can get into trouble because some old clothes are deceptive regarding sizes. For example, Victorian and Edwardian blouses and dress tops often appear to be larger than they are because there is so much room in the bust area. However, the shoulders, sleeves, and upper chest are often very small. People *were* smaller in those pre-vitamin, pre-healthy baby food days, and this means not just in height, but bone structure as well. It's embarrassing, to put it mildly, to find yourself in a strange dressing room stuck half in, half out of a Victorian top, not wanting to call for help, but afraid you'll rip the garment before you get out of it. Anyone who's found herself in that position will know whereof I speak; the rest of you may want to avoid this problem entirely.

Some dresses from the 1920's can also deceive the unobservant. For a few years it was the style to wear very loose dresses; these dresses may be as large as a size 14 in the body, but the armholes and sleeves may be a size 7. Again, it can be a touchy situation to get stuck part way in or out. If you've got any doubt, borrow the tape measure.

I know none of you will toss vintage clothes on the floor when you take them off and will always ask for help with tricky fastenings or unreachable back buttons. Not everyone is so thoughtful, however.

I know a shopkeeper who gets crazy when a button falls off and the customer doesn't tell her. Usually the customer feels embarrassed and sometimes will walk out with the fallen button. Most shopkeepers will be grateful, rather than angry, if you give them the button, which they can replace easily. What's hard is to have to replace an entire set of buttons, because the remaining buttons can't be matched.

It is not only bad form but also does no good at all to walk around a vintage clothing store and say things like "There's stuff just like this at the thrift store, and it's cheaper." If that's true, the shopkeeper already knows it and doesn't care.

Another exercise in futility is to ask a vintage shopkeeper where the merchandise is from. Believe me, even if it's your closest friend, you aren't going to get a straight answer. I know one shopkeeper who says she'd rather give out her hip measurement than her vintage sources, and she won't even tell her husband her hip measurement.

It's not bad manners to talk about all the wonderful vintage clothes your Aunt Mabel gave away to the Goodwill three years ago.

It's just that the shopkeeper has heard that one and five others like it already today. If you become an old and valued customer and friend, then trade stories of lost opportunities with each other. This is a time honored tradition among vintage clothing lovers, but it ought to be a conversation, not a speech to a captive audience.

When looking through racks, move the clothes along by grasping the hanger, rather than a sleeve or skirt. There is less chance of damage this way. Find out whether the shopkeeper would rather hang things up herself, or if you should do it. Some feel strongly about where things go and how they're hung, so do it their way.

Is it okay to bargain? It's always worth a try. After all, even in the classiest of shops the shopkeeper is often a scrounger like you and me, turned professional, and used to bargaining. I've found it possible to bargain in the most elegant shops, and, conversely, have gotten a very cold reception in dungeons laden with cobwebs and dust. The only way to find out is to give it a shot. Believe me, you'll get the message loud and clear if it's not okay. It's almost obligatory to bargain at flea markets. Everyone expects it, and it's part of the shopping ambience.

How one bargains is the key. People who use putdowns and statements like "This is a piece of junk, so how much will you really take for it?" will get nowhere fast. Instead, armed with your knowledge about prices in the area and condition of the clothes, try saying "I noticed this hole. It'll cost twelve dollars to have it fixed. Would you consider coming down on the price?" Even if something is marked "as is," the seller may be willing to negotiate. If I think the price is high, and there isn't any damage, I will sometimes ask if the price is negotiable. Surprisingly often it is. If not, I usually take no for an answer. If someone is uncomfortable with bargaining, respect that.

Some shopkeepers welcome small children and others suffer cardiac arrest at the sight of anyone under the age of eighteen. Most moms and dads would rather go shopping by themselves, or with someone more their own age, but this isn't always possible. If you've got small cherubs along, keep them corralled and under your supervision all the time. Even if the dressing room is crowded, better to stack a child or two, than hear a rack topple to the ground and have to face a justifiably angry proprietor. Make sure the little ones' hands and faces are clean. One small, grubby pair of hands can wreak a disproportionate amount of havoc. Try not to be offended if you aren't welcome with your descendents and heirs in tow. A shop full of freshly washed and ironed Edwardian whites or fragile sixty-year-old beaded dresses is a high risk proposition at best.

It isn't necessary to display all your knowledge of vintage clothing while shopping. Even if there are some glaring mistakes on labels, it doesn't really help to march around correcting the seller. If the prices are totally out of line, you always have the option of going someplace else, and I strongly suggest that you do so. It's a much more forceful argument, and has better results, than complaining verbally.

Now that all the customers are well behaved, let's take a look at the impeccably mannered seller. I saw a vintage shopkeeper in action one time who earned my undying respect for perfect manners. A man with noticeably greasy hair asked to try on an expensive top hat. Everything in the shop was beautifully clean and in wonderful condition, so I knew she'd have to have the hat cleaned if he didn't buy it. I wondered what she would do, and even what I'd do in the same situation. She smiled at him pleasantly and got the hat down for him. Whether it bothered her or not, that man and I will never know. Here is a woman who has come to grips with selling vintage clothing to the public, with serenity and grace.

It's good manners to mark prices on all the garments. When I go into a shop and see clothes without prices marked, I feel as though I'm being sized up for price, rather than the clothes, and often that's the case. When I have to ask the price of each thing I'm interested in, it gets tedious, to say the least. I shop with a clear, personal price range in my head, and I'm frustrated when I can't tell immediately what the price range is in the shop. I'm realistic enough to know that there are things that I can't afford to buy, and I prefer to know that before I get hooked. Because of that, I make it a policy to walk out when I find a shop without price tags.

Price tags should not be stapled to the garments. Staples make little holes that are most unpleasant, and those little plastic tag holders that work fine for new clothes can cause trouble for old ones. Safer alternatives are tiny safety pins or attaching tags with a needle and string on the sleeve or neckline facing.

I appreciate that shopkeepers have to be protective about very old, fragile clothing, but it's silly to think anyone is going to buy something, especially if it's costly, without trying it on. Is it a shop or museum? If a shop, you've got to expect customers to touch, handle, and try on clothing. Shopkeepers who can't deal with that should consider selling something other than vintage clothing. There are protective measures that are possible. For instance, hanging the more fragile pieces out of reach so the customer has to ask to see them. If someone asks, it's often because she is considering making the purchase and isn't taking an idle interest. When you've got merchandise for sale, the buyer must be expected to have access to it.

People vary in how well they tolerate hovering salespeople. My own tolerance is zero, and from what I hear, that is the case for many others. A friendly interest and a reasonable watch to make sure nothing is stolen is okay. What with all the shoplifting that happens, it's expectable that a seller would take some precautions. Otherwise, some folks like more attention than others. When you're being solicitous, pay attention to the reception you're getting. If it isn't enthusiastic, retire gracefully.

If it's at all possible, try to arrange a space for small children to play while their moms or dads shop. I know how much you pay per square foot, but this is an investment that could return big dividends. Women who are marooned with young children are desperate for a good time out, and if you can arrange things to give them a reasonable place to go, you'll get their money.

I have found that the most knowledgeable sellers of vintage clothing are also the least afraid to say, "I don't know." "I don't know if it's a hundred percent silk." "I'm not sure if it's late teens or early twenties." This is deeply appreciated, by me, because when that person does say "I know," it's likely to be accurate. Don't make wild guesses and state them as fact. Especially refrain from putting dubious information on price tags.

Basic good manners is to assume your customers are intelligent, knowledgeable people. Before dispensing information ("That's a thirties dress," "That jacket is supposed to be buttoned") make sure the customer has a need to know. Some probably do. Others already know everything you're saying, but can't stop your over-helpfulness without being rude themselves.

People who buy vintage clothing regularly are used to bargaining, so it's a reasonable expectation that customers will at least make a stab at it. If you don't choose to bargain, respond pleasantly that you don't. To feel or act upset or offended does nobody any good and can create an uncomfortable situation.

THE LAWS OF VINTAGE CLOTHING

There are certain laws of vintage clothing that we've identified over the years. Those people who know the laws and accept them will find the whole world of vintage more comprehensible and infinitely easier to navigate.

1: You *will* find what you're looking for. It may take years of searching, but someday it'll show up; the perfect silk teddy; the ideal pinstriped, nip-waist suit; the Victorian skirt of your dreams. Keep your faith, keep looking, and think of all the wonderful things you'll find along the way!

2: If you've looked high and low for an item for years, and finally break down and buy something that is almost, but not quite right, you will find exactly what you wanted a short period of time afterward. This is particularly true if you spent all your money on the "not quite right" one.

3: Help someone else find something he is looking for, and you'll find something that *you've* been looking for very soon thereafter. Actually, this works so well that I've found things I never dreamed I'd own shortly after giving a hand to another vintage lover.

4: Never go shopping for vintage clothing with someone who wears the same size and likes the same things you do. Neither of you will choose friendship over a perfect vintage garment, so you're almost certain to lose a friend.

5: With vintage clothing as in romance, there are some things that are "meant to be." Here's a typical example: the hat of your dreams appears in a shop window, but payday is far away. You're already living on peanut butter sandwiches, the next paycheck is dedicated to such trivialities as mortgage payments and groceries, and your VISA is charged to the limit. So you do everything you can to avoid going past the window. Then you get an unexpected bonus, race to the shop, and the hat is still there, waiting just for you. You can use this to your advantage when shopping. If you're not sure, you can say, "I'll come back later and if it's 'meant to be' it'll still be here."

6: Finds come in streaks. There are periods of time (sometimes they last for months) when everywhere you turn you find some wonderful vintage treasure. Make full use of these opportunities, as they give you something to fondle during dry spells. Other times no matter how hard you look, all you can find are tattered, ugly clothes that don't fit. No need to worry, these times will pass.

7: When you are completely, totally, and absolutely broke you are certain to find vintage clothing that you would die for. That's why so many vintage clothing lovers live on peanut butter sandwiches for long periods of time. Inventive layaway programs, second and third mortgages on the house, as well as tears and sobs are some of the solutions regularly employed. No one likes this law, but there it is.

CHAPTER TWO

LET'S DRESS UP THESE MODERN CLOTHES OR CAN YOU WEAR VINTAGE CLOTHING AND STILL LOOK UPTIGHT AND RESPECTABLE?

Getting right down to the nitty gritty, the enchantment one feels while shopping for vintage clothing can fade when you get home and find yourself looking for excuses to wear it. After all, vintage clothing, no matter from what era, *looks* different. When it comes down to walking out of the house wearing a dress, suit, or fur from another period, you may decide that the better part of wisdom is to take it off and put on your old reliable jeans. Before doing that, take a look at some of the ideas in this chapter. You may find something here that you haven't thought of, or, better yet, find your own creativity is sparked. Creativity and fun are the fundamentals of wearing vintage clothing. Bring yours along and you'll never look back.

The first and most important thing to put on with your vintage clothing is a sense of humor. If you catch yourself on the way out the door all dolled up in beads and feathers without it, return, and put it right on. Vintage clothing is fun, and you'll ruin the whole effect if you're too serious.

The trick is to bring the vintage pieces into your wardrobe and let them mingle, rather than take over, as they are wont to do. Like most of you, I often have to appear respectable and uptight. It's possible, thanks to various vintage accoutrements, at least to have a small private chuckle and keep our perspective while going around being official. For example, one day I popped into a store and was looking at something with my back turned to the clerk. She called my name and said, "I knew it was you. Who else would wear a business suit and seamed stockings!"

Some folks are comfortable going the whole hog, wearing vintage outfits complete from soup to nuts, shoes to chapeaus. Others, and I'm one, prefer mixing vintage with modern clothes. I like to wear vintage clothing frequently and find that I feel too "costumey" for my own comfort in most situations if I'm hatted, dressed, and shod completely in a vintage period. Of course, when an occasion for dress-up arises, I take every advantage of it.

As modern styles change, the types of vintage pieces that work with your wardrobe will change as well. For example, many of my 1940's suits were simply too padded in the shoulders to be worn on "non-vintage" occasions in the late 1970's and early eighties, but I was able to pull them out in the mid-eighties and wear them comfortably to business meetings. No one even asked if they were vintage! As skirt lengths change and shoulders expand and contract, as waistlines move around and sleeves go from plain to puffed, keep track of your vintage options at all times.

At the beginning of each season, after you've looked through fashion magazines and stores to see what's new, keep vintage clothes in mind as you pull together your wardrobe. You may already have some vintage pieces that you haven't been wearing. Get them out and see what you've got. This might be the year that navy polka dot shirtwaist from the thirties is going to perk up your life. Do some shopping in vintage stores, armed with a vision of what you are going to be wearing this year. Look for vintage garments or jewelry that will add a touch of spice and individuality to your modern clothing. Then have a grand try-on with your new clothing, modern carryovers from last year, and vintage clothes. Don't be afraid to go a little wild; it's in the privacy of your bedroom, for goodness sake! Try denim with beads, furs with gray flannel, lace collars with sweaters.

Are jabots being shown in the fashion magazines? Rather than buy one that looks like all the others on the street, how about an antique silk lace handkerchief, gathered in a vintage pin, and tucked at the top of a silk shirt? Are print rayon dresses the latest thing? An authentic forties version might be exactly right for you. It could be just the thing to make your wardrobe special, individual, and worth a second glance. Are men wearing vests this year? There are hundreds of vintage vests around, and one of them may fit into your life perfectly.

An unusual, well cut jacket is often central to a modern wardrobe. Unfortunately, every year seems to bring a slightly different length, shoulder line, or lapel shape. It's painful to see last year's elegance go out of fashion, not to mention the money you spent on your "investment jacket" that was supposed to last for years. Before racing out to spend more on a new jacket, take a look at the vintage jackets in your closet or the vintage clothing store. Vintage jackets can be found in at least as many style variations as today's designers can come up with and for considerably less money. When long line (to the knee or below) suit jackets came in, I found a knee-length silk coat from the late 1950's in a very fashionable cream color. I added shoulder pads and a long, toast colored linen skirt. The result was a suit that would have cost four to five times as much new and was one of a kind. And when short skirts reappear, I can quickly turn my silk suit jacket back into a silk coat.

When you're trying on vintage clothing, at home in front of the mirror or in a shop, don't forget to keep some shoulder pads with you. Shoulder pads can change the look of a dress, shirt, sweater, or blouse to an amazing degree. A jacket, blouse, coat, even a sweater, can pop right into an up-to-date shape in seconds and immediately become a part of your everyday wardrobe.

If your last year's wardrobe was notable for conservative colors and styles, but this year's brightly colored clothes feature red, pull out vintage silk and rayon scarves and see if you can update some of your existing clothing. Try tying a large scarf into a mock-blouse to wear with a dark colored suit. Men used to chuckle at the bright, wide, neckties from the forties, wearing them only to costume parties. No more. Some very conservative businessmen are putting on ties every morning for work that look very similar to the 1940 legends.

There are a million ideas, many of them already fomenting in your own head and wardrobe, others a pleasant shopping trip away. If you're still a bit nervous about venturing out bedecked in vintage, I have a word of reassurance. People really *enjoy* seeing vintage clothing. I don't know how many times someone has approached me and said, "Is that an old blouse [or suit or dress or hat]? It looks wonderful." You're going to give this dull old world a bit of pleasure, so have fun doing it!

While I have eclectic taste in vintage clothing and can find something to love from almost any period, I know that many people feel drawn to one time period. They will choose their vintage clothing exclusively from one era and seem to have an almost mystical attachment to that time. Despite my general love for vintage clothing, I have found that I look particularly "right" in clothing from the 1920's and 1940's, and that I have been able to fit clothing from these periods into my wardrobe most easily. You may have a natural affinity to the thirties or the teens that you've never even suspected. For that reason I've grouped ideas for wearing clothing by era, rather than categories, like blouses or suits. I'm hoping to broaden your horizons and suggest ideas for garments and about whole periods of clothing that you haven't considered previously.

For practical purposes most clothing up until the 1930's is best merged into a modern wardrobe by bits and pieces—blouses (waists), skirts, petticoats, jewelry, fur pieces, hats—rather than aimed for the full effect. That is because of line or the overall effect of the way the body looks in the clothes. A look that features an enormous hat and bosom with long flowing line to the ankle (typical of early teens) is so different from what we're used to seeing that you'll look costumey. There's nothing wrong with that look if it's what you're after. However, the main purpose of these chapters is to spark and suggest ideas for putting vintage clothing into daily use and for that purpose this advice stands.

Another drawback to older clothing is condition, which must be checked carefully before wearing. Pay special attention to anything made of silk (this rule holds true with clothing through the 1920's), which has a tendency to crumble without warning under any undue stress. Use good judgment. If you've got something you feel simply terrible about losing, put it in the lovely-to-look-at but risky-to-wear pile. If drawn to these early periods but your body size is just impossible to squeeze into the common petite sizes of the time, think about making, or having someone make, reproductions for you.

VICTORIAN AND EDWARDIAN, WWI, 1919— THE LADIES GET THE VOTE

Women's clothing changed dramatically between 1900 and 1919, reflecting the enormous changes that were going on in the world and in individuals. Women started this century wearing clothing that twisted their bodies into impossible shapes. They ruined their health with tight laced corsets, boned bodices, and sleeves too snug for easy movement. Even their shoes were commonly a size or two smaller than their feet. Twenty years later (and twenty years is a fairly short time for all these changes to have taken place) corsets were out of style and dresses were hanging loose. The same ladies, or at least their daughters, were driving cars, going to college, and holding responsible jobs. They could vote. Men's clothing also changed—from the high starched collars and bowlers of the turn of the century to the soft collared shirts and felt fedoras common in the twenties.

A big factor in causing these changes was WWI. A number of women went out to work during WWI, as they were to do again twenty-five years later in WWII. They demanded, and got, tailored suits, comfortable dresses and blouses, and shoes they could walk in. By the end of WWI they also got the vote, although, after trying on a turn of the century corset, I wonder which mattered more!

Clothing from the teens has been largely ignored by vintage clothing people, with the exception of vintage car enthusiasts, although there are droves of women who adore the earlier tight bodices and long full skirts. I suggest that if you haven't already explored clothing from the middle and late teens you take a closer look; and, incidentally, a woman who has come through the turbulent feminist battles of the sixties, seventies, and eighties may feel a natural affinity to them.

There are many pieces from the early century that have potential for adding an individual touch to a 1980's wardrobe. The tricky part is finding something that will fit, as not only were people generally smaller then than now but clothing was shaped differently. However, there are so many charming pieces available that it will be hard not to search out at least one to play with. Much of the clothing of this era featured lovely beaded designs, lace, and spectacular embroidery, which most of us would never have an opportunity to own and wear otherwise. Unless, that is, you've got the kind of budget that allows for handmade or designer clothing. For most of us vintage is our chance, and we should take advantage.

One of my favorite things about vintage clothing is how it can be used for contrasts. Victorian and Edwardian boned jackets combined with modern softly pleated below mid-calf skirts are a wonderful way to do that. The look of a small jacket, fitted at the shoulder and waist, usually slightly puffy in the sleeve, contrasted with the soft floating line of the skirt is elegant and unexpected. Add classy modern boots, and you'll not only look good, but you won't meet yourself five times when you walk down the street. At the times that an evening jacket is called for, a Victorian jacket is a good way to be "the same, only different." Try one with a plaid taffeta, tiny floral print, or gray wool knit skirt. Another unusual and modern look for Victorian jackets is to wear them with a boot length divided skirt. I've also seen them worn with flair complementing good old jeans. Of course, the wearer was thin as all get out, but did she look great! Incidentally, if the jacket fits across the shoulders and upper back but won't fasten because of the tiny waist, wear it open over a bright silk T-shirt.

Jackets from the late teens have an unusual shape that until recently I had found difficult to blend with modern clothing. They tend to be cut in a long, loose style with only a suggestion of a waistline and a narrow shoulder line. On the other hand they often have remarkably nice detailing worked in braid, beading, or embroidery. I considered this issue for some time, as I have a couple of these jackets that I wanted to wear on an occasional outing. Adding shoulder pads (my normal solution to this sort of problem) threw the shape out of whack without improving it. One day I stopped thinking and tossed the jacket on over a very plain silk shirt and below mid-calf skirt. It looked great. It's a different style, but fine for a play, movie, or informal concert.

Linen and cotton dusters (long, lightweight coats worn for protection in the early days of automobiles) are much sought after by the vintage car crowd. Some of them are plain and utilitarian, others have an especially attractive cut or unusual braiding. Most are sturdy despite their age. If you find one that is especially appealing, try it in the spring with different combinations of shirts, skirts, and slacks.

One of the best accessories to bring out the new-old ambience of vintage clothing is a spectacular modern pair of boots. With most of my vintage clothes that are mid-calf or longer I wear boots, whatever the era or style of the garment. Boots make a statement about what's going on by saying that you're enjoying yourself and the clothes, and then set a tone of "this is for fun, and ain't I pretty?"

People who like vintage clothing and have lots of evening obligations should invest in a relatively plain, sleeveless evening dress in either black, gray, or white. I've got several suggestions for dressing up a simple evening dress with vintage jackets and accessories. The first is to add a Victorian jacket, fastened or open. The problem for most of us is that evening clothes should look spectacular, but few of us have enough money to invest in more than one or two outfits. I mean, with the price of jeans being what it is, it's hard enough to cover yourself decently for trips to the grocery store, let alone business clothing. Unless you've got some way to look totally wonderful on little cash outlay, creating a splash in the social world can break the bank faster than raising teenagers. That's where vintage clothing can dig you out of a hole fast. Another Victorian-Edwardian piece that adapts well to this system is a black velvet cape. These are common finds, and normally feature beading, embroidery, and appliqué. They are intensely dramatic looking, although originally worn during the day, and look spectacular in the evening. I know one woman who tosses one on over jeans and a silk shirt—she adores making a grand entrance.

Skirts from 1895 to 1909 are graceful, fitted at the waist and hips and fully flaring at the hemline. Often there is also braiding along the seams and hem, which can be dramatic. It's not uncommon to find wool, linen, or cotton skirts from this period in very good condition. They can look charming with a blouse from the same period, but also take beautifully to a tailored silk or cotton shirt. As I write this, long evening skirts are definitely not the thing, outside of an occasional bridge club, and even there the style is fading. The style for long skirts does go in and out over time, and I can't imagine a more glamorous, individual evening skirt than one from the turn of century. If you find one, you might consider buying it and tucking it away for a future fashion piece.

Blouses (often referred to as "waists") from this period are especially wearable. If you want one really usable piece of clothing from the early twentieth century, a "lingerie blouse" is probably your most versatile investment. They tend to come in more wearable sizes, because they were standard dressy daytime apparel, and were worn by women of all ages and sizes. It's easy to find them and, more importantly, it's possible to find one that fits! Made of white cotton lawn or batiste (occasionally linen) with lots of embroidery or lace, lingerie blouses were popular from the turn of the century to the 1920's and are lots of fun to play around with right now. They look wonderful with denim, either jeans or skirts; elegant with drapey mid-calf skirts; romantic with print dirndl-type skirts; formal with black silk or velvet; and playful with striped or plaid loose jumpers.

In addition to the lingerie blouse, black silk blouses trimmed with lace or beading are common finds from this period. These often feature high necklines and long sleeves, and, since they were worn by older women, frequently come in larger sizes. They tend to have a distinctive look, which can be the focal point of an outfit. In other words, just put on a black silk blouse with a divided skirt and boots, and let it dominate the situation. Another type of blouse that one bumps into often is the silk georgette (a sheer crepelike material) overblouse, originally worn 1917–1920. These are nearly always embroidered, sometimes beaded, and have a light, delicate appearance. Strong measures have to be taken in terms of undergarments however, as they are decidedly see-through! A camisole (modern or period) will do you nicely. I have a georgette blouse in peach with a sailor collar and blue silk embroidery that I wear with a mid-calf skirt and boots, and never fail to get compliments.

The high lace top or button boots of this time are much sought after and can frequently be found in respectable, wearable condition. When you finally find one to fit your foot, however, it can be a shock to discover that it's virtually impossible to close it at the ankle! How did they ever wear them? The same way they wore those miserable boned waists—by suffering inhuman pain so that their ankles would appear tiny and trim. This style of boot is so unique and attractive that most vintage lovers look high and low for a pair of their own. Help is at hand if you've about given up. In the Appendix is the name of a firm that makes reproduction vintage boots and shoes. For an amount about the same as you'd pay for a good vintage pair, you can have a brand new pair, sized to fit a modern foot and ankle. A pair of high top shoes, either button or tie, are as individual as shoes get. While most folks wear them "in period," so to speak, I've seen them paired with some jeans and a shirt to give a new look to an outfit. They also look good with a modern longer length skirt, just for fun. Some young women like them with short skirts, although you have to have a slightly funky turn of mind to pull this look off.

Young women like to wear old camisoles and petticoats together as summer outerwear, and for that they are lovely. This tends to be a look that is on the young side, although these things are up to one's own conscience and comfort level. Having grown up with an English grandmother who was given to making cracks like "mutton dressed as lamb" to describe women who were wearing clothes too young for them, I may be more sensitive than most. I like to wear petticoats as petticoats with big loose jumpers or button front skirts. I leave the bottom buttons open so that the pretty lace shows when I walk and sit down. This looks especially good with high top shoes or boots.

Camisoles or corset covers, when you can find them with long enough waists, work very nicely under sheer white cotton blouses and dresses, just as they were originally intended. In fact, a good opaque camisole is a must under the sheer blouses. Often you'll come across an undergarment that is a combination of a camisole and bloomers. This was called a "combination" or "all-in-one" and is a remarkably practical and comfortable undergarment. After I bought my first and realized what a delightful way they are to complement sheer or lacey clothing, I've been picking them up whenever I find them. Made of cotton or linen (less frequently of silk), they are cool and comfortable while giving no hint at all of whatever else one is, or is not, wearing underneath.

Many people are introduced to vintage clothing by finding, or seeking out, the white lacey dresses from this era. Sometimes called "lawn dresses," or "lingerie dresses," they are totally pretty and usually totally tiny. These pretties were commonly worn by young women who took great pride in having eighteen inch waistlines. Some of the dresses that come from later in the period (mid to late teens), when a more natural line was in style, have larger waists and shoulders. Lingerie dresses have been in vogue as wedding dresses for modern young women for a number of years now, and this is the most practical use for them. But that doesn't stop the rest of us from lusting and looking for the elusive one that will fit. Unless you're a blushing bride or high school graduate, once you've got one home you may find occasions for wearing it few and far between. I wore one to a folk festival last summer, for which it worked beautifully. Other summer occasions to look feminine and charming sometimes turn up. Incidentally, these dresses are often very sheer, so you will need to find appropriate undergarments. This is a perfect time to pull out your camisoles, corset covers, petticoats, and combinations, because modern underwear looks like the dickens underneath.

Unfortunately, women's hats from this time generally tend to look off balance with modern clothes. Hats were often very large and featured lots of trim. You can sometimes find them with the entire body of a bird adorning the crown! Fun and silly, and absolutely charming, but not an everyday sort of hat. An exception are the straw hats, either wide or narrow brimmed, which are often usable. If you don't care to wear one, you can carry it with you and drape it carelessly over your lap when you sit down. This is a great effect with full summer skirts and dresses, particularly if you've got an old petticoat peeking out from under. Because it was then the style to have lots of hair, and false hair pieces were common, women's hats from this period tend to be huge inside the brim where they fit on the head. Often you'll find a separate piece of lining, gathered to form a small sack. You can stuff tissue paper inside to fill up the space and make it fit your head, which is exactly what the sack is for.

Jewelry, beaded bags, lace pieces, and beaded motifs may be your best buys for this era. Do a lot of comparison shopping before investing in Victorian or Edwardian costume jewelry, as it has become a popular collectible and is often priced very high. On the other hand, while I've seen pieces starting at $100 in some shops, I've also seen equally lovely pieces ranging from $30 to $50 in others. It's a good idea to proceed with some caution when spending a lot of money for vintage costume jewelry, as some firms are making reproductions, often using the original molds. Unless you know and trust the person selling the jewelry, or are knowledgeable yourself, keep your spending in this area modest. I don't mind the reproductions myself, as I like the look of the pieces, but a reproduction should never cost as much as an original piece. Reproduction or original, jewelry from the early century looks simply smashing with modern clothing. I nearly always wear a vintage necklace, pin, or watch fob, no matter how modernly I am otherwise dressed, and I never fail to garner compliments on my jewelry. Vintage costume jewelry of any period, but this one in particular, is just what ordinary business suits need for a bit of style. Much of the jewelry of the early century is relatively simple but distinctive. Lockets and cameos on necklaces or pins, Italian mosaics, carved ivory and jade on gold chains, amethyst and amber beads, are all easily wearable with modern clothing. They are seldom distracting, but always interesting.

Now that vests are coming back for men, pocket watches with chains and fobs are reappearing, and they look very special. Men's jewelry is starting to make a serious reappearance as dressing up becomes more and more acceptable. The pleasant but unobtrusive touch that Victorian or Edwardian jewelry provides is a perfect way to enjoy this trend, even for fairly conservative men. Other fun jewelry for men includes the little gadgets that were designed to cut off the ends of cigars, and unusual tie clasps and stick pins.

Beaded bags have acquired a following all their own, and for good reason. They're often amazing works of art. If you plan to use a vintage beaded bag, rather than just look at it occasionally, be sure it is sturdy enough to do what's required. It should also be large enough to hold what you need. Like jewelry, the bags are collectible, although they are not being reproduced. When something becomes collectible, it means that prices shoot up. Books get published listing prices and everyone decides that every piece, no matter how humble, is worth lots of money. In practice, prices for beaded bags (as for other collectibles that we touch on in the vintage clothing world) vary widely. Beaded bags of various styles were popular throughout the last century and the first thirty years of this century. There are thousands of them around, of all levels of workmanship and degree of delicacy. Many were homemade and all were handmade. Most are lovely, and few are actually usable at this stage of their lives. Those that are tend to be made of larger beads and stronger threads, and are of more recent manufacture (usually well into this century). For these reasons they are often less costly. Vintage beaded bags add a piquant touch to modern clothes, and are lovely to use for evening.

For those who sew, or those who prefer to use reproductions, the beaded motifs, lace collars, crocheted yokes, and other needlework pieces that can be found in fairly respectable numbers are valuable purchases. Most Victorian clothing had beads in motif form (a design that was made as a separate piece, appliquéd to the garment and later removed), rather than worked into the clothing itself. The thrifty ladies expected to take everything usable off a garment before it was discarded, so that it could be reused on another. The bead motifs made that easy for them, and because they often survive in excellent condition, lucky for us. Almost always black, they can be worked into creative sewing beautifully, as well as making the reproduction of authentic looking Victorian jackets and skirts possible. The same can and should be said for the lace collars and yokes, which are very available and usually modestly priced. A Victorian or Edwardian lace collar can transform an off-the-rack modern garment into something remarkable and original. Keep them in mind for using with sweaters, over plain gray and black dresses, as well as paisley and plaids. Tie the longer ones loosely over a blazer to tone down the dress-for-success look when you're away from the office.

Fun accessories like parasols, lorgnettes, pocket watches with chains, gentlemen's canes, monocles, and so forth are for playing dress-up in a big way. A parasol can make you feel like a real "lady," but I have to admit it's hampering. I took a silk parasol to an outdoor event this summer, and it made a big hit. However, I got tired of carrying it around after a while and was faced with the question: What do you do with a ninety-year-old silk parasol besides carry it carefully? The answer: keep on carrying it!

Men's suits from this era are mostly unremarkable, because they're too similar to modern ones to provide an interesting counterpoint. An exception is the morning coat, a daytime suit jacket, normally worn with striped pants by the top executives of that period. Men adore them for costume wear, when they can be found, although I've yet to see the president of General Motors wear one to work. Maybe next year! The hats, bowler, straw boater, and felt, can be fun to wear, as can the vests. Shirts were roomy and had long tails. Many shirts had detachable collars, leaving the shirts themselves with just a band. All men's shirts were made of 100 percent cotton, linen, or silk, so they are comfortable as well as good looking. While men enjoy them, the biggest fans of these shirts are women, who can wear them as tunics, maternity tops, nightgowns, or, with shoulder pads attached, as big shirts. Here is one case where the smaller size of people then comes in handy, as an Edwardian man's shirt will often fit a modern woman across her shoulders. Women also like men's vests from this era, especially festooned with watch fobs and dangly jewelry.

Men's vintage formal clothing, including tuxedos, tailcoats, evening vests, and wing-collared shirts are becoming increasingly popular. With men! Evening wear is an important part of the big trend toward men's vintage clothing, and an authentic top hat is considered a most desirable find. Evening clothing has changed little since the turn of the century, so the very early clothing (when found in good condition) is much in demand.

At various times a romantic look comes into style, and when this happens nightgowns from the Victorian and Edwardian period often enjoy a period of popularity with women. Usually of white cotton, fairly full, with lace and tucking, they are pretty, comfortable garments. However, when the romantic look is out, you tend to look as though you forgot to get dressed in the morning when you wear one. The shorter ones, and some of the more decorative men's nightshirts, can be worn under loose jumpers or long, full skirts. This gives the effect of a blouse and petticoat all in one piece, and is very charming with the right nightgown. When they are popular they become very pricey, but when out of style they can often be picked up at a fairly reasonable cost. I wore one to a Christmas Eve party one year, complete with my beloved boots, and someone said, "I don't know what you're wearing, but I sure like it!" The sleeveless versions are wonderfully comfortable to wear around the house in the summer time. Sort of the Edwardian version of the muumuu. (All vintage purists will please refrain from throwing tomatoes at me!)

Fur muffs, detachable collars, and fur capelets are sometimes found in usable condition, but more often than not the fur is too old and brittle to be practical. Fur muffs are pretty, practicable items and add immeasurably to a charming look for evening wear. Men's coats with fur collars are great treasures, but most were worn out at the time and few survive.

Some of the most popular vintage items right now are beaded silk georgette dresses from the teens. They are breathtakingly beautiful, high on the search lists of vintage collectors, and priced accordingly. In my opinion they have limited value as wearable garments because the dresses are extremely fragile. A friend invested three month's worth of spending money on an irresistible one, only to have it fall apart after two wearings. It now resides in a drawer, waiting for her to save up enough money for extensive renovation.

Not anyone's definition of a good bargain! If you found one and were tempted, I won't blame you if you fell, but don't say I didn't warn you. Wear it with modern shoes, but few accessories as it is very decorative on its own.

THE FLAPPER ERA, ROARING TWENTIES

Women's vintage clothing from the twenties is usually light, airy, and charming. On the surface, at least, it was a happy time, and women were enjoying lots of physical activities and freedom. Actually, while it's unusual to find tailored suits and dresses from the twenties, there were lots of them around at the time. There were women lawyers and doctors, school principals and shopkeepers, and it's interesting to keep an eye out for the clothing worn by these businesslike women of sixty years ago. For the most part, though, twenties vintage clothing will contribute more to the fun part of your wardrobe than the serious side.

Whenever styles change dramatically, as they did in 1909 and again in the early 1930's, there were not many options for altering the old styles into new ones. I realized that it was a hardship on the people of that time, but as a vintage clothing lover, and devotee of twenties clothing in particular, I am eternally grateful. The lowered waistlines, straight lines, and skirt detailing common to dresses from the twenties made them difficult to restyle into thirties fashions and therefore (comparatively) easy to find now in reasonable wearing condition.

I've rarely met a woman who wouldn't love to own a beaded twenties dress. This style may be considered one of the true classics in clothing. One dress can be worn, stored away, worn, then stored away, again and again. It isn't that they don't go out of style, they've been out of style for sixty years. They are unique enough, however, in that they transcend style. More importantly, they are fun. That's the good news. The bad news is that, like the silk beaded dresses of the late teens, they often are terribly fragile and expensive. However, there is more good news. Some of the twenties beaded dresses were made of rayon, which came into common use about this time, and those dresses are much sturdier. Even more good news is that the rayon beaded dresses are often less expensive than the silk ones. Some vintage clothing collectors still turn up their noses at rayon dresses, which clears the field for those of us who require durability. Take advantage of this, it may not last long.

While beaded evening dresses from the twenties are the most sought after, don't limit yourself to them. Other evening dresses from this period are also wonderful for playing dress up and usually far less costly. I have a darling blue chiffon velvet with a cascade of taffeta flowers on the skirt, and a black rayon crepe with draped skirt and rhinestone flower, that look as distinctive as any beaded dress. They are loose and comfortable, and are among my most beloved and wearable vintage garments. When you want to look absolutely individual you can't beat twenties evening clothes.

Day dresses from the twenties tend to look uncompromisingly like what they are. That's no reason not to wear one, but I'm not going to pretend that it'll fit right in without exciting some comment. On the other hand, many of the dresses feature embroidery and lace that looks wonderfully charming. One of the beauties of dresses from the twenties is that you don't have to be slender to wear them. They look wonderful, classy, and unusual on all body shapes. Even though the desirable body shape in the twenties was slim, bustless, and hipless, those lovely baggy dresses do disguise a variety of figure blips and bloops. I've seen twenties dresses that look great on women from size 9 to size 16 (and rising). It takes some looking to find the larger sizes, but it's worth it.

Remember that, while the twenties was a different world in terms of clothing and technology compared to the turn of the century, it was, after all, only twenty years later. A woman born in 1890 and trained to do embroidery, beading, and lacework at her mother's knee was only thirty years old in 1920. Much of the clothing and underwear, while different in overall design, still featured the beautiful handwork that these women were accustomed to. Since the clothing is twenty years newer to us, it's more likely to last for a while. In the realm of wearable old clothes every year counts.

Beaded blouses were very popular in the 1920's, and a number have survived intact. These blouses are very loose and floaty, usually of silk or silk georgette, and feature a very simple shape. Herein lies the rub: they often look much larger than they are. Before trying one on take a look at the sleeve, because it may fit a size 7, while the body is big enough to float loosely on a size 14. They look fabulous with Turkish harem pants or pleated silk pants on a day when you are feeling at least slightly glamorous and offbeat.

Once you've worn underwear from the 1920's, you'll wonder why women were ever willing to give it up. We're talking comfort on a high level. Now, you've probably seen the teddies that contemporary lingerie shops sell today, usually very sexy and certainly fitted to the body. If so, you're in for a culture shock when you see and wear a teddy from the 1920's. A direct descendant of the combinations or all-in-ones that we encounter from earlier in the century, the tops are skimpier and the legs shorter. They are designed to hang straight down from the bust and are extremely loose. Often they are hand embroidered and have lovely lace on them, and that includes the white cotton ones as well as the silks. A great fuss was made about them at the time, and they were considered sinful in many quarters. Sinful or no, women of all ages and shapes grabbed them up, and they were widely available. In the summer I wear teddies almost exclusively for underwear, because they cover up the essentials, while allowing a lot of airflow around the body. They make wonderful summer nightwear, if you can't quite get used to them as underwear.

I'm not forgetting silk and rayon stockings from this and earlier periods, in case you're wondering. I'm simply ignoring them. The reason is that they will usually fall apart under the stress of being put on. I'm all for old seamed stockings, but better to wait until we hit the forties and fifties, where there's a better chance for survival.

On to hats, cloches to be exact. I adore cloches from the 1920's and have enough to cover all of my heads, and then some. I also have to admit groaningly that they are one of the hardest hat styles to wear. First, because a hat that completely covers the head and allows little if any hair to peek out looks funny today. It can make you feel as though your face is hanging out, all naked. Second, cloches made the head appear smaller, which is the idea, but not a line perspective that we're used to. This is true, incidentally, even when wearing cloches with clothing from the 1920's. At fashion shows I find that models often will feel uncomfortable about the way a cloche looks, although they'll love it before they put it on. I think, however, that it is as much a matter of getting used to the look, as anything. I have a fabulous purple velvet cloche that I wear with a silk kimono, a line combination that works together and that can be worn for relatively informal sorts of occasions. A cloche also makes a good addition to the beaded blouse and Turkish pants outfit mentioned earlier. The cloches designed specifically for evening wear, made of luxurious velvets, satins, and brocades, with beaded or rhinestone decoration, make an enormous splash. Also look for crocheted evening hats, often beaded, a silly, lighthearted accessory. We've gotten so serious about everything, including our play, that you'll do everyone a favor at a party if you can pop in with a twenties evening hat and remind them that parties are supposed to be fun, for goodness sake!

The twenties were a time of glitz and glitter. Coco Chanel popularized costume jewelry, and most women had lots of it, so there's quite a lot available now. Most of us think of the long strings of beads, often in iridescent colors or jet, but there is much more to consider. Rhinestones were very popular in the twenties. Plastic jewelry also began to appear, and long gold chains were often worn, as well as beaded and feathered headbands. The headbands are an unexpected and elegant accent for a modern cocktail dress. The wonderful Art Deco jewelry of the twenties can be used as a focal point for any modern outfit with simple lines. Beaded bags were also popular in this period, and gold and silver mesh bags were a big part of the general love of glitter. Any of these fun accessories can be used to make clothing that we buy off the rack look original and unique, although the more dramatic and different looking pieces should be worn with very simple clothing. Let that one Art Deco necklace, feather headband, or string of lead crystal beads be the central feature.

A special mention should be made of the embroidered silk and rayon shawls that enjoyed popularity during the twenties. These are great buys, as they were seldom worn out (how do you wear out a shawl?), and are bright and charming with everything from evening clothes to jeans and a shirt. Bette Midler gave these shawls a moment of popularity in the seventies by sometimes wearing one tied around her hips, but they work just fine thrown casually over the shoulder. They are, I should warn you, the sort of thing that completely takes over, so should be worn with something simple. Here's a buying tip for them: Embroidered shawls that were identical to the ones from the twenties were popular as piano throws during the thirties and forties. They can sometimes be found in antique stores, labeled "piano scarf," for about one third the price of one labeled "embroidered shawl."

Shoes from the 1920's have a graceful shape, and although they usually have pointed toes, are comfortable. That's because, my dear, unlike the pointy toes of the late fifties and early sixties, the pointed part is designed as an add-on, sticking out past the toes. You weren't expected to cram the operating portion of your foot into a point. When you can find them in good condition to fit, you'll have a good looking shoe that you can wear not only with clothing of the period but with regular everyday clothes as well. If you can't find them, look into reproductions because no one should miss a chance to wear such a pretty style.

The men's look that we associate with the thirties and forties actually first appeared in the twenties. The pinstripe suit, single or double breasted, with nipped-in waist, was worn with little variation in cut for the next three decades. While you hear people talk about the gangster look of the thirties and forties, in reality the gangsters all got their start in the 1920's with prohibition. George Raft and James Cagney were carrying violin cases and rubbing out the opposition on the silver screen, while Al Capone and Arnold Rothstein did the same in real life. The felt fedora, wing-tipped shoes, and tuxedo adorned the stylish male and did for many years to come. The straw boater hat was still popular during most of the twenties and did continue into the thirties. When these are found in good condition, they can make a fun summer topping. Cloth caps were sportswear toppers, and some men are beginning to enjoy them again. However, men have to look hard for vintage versions, because women are picking up on them as well. Knickerbockers were common sportswear for both men and women, but few men can be coerced into wearing knickers now. The female of the 1980's has taken over vintage knickerbockers from both men and women's wardrobes. I like the men's best, baggy bottoms and all, because they are so roomy.

Few furs survived in good condition from this era, but of those that did the man's raccoon coat is probably the most popular and sought after. I don't know anyone who wears one around town, but these coats are enjoying a renaissance for cold weather football games and related events, and the vintage car enthusiasts always get a kick out of them. For women, muffs, which are more durable than earlier ones, are a nice find. Fur pieces complete with head and tails were worn all through the twenties, thirties, and forties. One day someone may figure out a creative use for these things; meanwhile, they're for wearing around your neck when you want beady, reproachful little eyes staring at you.

THE SAD, SILLY, SOMETIMES GLAMOROUS 1930's

We can still feel the effects of the Great Depression in the vintage clothing that we find, or more accurately, don't find from that era. Millions of people lived in poverty, so their clothing was worn until it fell apart. A woman I know told me this story about the thirties. She worked full time for $25 a month, and her husband made $40 a month. They supported four people on this income. In a moment of madness she went out and spent her full month's salary on a wonderful wool dress. She wore it almost daily for years, altering the neckline and cutting off the sleeves as they began to show wear. When it was finally completely worn out, the buttons were moved to another dress, and the fabric that was still in one piece used in a patchwork quilt. She claims that was the best dress she ever owned, and she never regretted her extravagance for a minute. This is typical of what happened to much of the nicer everyday clothing in the period. Scarcity is therefore a big factor when we look at vintage clothing from this period.

Dresses that we find from the thirties vary wildly in quality and style. Clothes worn by the rich were wonderfully designed and of good fabric, while the poor settled for cotton print house dresses or cheap, sleazy copies of designer models. The best of the dresses, when you can find them in decent condition, approach wearable art. They often feature intricate cutting and elegant, but unobtrusive, details such as pieced sleeves, skirts with bias cut panels or full bias cut, or unusual trim. Unfortunately, these unique dresses are not only rare, but they are also snapped up by collectors, so you are lucky indeed to find one. People new to vintage clothing often pass over them because they may look shapeless or straight on a hanger. But because of the bias cut, as soon as you put it on the dress will shape itself to your body. Wear these dresses with simple modern shoes on occasions when you want to project a distinctive, unusual, but sophisticated look.

The bias cut is basic to the long, slinky outline common to the

1930's. It was used to shape dresses from the humblest cotton to the most fabulous evening gowns. Bias cut means the fabric is cut diagonally across the grain, instead of the more standard straight up and down method. When the fabric is cut this way, it can stretch out enough to be pulled over the head, but clings gracefully to the body once it's on. Cutting on the bias requires more fabric and workmanship, and is therefore considerably more expensive than the more traditional cut. In the thirties, when prices and wages were low, it was possible to mass-produce bias cut clothing for a reasonable cost. That's something we'll never see again, so we have to take advantage of bias cut clothing from the thirties.

A picture of Jean Harlow in a clinging satin evening gown is the ultimate example of the bias cut, although it was also used for day dresses, nightgowns, and slips as well. The one drawback to a completely bias cut gown is that you need a perfect figure (and few or no undergarments) to carry it off—it clings to *every* curve whether you want it to or not. Happily, there are a number of dresses in existence that use bias cutting in lower skirts and sleeve inserts.

Print dresses are common finds from the thirties, replacing the beading and embroidery of previous times. Some of the prints are wild and wonderful with huge brightly colored flowers or silly scenes. I found a navy blue dress printed with birds sitting on signposts, and a friend treasures her thirties dresses that feature fruits and vegetables in gay profusion. The wilder ones are best worn with very plain shoes or boots at times when you feel up to being the center of attention. Quieter versions can look funky or elegant, depending on the print, with a jacket or lace collar and low heeled shoes.

Romantic pastel print dresses, most often of filmy silk cotton with huge floating collars and bias cut shaping, turn up occasionally. They are definitely for summer tea party sorts of events, complete with gloves and hat. There are people who adore the lowly print cotton house dresses of this period. They claim there is no vintage garment as cool, comfortable, and easy to wear. Vintage thirties addicts are the most dedicated and single-minded of all vintage lovers. Some wear no other clothing and swear that clothes from the thirties are the most attractive of all.

Despite the Depression (perhaps because of it), one area where clothing from the thirties shines is in evening clothes. Thanks to Hollywood and all those glamorous movies and movie stars, evening gowns were a real focus of the period. People who had any income at all owned evening wear and often surprisingly elegant stuff at that. The bias cut gave them sleek and flowing lines, and they were often deceptively simple in design. When detailed, the back was often the focal point.

Whether or not cut on the bias, a thirties evening gown is a wonderful investment. Outside of haute couture, there is no modern source of women's formal clothing to match the soft chiffon velvets, satins, taffetas, and laces inherited from the period. Don't neglect the rayon crepes with unusual sleeve treatments and intricate beading that will also turn up. We have been moving toward dressier looks for evening in recent years and thirties evening wear is perfect for the most dressed up of modern occasions. The styles are more modern in appearance than earlier dresses, but are still different enough to be unusual and distinctive. I've seen more than one authentic vintage thirties evening gown on actresses and other notables on the Academy Awards show on television. A bonus is that thirties dresses are available in a variety of sizes; small sizes still predominate, but medium and larger sizes show up regularly.

There are a couple of thirties evening styles that can be worn in more casual surroundings. One is the black velvet dress with a white lace collar, popular in the late thirties. These appear to have been worn primarily by older women and usually are mid-calf length with short sleeves. I have one that I've been able to wear on several occasions, appropriately toned down with my boots, and accented with a pink lead crystal necklace. My teenage daughter has a similar dress that she wears to semiformal dances with pumps and rhinestones. A versatile style indeed! Black lace evening dresses with matching jackets were a fad at one point, and often we bump into the lace jackets by themselves. The jackets can be paired with a silk T and skirt or slacks, or a plainish evening dress for a look that is formal but not too.

Men's evening clothing from the thirties is highly desirable right now and bodes to continue to be for the next few years. Similar in style to earlier clothing, it's easier to find in good condition and wearable sizes than the older versions. Rare is the man who can resist becoming suave, debonair, and charming under the influence of a well tailored thirties tuxedo. The demand for vintage men's evening wear is currently so high that reproductions of the suits and accessories are being manufactured. This means the lucky man who finds an authentic vintage tailcoat that fits can purchase reproductions of the appropriate shirt, vest or cummerbund, bow tie, and shoes to go along with it.

It's unusual to find a woman's suit with both pieces from the thirties. More often the jacket survives alone and can be worn exactly as you would a blazer with a shirt and slacks or skirt. The tailored suit as we know it comes from this period, and often a genuine thirties suit jacket is indistinguishable from a modern one, with its lightly padded shoulders and long, lean lines. Those lucky enough to find an entire suit in good condition can usually mix it with up-to-date shoes and purse.

Pretty silk or rayon crepe tailored blouses of this era are very similar to the ones we wear. They sometimes feature a subtle touch of embroidery or lace, seldom enough to detract from the businesslike effect. My favorite vintage blouse is a tailored cream rayon crepe with cream embroidery. It was in shaky condition when I bought it five years ago, but is so lovely that I've been nursing it along carefully ever since. The longish straight skirt of the thirties had a kick pleat for easy movement. These skirts are often cut beautifully, and give a long, leggy look to the wearer. This style of skirt comes in and out of fashion fairly often, so I wouldn't pass one up if I found it to fit. If you can't wear it this year, I'll give odds you can pull it out in the next season or two.

Men's suits were essentially the same style throughout the twenties, thirties, and forties, although the majority of those we find actually date from the forties. Some discussion of them belongs in the thirties section, because this is the decade that gives the ambience to the pinstriped suit, fedora, and trenchcoat. A man dressed in vintage style is projecting the tough sexiness of Humphrey Bogart, the masculine sexiness of Clark Gable, or the suave sexiness of Cary Grant, as they appeared on the silver screen in the thirties. This was the era of the gorgeous but highly individual male, and it's a rare man who doesn't look wonderful and feel even better dressing up in vintage clothing from this period. The thirties saw the addition of the colorful wide necktie, often handpainted. These ties are sought after by women as well as men and are currently enjoying a renaissance with teenage boys.

Sunsuits from the thirties and forties are considerably more covered up than we're used to, but have a charm all their own. Shorts were usually cut with wider, longer legs and are flattering to those of us whose thighs are better hidden. Halters and shorts usually came in sets, although we normally only find one or the other intact. They are often of soft cotton and feature the bright, charming thirties prints. I know someone who found a complete halter and shorts set from this period and liked it so much that she made a pattern from them, and has made all her summer sun clothes from it ever since.

Hats from the 1930's fit right in with modern clothing. Some of them are a touch on the extreme side, granted, but for the most part the straws and felts, particularly the fedora and slouch hat of the period, are the styles being copied by modern hat companies. These hats are good "starter" hats for when you first begin to venture out wearing a hat and want one that is not quite as distinctive as those of earlier periods. An exception is the little tilty hat, which appeared in the late thirties, and never fails to draw attention to itself. I have faith, however, that at some point the rest of the world will come to its senses about hats, and we'll feel just fine with a bunch of flowers cocked happily over one eye. It's hard being a fashion torchbearer! Wear thirties hats with suits and day dresses, as they nicely complement the lines of modern clothing.

One of the things that lured me into vintage clothing in the first place was the luxury of silk underwear, specifically the thirties tap pants and bias cut slips. Price silk or rayon satin underwear at a lingerie shop, and you'll hussle right out to buy some vintage versions. Now, some folks feel a little uncomfortable at the thought of wearing used underclothes, particularly such intimate versions. However, they are so comfortable and sensible that if you can overcome your reluctance you'll be glad you did. Silk and rayon bias cut slips are the last word in comfort; there isn't a nylon tricot slip in existence that comes close. Even when I'm dressed to the teeth in modern gray flannel, I always have silk bias cut underthings from the thirties on my person as a reminder that the real me is a creature of luxury.

Some silk and rayon bias cut nightgowns are pretty and opaque enough to be worn as slinky evening dresses by the brave. I admit that I'm not up for this myself, although Jean Harlow got her start this way. It really depends on you, your figure, and the circles you travel in. In my crowd you'd be taken aside and tactfully told that you forgot your dress. However, for use as intended—sleepwear—they are the ultimate in comfort and looks. During a serious illness I entertained visitors clad in a pale blue silk bias-cut nightgown, covered by a matching bedjacket edged in lace. I looked much healthier than I was, and the soft silk gown felt wonderful on my aching body. Bias cut silk and rayon sleepwear are an ultimate sensual experience, and you owe it to yourself to try them out. Men's silk and rayon pajamas can be found occasionally. Women have been grabbing them up all along, but when the gentlemen among us started developing an interest in vintage clothing, the competition for these items became fierce. A man enjoys a touch of luxury too!

Silk and rayon bedjackets are nice for reading in bed. Since they have to be handwashed and carefully pressed, most of us prefer to use them sparingly for that purpose. During a hospital stay, when you know visitors are going to see you doing your best Camille, they can be a boon. And they feel one heck of a lot better than the cotton hospital gowns provided by our local healers! Depending on the general frilliness of the particular bed jacket, consider popping one on with a silk T-shirt and skirt or slacks. They also have possibilities for evening wear, again frilliness and pastelness being a consideration.

Some people are establishing serious collections of plastic jewelry from the thirties. Leaving them to it, you and I can have some fun with the wide plastic bracelets, necklaces, and pins as wearable items. It takes an expert, incidentally, to tell the difference between plastics of the twenties, thirties, or forties. So I'm going generic on this one and putting them in the middle. Some of the plastic pins are miracles of whimsy and charm. You'll find them shaped like fruit, animals, birds, umbrellas, cartoon characters, and innumerable other delightful images. Just for fun, they look delightful on suits, coats, denim jackets, and sweater vests. They can also be tucked on plain felt hats to add some variety. I saw a woman wearing a fur coat with a huge, gorgeous, thirties enamel and rhinestone pin and the effect was glamorous. I couldn't bring myself to poke holes through any of my furs (I'm casual only to a point), but if you don't have the same hesitation, you might try it. This jewelry looks playful and should be used in that way. Other, more serious, plastic pieces are made to resemble jade, ivory, or tortoise shell. The necklaces can be charming, but subtle, with contemporary clothing.

There was a fad for old-fashioned looking costume jewelry in the thirties, and lots of the pieces we find that look old really date from this period. These pieces cost less, or should, than the real Victorian jewelry, but look every bit as lovely. Amethyst, amber, ruby, green, and bright blue glass imitation stones tend to look delightfully fraudulent in intricate imitation gold settings. Wear them with a suntan and a simple white blouse, and you'll look divine. Carved ivory (real or fake) bracelets and necklaces from the thirties are subtle, elegant touches with suits or silk shirts and slacks. Jewelry companies are currently making imitations of these imitation antique pieces, and it's very difficult to determine whether you've got a modern fake or a thirties' fake or even an early 1900's fake. Unless you're sure, don't spend too much money on any one piece.

Rhinestone jewelry is on its way out of style at this point, and it will be interesting to see what happens to the prices in the next year or so. Rhinestones were popular from the twenties through the fifties, then disappeared into children's dress-up boxes and junk drawers until the early eighties. It was common to pick up a handful of rhinestone necklaces and pins for a dollar or two at rummage sales, and many were thrown away. Then they became so popular that imitations were made by several large companies, some types of vintage rhinestone jewelry became collectible, and prices grew astronomical. Now rhinestones languish in vintage stores and the fickle public is finding the plastics and antique-looking pieces more to their liking. However, if you like the glitz and glitter of rhinestones, don't let this trouble you a bit. As a long-time vintage clothing lover said, "I wore rhinestones before they were popular. I wore rhinestones when they were popular. I intend to wear rhinestones after they go out of style. I may be buried in my rhinestones. I like rhinestones!" A noble attitude, and one well worth emulating. If there's anything this world needs, it's an occasional touch of glitter. So grab it where you can and ignore those who try to dim your light.

I want to mention gloves at this point, because there were some particularly nice glove styles dating from the thirties. Gloves older than the thirties rarely will stand being worn, no matter what they're made of. Gloves have to stretch to go on the hands, and very early gloves will often fall apart when you put them on. However, the crocheted cotton gloves that were popular during this time seem to hold up to being worn, and they are pretty with summer clothes. Gloves with wide, flared cuffs, known as "gauntlets," became popular in the early thirties. These are the most elegant and charming of all gloves, whether made of crochet, cloth, or leather. They make a perfect accent piece with modern suits and coats. Gloves are returning to the fashion scene in a big way. Unique and interesting new gloves cost a fortune, but vintage versions can still be found at comparably low prices. I suggest keeping an eye out for vintage gloves and stocking up while you've got the chance.

Fur coats from the late thirties are just barely within the fifty year wearable range for fur coats. The waist-length fuzzy chubbies (usually made of fox or raccoon) from this period are much coveted by vintage clothing devotees. They have a regrettable tendency to make you look short and squatty unless you're six feet tall, but that apparently was the purpose. Most women nowadays wear them with slacks, which helps considerably with the appearance.

The thirties produced some glamorous and wonderfully shaped fur collars. If you're thinking of those miserable baggy coats with a three inch wide strip of mink sewn to the neckline when I mention fur collars, think again. Those are fifties and sixties relics and dull as dull can be. In the thirties the most elegant suits and coats were often accented with fur, not only collars, but cuffs, pockets, and even partial bodices, as well. Rare indeed is the fur trimmed suit or coat that has survived, but many of the trims were removed when the garment expired. These trims constitute one of the best buys in vintage clothing right now, as they are usually priced reasonably and there is currently little demand for them. I predict that this will change in the next few years, and recommend you keep an eye out for fur pieces that you like and buy them now.

THE FABULOUS FORTIES, WWII, PROSPERITY RETURNS

The style of clothing that we associate with the forties actually covers the years from 1938 to 1946: from the beginning of World War II in Europe to the return of most of the American troops from the South Pacific. For the sake of concise communication, however, I'm going to use the term "forties." With World War II came more jobs, higher paying jobs, and more spending money. To us that means people bought more and better clothes, and were less likely to wear them into rags. Thanks to this circumstance, there are great quantities of forties clothing available, much of it in very good condition.

WWII affected the clothing we've inherited in other ways as well. Cloth and metal were rationed, which made a difference in things like skirt lengths, types of fabrics (silk was used for parachutes, not dresses), jewelry, and hat trims. Most important of all was the effect on style. There is a strong connection between women's lifestyles during the war years and during the present. Millions of women today are the only adults in the household, and millions more work for a living, married or not. During the forties that was also true for the first time in history. Much of the clothing that women wore then is exceptionally suited for our current way of life; well tailored, businesslike, practical to care for, and attractive. A woman who admires vintage clothing, but knows lace and frills are not for her, owes it to herself to look carefully through forties vintage garments. This might be just what she's looking for.

Then as now, suits were a major item in most women's wardrobes. You stand a reasonable chance of finding both jacket and skirt intact, which is something to celebrate. Many of the suits can pass for modern, and the especially well designed ones look like current designer models. One dedicated lady I know wears nothing but forties gabardine suits to her office. She must own thirty of them! You're more likely, however, to encounter the jackets by themselves, and there seem to be millions of them around. Forties jackets are a major vintage clothing item. You are likely to find one or more to fit; they will wear well, and they fit nicely into our current lives.

The term "forties jacket" is wildly generic and covers a multitude of styles. Padded shoulders are always included but they can vary from the super football type to a more natural line. A forties jacket can have standard lapels, asymmetrical lapels, beaded lapels, or no lapels. It can be long and full, long with a nipped in waist, end just below the waist, or have a peplum. It can have velvet inserts, fur trim, shoulder detailing, full sleeves, cuffed sleeves, or fitted sleeves. In other words, the possibilities for finding a forties jacket that will accent your wardrobe are almost limitless. Get into the habit of searching them out and always, always try them on. A jacket may look relatively plain on the hanger, but jump into a spectacular and stylish shape on you. I must own thirty of the little darlings and move them in and out of my current wardrobe as fashion changes. I wear them with jeans to the grocery store; sometimes to parties; with modern skirts, straight, pleated or full; for everything from board meetings to wedding receptions.

One year I lived in a short black wool forties jacket that had velvet inserts along the front, no lapels, and was fitted to just below the waist. I wore it with mid-calf length print skirts, either with my beloved boots or with black suede ankle strap forties shoes. It went everywhere and always looked wonderful. The following year I noticed a layout in Vogue showing an outfit that was almost identical. By accident I had made my mark as a person on the cutting edge of fashion. Imagine! The lovely thing about these pieces, aside from their versatility, is that they are usually remarkably sturdy. You get the fun of wearing them, without having to be careful about moving your arms. It's also reasonable to wear one for a year or two, then tuck it away when it goes out of style for a while, in the confidence that you'll find it in good condition when you want it again.

There was a clothing item called a redingote during this period that you may come across. It is long, cut like a coat, but slightly more fitted and of lighter material. This style was worn over a blouse and skirt, and is extremely flattering to less than perfect figures. Wear it as they did originally, with blouse and skirt, or in a more up-to-date look with slacks. I noticed that some of the fashion magazines are starting to mention them as a coming style, and one major designer showed several in his collection, so do prepare for them to be a fashion item again.

Forties dresses can be as variable as the jackets. With fabric rationed and federal regulations controlling how much cloth could be used for what, some of them are remarkably plain. While you may run into more brown crepe shirtwaists than you have any need of, you will also bump into dresses cut with peplums, side drapes on the skirt, and wonderful tucking and gathering on the bodice. Length can be the biggest problem, as most day dresses from 1939 to 1947 were knee length. Modern skirt lengths tend to move up and down every few years, and when they're down, the knee length forties dresses feel off balance in shape. When knee length is in, forties dresses look wonderful, and the print ones work well with modern blazers. Some forties day dresses are longer, particularly the ones toward the end of the period, and these can look equally good when fashion dictates longer skirts. Wear a forties dress with current shoes and accessories just as you would a modern dress. For sort of dressed-up evenings, when you don't want to be too formal but do want to look special, a forties day dress with ankle strapped shoes, outrageous hat, bag, and gloves all in period is perfect. This is one time when a period costume look works perfectly for noncostume occasions.

The beautiful print fabrics of the thirties were still available, although most forties versions are somewhat toned down. In recent years we've been unable to buy off-the-rack print clothing in dressier fabrics. Women who like prints have gone without or been reduced to cotton dresses, which can be terribly tacky in the business world. Forties rayon crepe print dresses can fill the void, as not only is the fabric more suitable, but also the prints are more sophisticated. I know a lady who wears forties print rayon dresses to the office, tactfully tucked under up-to-date blazers and jackets. She's done this for years and the only comment she hears is "How do you find such fabulous print dresses?" No one has ever suspected they are forty-plus years old!

Despite wartime rationing, there are a lot of wonderful evening dresses from the 1940's. Most are full length, but there was a period when mid-calf skirts were in style as well. Often beaded, frequently featuring draping and pleating, tucks and gathers, they look totally beautiful. Many modern dress shops sell evening clothing now that is similar to these dresses. Evening clothes of the forties was made for adult women. These dresses have a sophisticated aura about them and tend to be less dressy than the thirties. For a long time I wore these dresses with my boots, in an effort to keep them from looking too dressed up. Everyone else was wearing jeans to the symphony, for goodness sake! But in the last couple of years I've been wearing them with forties or modern evening shoes and not feeling one bit out of place. This is a good example of how changing modern styles affect the vintage styles and make them wearable.

Depending on the type of fur, fur coats have an average lifespan of up to fifty years, so forties era fur coats usually have a few years of life left in them, making them a worthwhile investment. Oftentimes forties fur coats were imaginatively styled. They nearly always had the wide padded shoulders, and many had unusual sleeves and collars. The linings and buttons of forties fur coats were sometimes their most appealing features. It's not uncommon to find a coat with a lining that is embroidered and appliquéd, and others come with lovely brocades. Length can be a problem, as forties furs were knee length, and the first batch of modern fur coats has been mid-calf. Some women have tackled this problem by cutting off forties coats to make jackets, but I urge you to think before doing this. Skirt lengths go up and down like window shades, and two years from now you may regret taking such a drastic step.

Fur jackets, capes, and stoles are common finds from the forties era. Jackets are very desirable right now, meaning, of course, that the prices are going up, but stoles and capes can still be purchased for relatively modest prices. Capes and stoles are not in fashion at this time, but that will likely change in time. When you find one you like, consider purchasing it now to be used later.

For many styles of hats it's impossible to tell whether one is from the thirties or forties. This is particularly true of the felt fedoras and other styles that we see in new clothing stores right now. Some of the more distinctive forties hats have feathers shooting up at improbable angles or are immense sculptures of felt that stick straight up from the head. These hats come under the category of fun hats. I like to wear them when I'm going to a play, with an appropriate forties dress and bag, or out for cocktails or other semiformal occasions. There is certainly no way to claim these hats look modern, so if you like them, you have to make occasions to wear them. I must say that they never go unnoticed, so you'd best be prepared to arouse some curious glances and friendly comment. Turbans often date from the forties, and they're occasionally festooned with fruit or flower trims. Turbans are extremely practical for days when your hair absolutely refuses to behave itself properly.

Jewelry from the 1940's is for the fun and young at heart. During the war metal was in demand for airplanes, ships, and bullets, so much of the jewelry was made of plastic or wood. You'll find chokers made of plastic strawberries, necklaces of wooden flowers, and big plastic bracelets. Certainly there were also pieces made of metal, but not as frequently as other materials. My very favorite forties piece is a 7 inch long enameled parrot, with rhinestone feathers. The silliest of the forties costume jewelry pieces are fun to wear when everything else you've got on is far too serious.

When they came home, American servicemen stationed in Hawaii often brought back Hawaiian print shirts for themselves, and dresses for their wives and sweethearts. Hawaiian shirts of the forties have been popular with men and women for years. Some of the silk and rayons from that time are now considered collectible, and hence very valuable. The Hawaiian print dresses have been largely ignored until now, but are just beginning to be discovered. Some have sarong-type skirts and small jackets, others a simple, almost Oriental appearance. Made of lightweight rayon crepe, these are fun, cool summer dresses, worn with modern sandals and silly jewelry.

There were other fads and passing clothing fancies in the forties, remnants of which appear in vintage clothing stores today. The popularity of the western movie in the forties brought on a bout of cowboy clothes. Fringed suede or leather jackets, boots, cowboy hats, and western style shirts can still be found, and go through periods of being in style. These were garments that seemed to be competely without charm or merit for years, then all of a sudden everyone wants them. Aviator jackets and military style clothing also go in and out. Admittedly, one has to have either a certain flair or a love of funk to wear them successfully, but if you've got one or t'other, stock up during the slow periods. Then pair a leather aviator jacket with your jeans and swagger around with class.

Alligators and crocodiles were put on the endangered species list in the sixties and have only recently been taken off. I guess the powers-that-be realized that these giant lizards are much pleasanter company made up into shoes and purses, rather than roaming the countryside eating small children and dogs. Alligator and crocodile make elegant looking, and remarkably sturdy, shoes and bags and these were very popular during the forties. The shoes and purses that have survived are often in very good condition and surprisingly current. With new alligator and crocodile shoes and accessories selling for hundreds of dollars, these very usable forties vintage pieces are definitely bargains. Lizard was also popular then, as it is now, but tread carefully when buying vintage pieces made of it. It is less durable than alligator and crocodile and won't last as long.

Another typical forties purse is the corde bag. The fabric is constructed of rows of braid (black, dark brown, or navy blue) sewn together, and it is very hard wearing. The most desirable have enormous clasps or decorative zipper pulls of clear plastic. I love these bags and use them most of the time, never failing to get compliments on them. Lots of people have never seen a corde bag and always want to know where to get one as soon as they do.

Shoes from the forties are sturdy and wearable, often very clunky looking, but very comfortable. Shoes were made with some regard for the shape of the foot, so the front of the shoe will actually hold a human foot. You may find that you wear a full size, or at least a half size, smaller in a forties shoe than you do in a modern shoe. Forties shoes will also amaze you by how long they wear—during the war it was hard to get new shoes and the ones people bought had to last. The evening shoes, however, can be more graceful looking and are well worth having. Most of us adore the ankle strap wedgies, known in some circles as "Joan Crawford go to hell shoes." We are talking sexy shoes here, and they look fabulous with all kinds of outfits from daytime to evening. Spectator pumps and slings (two tone shoes most often of white with navy, brown, or black) are becoming popular again, and the forties versions fit right in.

By now I hope I've convinced everyone that men's clothing from this period is perfect for modern dressing. I know, you conservative old things, that it takes a bit of crust to try them out, but I promise you won't be sorry. Here's a case in point. I have a friend who rented a forties suit for Halloween and liked it so much he asked me to look for one for him. I found a nice navy pinstripe that fit perfectly. He thought it was great—but never dreamed he'd use it for a serious occasion. Last year he wore it to a big company party and was *the* fashion hit of the evening. Everyone, male and female, oohed and ahhed and generally carried on about how wonderful he looked. For men, like women, vintage clothing is a hit. Men's vintage overcoats from the forties have also jumped into mainstream fashion in a big way. Women first discovered them as the good-looking, well made items they are, and more recently men themselves have begun snapping them up for everyday apparel.

THE FIFTIES LOOK, THE SOLDIERS ARE HOME AND MOM IS BACK IN THE KITCHEN

In 1947 came the Dior look, which took the world by storm and is the look that we generally mean when we talk about the fifties. The shoulders on women's clothing were narrower and more rounded, waists were tinier, and longer, fuller skirts became fashionable. Nylon was the new miracle fiber, replacing silk and rayon in women's underwear, stockings, blouses, and dresses seemingly overnight. As wearable clothing today, some of the fifties fashions are especially timely, since some major designers are taking ideas from that period and using them with a lavish hand in modern garments. The fifties are the most recent vintage period to come into style, and there are a lot of fifties treasures around. Most of the things we'll be talking about are easy to find, and nearly as important, less costly than many early vintage pieces. Their condition is also uniformly better so care is easier. If you've been thinking about buying something vintage but are hesitant to take the plunge, clothing from this era may well be a good way to get your feet wet.

Teenagers were the first to appreciate fifties vintage clothing, and clothes from this period continue to be very popular with them. Those of you who have teenage friends or relatives for whom you occasionally buy presents, might make note of some ideas from this chapter. On Christmas and birthdays when you're stumped for a gift (short of a Ferrari, which always goes over well with this age group), a garment from this era might be an answer.

The fifties saw the last of the beautifully tailored women's suits. Well designed suits didn't reappear again until our own era. Many women prefer the fifties suits and jackets to earlier styles, because the shoulders aren't so padded and they look less extreme for business wear. Suit jackets from the fifties have less versatility than earlier ones, because they look like *suit* jackets. Most forties jackets work well with slacks, but the fifties variety have a tendency to look as though they should have a matching skirt. They are usually cut to emphasize the waist and are cut short (a little below the waist) with lightly padded shoulders. When you find a jacket you like that's missing its skirt, try a plain, straight skirt in a contrasting color. Pleated skirts sometimes work very nicely, as do long full skirts. These jackets look best with skirts mid-calf or below and very simple, collarless blouses.

When we think of the fifties, circle skirts are often the first things to pop into our minds. Appliquéd felts, particularly the ones with poodles or scotty dogs, are almost a cliché and much in demand for costume parties and fifties retro events. While these are charming and fun, circle skirts that are handpainted or resist-dyed are more practical. Many women leave circle skirts to the young, but I'd like to make a plea for this attractive skirt among the less youthful and funk oriented. The style is flattering to many figure types, and the variety of prints and colors is almost endless. They look good on the slender and also on those who come equipped with hips. Many of the designs are really gorgeous and can be fashion assets. Pair your bright print circle skirt with a modern or vintage short jacket and add boots or flat shoes. For summer a sleeveless silk T-shirt and pretty sandals are nice, undemanding accessories.

Fifties sweaters are wonderful for now. Cashmere pullovers and cardigans from that era vary little in style from their modern derivatives. Sweater sets, when you can find both pieces in good condition, are completely usable. Bring them home and put them on with a pleated skirt or your jeans. Add fake pearls (real if you can afford them), and you'll look wonderfully ladylike. Men's cashmere V-neck sweaters are popular with men, women, and teenagers of both sexes.

Beaded sweaters are probably the most consistently in demand vintage item. Vintage dealers tell me they can sell as many as they get, and this has been true for a few years. Be wary, beaded sweaters have a way of creeping up on you. They come in a variety of different colors, with all sorts of beading designs. If you're not careful, you'll find yourself buying "just one more, because I don't have a red one," and pretty soon you'll have a dozen. I know someone who wears them with full fifties paraphernalia, and another friend who has a couple that are strictly for evening wear. They are also fun with jeans and a shirt, and look good with a simple skirt and blouse for casual events. This is another fifties style that teenage girls adore. You'll win a friend for life it you give your favorite fifteen-year-old (or even twelve-year-old) one as a Christmas or birthday present.

Men's fifties suits and sports jackets were cut long with broad shoulders. They were single breasted with wide lapels and while cut loose, designed to suggest a narrow waist. The trendy young like to wear these jackets with casual slacks or jeans and the sleeves pushed up to the elbow. Teenage boys are devouring jackets from this period, and some young women enjoy wearing them as well. At the end of the fifties came short, straight suits and jackets with high lapels, which are now also coming back into style. The skinny necktie also dates from later in this period and is enjoying a renaissance. Saddle shoes,

V-neck cashmere pullovers, and button-down oxford cloth shirts are all fifties fashion items that men are picking up on. Letter sweaters and jackets from the 1950's are being grabbed up by some eighties teenagers, especially boys with crew cuts. (The new name for the crew cut, I'm reliably informed, is "astro turf.") Don't neglect the white sports coat (with or without pink carnation) for dances.

Until recently I would have dismissed dresses from the fifties as too recent to be interesting. Okay for the funky but not really right for anything else. Then I bumped into the most elegant women I know who said, "Do you like my dress? It was my mother's in the fifties!" It was gray wool with a V-neck, three quarter sleeves, and had a full mid-calf length skirt. The original dickey (a detachable collar that fits inside the neckline) was missing, so Beth had used a paisley scarf in its place. She looked her usual elegant self, and frankly, unless she'd said something, you'd never have known it was an oldie. This is how trends get started, and I have to admit, I'm ready to be converted. Look for tailored dresses from early in the period, as later dresses are usually of the fitted sheath or chemise type and are not yet ready to take their places as modern fashions. I should qualify the last statement. I've noticed a few teenage girls wearing fifties sheath dresses lately, so we may see a revival of this style in the next few years.

The little black dress was an important evening garment. Whether fitted, with draping on the skirt, or with a full ballerina skirt, these dresses look perfect right now. They are suitable as evening wear for professional women who like a tailored look, because they are usually simply styled but still definitely formal. Strapless, full-skirted gowns in florals and pastels, satins and taffetas, which are more feminine than the little black dresses, can be found fairly easily, so the chance to shine as a fashion leader is upon you. Grab the chance, and go shopping for your next evening dress in a vintage clothing shop. Evening suits for women were very popular, and when you can find one with both pieces, they work perfectly for the corporate executive. I can't figure out why modern designers have not come up with this sort of garment themselves. It makes such good sense for women who have to entertain for business.

Prom dresses from the fifties are selling like hotcakes, although this trend is still new enough that bargains can occasionally be found in thrift stores. Three years ago you couldn't give away a vintage prom dress, but the recent movement toward formal dances at high schools and colleges has turned this around completely. Formal gowns are nearly always in very good condition, as they were worn only once or twice and then stored away. The nylon lace versions are virtually indestructible, as I can testify. A few years ago I bought a white nylon lace prom dress for my youngest daughter's dress-up box (she was eight-years-old). When she was twelve her best friend wore it to be a princess in a school play, and this year my (almost) grown-up daughter pulled it out to wear for her first formal high school dance. It was still in perfect condition and exactly in style with the other prom dresses at the dance. I'd say I got my $5 worth, wouldn't you? Of course, now that prom dresses are desirable vintage items, it's not too likely you'll find one for $5, but they're still less costly than the newer versions.

In the early 1950's came the prettiest and most comfortable shoes ever made—even including the lovely twenties shoes. Frequently of the sandal variety, they have all the comfort and sturdiness of the clompy forties shoe but are more flattering. How anyone could have gone from these slightly rounded shoes to the toe-killing pointies in the late fifties escapes me! I could write poems to these shoes. As with other fifties fashions, they are easy to find and not yet especially costly.

Gloves are good fifties items to add to your current wardrobe. They were worn everywhere by everybody for every sort of occasion and survive in great profusion. You'll find beaded and plain evening gloves in lengths from short to long, medium length gloves with sheering, and short daytime gloves with buttons, bows, and lace inserts. They come in all colors from pastel yellow to black and occasionally in plaids or stripes. All the major modern designers are showing gloves, many of which are distinctive in style. Fifties gloves will give you a head start when this fashion accessory hits the general market. Vintage clothing stores always carry gloves, but they have not been a big selling item, so you may find a basketful stuck under a shelf or on the back of the counter. Ask if you don't see them. It's still possible to find decent looking fifties gloves in thrift stores; at a rummage sale recently, I found five pairs of very nice gloves for $1 each. This is a good time to stock up for the future.

Lingerie underwent a dramatic change after WWII, which is a blessing for vintage clothing lovers. Nylon became available and was used for stockings, slips, and nightgowns. Silk and rayon were relegated to the back of the closet. As a result, it is often possible to find old silk stockings and rayon or silk slips that have never been worn, sometimes in their original boxes. These finds are happening less as the years go along, but they still are possible. Silk stockings are *the* most wonderful thing that the vintage world offers. Imagine a whole day on your feet without feeling sticky or clammy. Even though you need a garter belt to hold them up, they're still worth it. Seamed nylons are starting to attract devotees too. Not as comfortable as silk or rayon, they do look nice worn with vintage fashions. Vintage nylons are only now beginning to move from the garage sale level to the vintage clothing store arena, so they're easy to find in thrift stores. Vintage silk and rayon stockings are harder to locate, but I've come across boxes of them at various times and they are well worth searching out. Because of the demand, some major stocking manufacturers are beginning to make seamed nylon stockings, and seamed pantyhose are also showing up in lingerie specialty shops. Modern silk stockings cost an arm and a leg, often $30 a pair or more.

FINALE

You are all asking yourselves "Is she really going to stop here? Aren't people wearing clothes from the late fifties and early sixties? How about minis?" Well, guys, one thing you've got to deal with in a book is the personal, unreasonable prejudices of the author. And you've bumped up against one. I think that both men's and women's clothing is terminally dull after the early fifties, with the possible exception of the mini skirt. Oh, how I regret my careless passing on of the cutest mini maternity dress that ever (barely) covered an expectant mother. It's a wonder the baby wasn't born with chilblain! However, we have to stop somewhere, and I'm gosh darned if I'm going to deal with ten-year-old clothing as vintage. A person has some pride!

CHAPTER THREE

HATS! YES, HATS. AH, HATS. HATS!

I suppose I'd best confess right up front that I love hats and that this is not an unbiased presentation. The world, if I may be forgiven a bit of philosophy, would be a better place with a few more hats in it. So what are we waiting for? There are many advantages to wearing hats: you feel like you look special (and you do), you have a reason to hold up your head and walk with a touch of class, and you'll get fewer traffic tickets. This last I report from personal experience. I don't know what the psychological reason is, but I know for sure that most policemen hesitate to give tickets to women wearing hats. Maybe it's because we remind them of their aunts and grandmothers. Whatever the reason, it's not to be belittled!

A glimmering of renewed interest in hats is stirring in the land, and I'm an advocate of pushing this along. Vintage hats, obviously, are a perfect place to start, as there are many more choices in style than are being shown in new ones. If you'll forgive a small tantrum, designers of new hats have gotten hung up on a few basic shapes. The only way they can achieve individuality is by making hats in a variety of colors, many of which look simply awful so close to the face. A choice between twenty hats, all pretty much the same shape, but varying from magenta to bright yellow to black is not much of a choice. Vintage hats are nearly always muted in colors but come in an enormous variety of shapes and sizes. There's still plenty of scope for color, but it's less likely to be a color that will drown out your face. A hat can be a wonderful accessory to make you look good. By picking the right hat, you can improve your appearance dramatically.

It takes a touch of dash to wear a hat because we're still not accustomed to seeing them out and about regularly. But who doesn't need some pizzazz in his or her life? It also helps to have some hat wearing tips. After all, many men and women in their thirties and forties have never worn a hat except as protection from cold or sun. Younger folks aren't sure that anything but a bandanna or ski hat is proper. Hats as adornments and flattering accessories are a brand new notion to lots of us.

A hat can quickly overwhelm an outfit, which can be good. People are so unused to seeing hats that they will often focus on the hat and won't notice that the suit or dress has been around the track more than a few times. However, you are supposed to be wearing the hat, not the other way round. Once you learn how to choose and wear a hat to suit your look and accent the clothes you wear, your comfort level will improve dramatically.

A hat can be a complicated piece of clothing because you have to consider both the close-up effect and the long range view. When you're talking to people, they will focus on your face, hat, and shoulder line. From a distance the hat will be a part of and will influence the overall shape you project. In both cases a well chosen hat can enhance your appearance and help minimize points you'd like to pass unnoticed. It isn't enough that the hat "matches your outfit"; that's a very small part of the effect.

Keep in mind that your hat will emphasize whatever shape it repeats or is exactly opposite to it. For example, if you have a broad, round face and wear a broad, round hat, you'll resemble a bowling ball rather than a woman of fashion. At the same time, put a tall, thin hat on the same head, and you've got an upside down, ice cream cone effect. A woman with an oval shaped face and regular features can wear any style of hat, and lucky she is! For others there are some types of hat that not only look "okay," but actually improve appearance.

A medium brim slouch hat, tilted slightly, will look wonderful on a round face. It will keep the eye from following the circular line of the face. Another hat that breaks the line and looks particularly pert and sassy on a roundish shaped face is the small, tilted hat of the late thirties and early forties. Designed to perch over one eye and often sporting a sprightly trim, it's a charming young look when worn by someone with definite cheeks. And if you've got dimples . . . expect to be admired! Rounded face women should avoid wearing a veil over the face, as it cuts the face in half and makes the lower part look plumper. Instead throw the veil back over the hat as though you've just tucked it up for a minute. Turbans tend to emphasize the shape of the face, particularly the lower part, so if you're sensitive about your cheeks and chin, don't choose one. Broad brims should be avoided by wearers with circular faces as they are unmistakably round. However, if you simply can't resist, choose one that can be tilted at an extreme angle.

For a thin face a half veil is a good choice, as it gives the optical illusion of widening the face. Thin faced women should look for a hat that gives a horizontal line, rather than a vertical one. When you tilt your hat, tilt it only slightly; then the eye will not travel straight up and down but at a crosswise angle. Hats that have trim that sticks out to the side are good for thin faces, as are medium brims worn as straight as possible on the head. Hats with very broad brims will emphasize the thinness of a face, and tilting them will not lessen the effect. Turbans are not a good choice for the same reason folks with round faces should avoid them: the face hangs right out with nothing to soften it or enhance the shape.

Women with a distinctive feature that they want to de-emphasize, like a distinguished schnozzola or a prominent square chin, have to tread carefully among hat shapes. As I said above, you want to avoid repeating the shape that you're disguising and also avoid the exactly opposite shape. Any trim that is long and narrow, like a single feather or plume, will draw direct attention to a long nose or chin. At the same time a too small hat will look out of proportion to a large or prominent feature and will force the eye toward it. Trims can help de-emphasize a large nose, as long as they cover the entire hat and don't point in any one direction. Look for medium sized hats with indeterminate shapes, no definite circles, squares, or points. The all purpose felt fedora hat, if it has a rounded brim, can be an excellent choice. A large nose is strongly emphasized by tilting a hat forward, no matter what the shape. If you've got a large jaw or square chin, make sure your hat is slightly wider than the lower part of your face and wear it at a very slight tilt. This will make your chin and jaw appear smaller. Broad brims should be studied on a case by case basis. Broad brim hats vary considerably in the depth of crown and in whether the brim turns down, up, or lies flat. It's difficult to make a sweeping statement about how to work with distinctive features, so I suggest you experiment whenever you find a broad brim that you love.

Oval faces with regular features can wear any style of hat. The turban that we've dismissed as undesirable for everyone else will look great on this face as will the 1920's cloche, which is difficult for many other face types. It's only fair oval faced women have a spirit of adventure, because they can take advantage of wild and wonderful trims that curve around ears, shoot up in the air, or stick out at improbable angles.

There is no reason to stay away from hats just because you wear glasses. I know many a lovely lady who wear both glasses and a hat and look every bit as wonderful as any other hat lover. Do avoid turned-down brims and veils, as these will create too much clutter around your eyes; but off-the-face styles work just fine. Small to medium brims, especially worn toward the side of the head rather than square on top, look great.

Once your close-up mirror tells you all is well, stand in front of a full length mirror and take as unbiased a look as you can at the whole. Blur the details a bit, and try to get the effect of the outline. Look at the hat from the view of your own body i.e., are you short and squatty, and does your hat make you look more so? Try tilting the hat and see if the line doesn't look longer, and give you a trimmer appearance. A very large or tall woman might find her silhouette looks silly, rather than elegant, with a too small hat; while a larger hat may actually improve the long view of her proportions by balancing her head with the rest of her body. A short woman who wants to look taller can get a boost from wearing a hat with some height in the crown or brim. However, a turned down brim will move the eye down and make her appear shorter.

Always consider the shape of the clothing as well as the body. For example, a very wide skirt looks best with either a small or a very wide hat. In between widths generally look out of balance. When padded shoulders were worn in the 1940's, it was rare to see a wide brim hat worn square on the head. It created a top heavy look that was not particularly flattering to anyone. Small or medium hats were more common, often with a trim or shape that was horizontal. When wide brims were worn, they were pinned on the head at an alarming tilt that created a perpendicular look above the shoulders. I think this bears consideration in light of today's fashions that also feature padded shoulders.

Because hats are so close to your face, color is critical. Choosing colors that flatter your skin is at least as important as choosing flattering colors for your clothes. Given the outbreak of Color Analysis in the last few years, most of us should have some idea of what colors look good on us. If you don't, you must have been hiding under the sofa somewhere. Now, keep in mind that your hair can add a buffer zone and help out an iffy color. For instance, I can't wear unrelieved black right by my face; but I'm a blonde and if the hat allows my hair to show, I *can* wear a black hat. Hats that are similar to your hair color tend to look awfully bland, no matter how spectacular they appear off your head. I've seen a totally elegant black hat, feathered and dreamy, completely disappear from view on the head of a brunette.

In the thirties and forties it was considered the thing to have all accessories, shoes, purse, gloves, and hat, match. This is no longer necessary, or even desirable; however your hat color should bear some relationship to something else that you're wearing. For example, if you're wearing a navy blue suit with white and red accessories, you might try a navy blue hat with a red flower; a white hat with a navy ribbon, or a red hat with navy and white trim. A hat that repeats the main color you're wearing will give a more compact appearance; whereas when you repeat an accent color, it will draw the eye and you'll appear larger.

Use more makeup than usual when you wear a hat, particularly on the eyes. This is especially important with a broad brim or a cloche. I don't mean you should gob the stuff on, but do make sure you eyes will be seen. A slightly brighter, or at least more noticeable, shade of lipstick will balance the tendency of the eye to look right past your face to your hat. Put your makeup on, then try it with the hat, then correct for the hat.

Trimmings (feathers, flowers, veils, and such) can change the shape of a hat and make it more wearable. A small hat with a feather trim looks very dramatic, and the feathers can add either height or width, depending on where they're placed. At the same time, trim can change the flavor of the hat and the effect you're aiming for. Flowers tend to look somewhat off with a wool business suit but right on target with a summer dress. I have a very small, plain navy straw that I wear with suits and dress it up with a big pink silk rose when I'm feeling in a more flowery mood. It's easy to change the trims on hats, usually a couple of stitches or a pin will put you right in business. In more hatty times women regularly retrimmed their hats, and I think more of us would enjoy hats if we felt freer to play around with them.

I usually wear vintage hats with modern clothing and no hat with vintage clothing when I'm not trying to look "vintagey." I also keep a supply of new hats, especially broad brim straws, to wear when the wind is up and I'm afraid my hat will blow off and land in the street. It's bad enough to run down the street chasing your hat (and I've done this many a time!) without having to worry about it being destroyed.

Keeping your hat on your head can be a tricky business. Hatpins are fine, assuming you've got something to stick them into, and I don't suggest a scalp! A woman with thick hair or hair long enough to wrap up into a knot can make good use of a hatpin; but those with fine straight hair or very short hair have to look into alternatives.

Many hats from the 1930's and forties come with small combs sewn inside the crown, a system that is very satisfactory for keeping small hats firmly in place. For hats that don't already have them, packages of combs can be purchased from craft stores and hair care departments of drug and department stores, so this sensible idea can be reproduced. Put the hat on your head and move it around until it looks the way you want it. Hold it with your fingers to find the best places to secure the hat, then mark with chalk or an air soluble marking pen. Sew combs in as many places as necessary to keep the hat stable. It's your hat, so if you need five combs to keep it on, that's just fine.

A simple way to stabilize too large hats is to stuff tissue paper inside the crown. It's easy to adjust how much you need, and take care that it doesn't show. Many hats of the early century and teens came equipped with a separate part of the lining that had an opening for just this purpose. Women then usually had long hair or wore false hair pieces, so the hats had to be enormous. Those who needed less room in the crown could stuff paper inside to take up the slack.

If the style of the hat doesn't allow for this temporary measure or you want a more permanent solution, look inside and see if there isn't a strip of bias or grosgrain ribbon around the edge of the crown. Make yourself another just like it (either purchase grosgrain ribbon at a fabric store or cut a bias strip of a tightly woven fabric), pad it lightly, and tack over the original.

I'll bet someone is saying to herself about now, "Egad, this is so complex, no wonder I'm not wearing hats!" Actually isn't it true that, with no clue at all to what suits you, you've tried on one or two hats and have decided that hats don't look good on you? Try again, using the tips I've given you, and you'll probably find that it's *those* hats that didn't work out. The world of hats is various and almost infinite; there must be millions of hats in the world! At least one is exactly right for you. What a sad, dull world to live in if you don't at least make an effort to find it!

Before I close, I must tackle the most important hat subject of all: whimsy. The hats we're involved with here are strictly for looking at. Most of them have absolutely no practical reason for existence at all. This is an excellent reason to have fun with them, to let the imagination flow, and have a good chuckle while we're at it. My vintage hats give me hours of delight and are a sure cure for being down. How can I feel bad when I pull out my brown velvet cloche with gold lace on its brim, two big pink roses, and bunches of lemons? I might modestly add that it looks absolutely divine on me. Another favorite is a small dinner hat from the 1950's featuring a complete blue bird, tail and all, curling around the edge, and a veil with tiny bows worked into the net. Then there's the love from the 1940's that has a gold cruet on top that contains several feathers reaching to 9 inches above the head. I could go on for hours describing wonderful old hats . . . perhaps I should, since it's such an intriguing subject. No, I must pull up my socks and get serious again. I hope I've made the point that a hat is a creation, a joy, something to be loved and to bring zing into one's life.

Of course we have our more traditional hats that are for wearing in the cold cruel world of the hatless. With hat wearing a new occupation for many, it takes a bit of working up to before appearing with purple velvet and rhinestones on the head. People are more prone to laughter than oohs and ahhs of appreciation. My own husband, a man famous far and wide for his tolerance, makes endless jokes about my hats. I can forgive him because I know he's doomed to live forever without ever having the pleasure of walking down the street with iridescent feathers dripping over his ear and around his chin. A fate I'm sorry about, but there it is. Don't let this happen to you, get out there and put on hats!

CHAPTER FOUR

VINTAGE FURS
OR
I NEVER SAW A LAVENDER SQUIRREL BEFORE

Expecting me to write a little bit about fur is like putting a fox in a hen house and asking it to show some restraint. However, writing is not anywhere near as bad as when I'm exposed to fur in the flesh, so to speak. Then I just go bananas. Some scientist should study the genetic makeup of fur lovers, i.e., is there a fur chromosome? Can it be detected before birth so that people will know what to expect from the small lover of soft, fuzzy playthings—like mink coats and ermine shawls? Be that as it may, when you've got a love of fur and live on a beer budget, you'd best learn to love the old ones! The good news is that you can learn to like vintage furs better than new ones. I visited with a furrier to get some background material, and as he showed me his gorgeous, shiny new coats, I realized something was missing. They didn't smell right. Yes, unless a fur has that distinctive musty odor that is "essence of old fur," it doesn't seem real to me.

I'm delighted to see fur coats returning to the fashion scene in a big way. They disappeared in the early 1960's, and frankly unless you were into conspicuous consumption or vintage clothing for the last twenty-five years we haven't worn fur in public. Jeans and sweatsuits, yes; mink coats, no. This created a problem for those of us who adore fur but traveled in conservative circles. For years I bit the bullet, hiding my furs in the closet and taking them out only for private fondling. About ten years ago I couldn't stand it anymore. I took my courage in my hands and hesitantly began to wear fur jackets. I got interesting reactions, from outright laughter to stares, with only an occasional nod of approval. But I persisted, and sure enough about two years ago the climate changed noticeably. Now I'm getting used to having perfect strangers comment favorably on my fur coats. This year the major fashion magazines are showing lots of fur, and while I'm not claiming that every other person on the street is covered in fur, it's certainly no longer risky to one's dignity to be clad in it.

For practical purposes it's best to stick to vintage furs from the 1940's and fifties. Generally speaking, most furs last about fifty years, conditions being favorable. Much older than that means you're going to have a liability on your hands. How much of a liability depends on how much time you're willing to spend fussing around with it. Once a fur starts to go, it can be patched here and there, but at some point it has to be laid to rest with appropriate ceremony, and we want that to happen after we've enjoyed it for a while.

Fortunately, new fur coats are being designed and cut in the styles of the forties and fifties. If you don't believe me, go visit a furrier and take a look. You'll see the padded shoulders and puffed sleeves common to the forties, and the full swingy jackets and wraps of the fifties. But, egad the prices!! To a person like me who thinks hard about spending $75 for a fur coat (I mean, it'd better be a good one before I spring for that much), I nearly had a cardiac when I saw how much new fur coats cost. All of my beloved fur coats added together couldn't buy the sleeve of a new one! I should qualify this statement by saying they couldn't buy a *good quality* new one.

There are inexpensive (as in a few hundred dollars) fur coats around in department stores; however, they are made with fewer pelts, eked out with strips of fabric or leather. Compare one of these with a fur coat that costs several thousand dollars and you'll find an unmistakable difference. A good vintage fur coat, in decent condition, is comparable in quality to a better fur rather than a cheap one. But, before you get all excited about finding a $100 1940's fur, thinking it's the same as a $10,000 new fur, don't forget the longevity factor. That $10,000 fur coat is an investment that will, with good care, last fifty years. Your vintage coat is something of an unknown. If you've shopped carefully, bought wisely, and allowed for maximum care, you're hoping to get up to five years use from it. With luck you might get more, but there's no guarantee that it will last out a year. You may find it coming apart within a few months. It's a gamble. On the other hand, it's one heck of a lot less of an expenditure too.

How much should you pay for a vintage fur coat? I'll answer with a firm "that depends." I've seen vintage furs priced at several hundred dollars, some even in the thousands, and others for $25. How much you can afford, coupled with what you can find, the condition and sturdiness of the coat, and (to come down to the nitty-gritty) appearance, all have to be considered. My own budget allows for the under $100 variety, so that's where I do most of my buying. I've indulged my fur fetish to excess and have been able to stay within my limit most of the time, so I know it's possible to find usable old furs at a low price. And thank goodness, or else I'd be a basket case! The prices on vintage furs depend a lot on where you live, how popular fur coats are in that location, and how much of a scrounger you're willing to be. If you're willing to do some mending, live with some worn spots, and enjoy furs like squirrel and muskrat, there are still some inexpensive options. If you insist on a perfect mink, be prepared to pay for it.

Many times people who sell vintage furs don't know much about them. They may put unrealistically high prices on a fur in unusable condition, just because it's fur. At the same time, furs that are basically in good condition, but have tears that can easily be mended, might be priced in the bargain category. Do some practice fur repairs on old fur that you might have around (if not a coat, a collar or other piece) so you get an idea of what you can fix easily and what you can't. Then you'll know when a good deal looms near. Learn to be a careful shopper, and save up your hard earned dollars for one that's just right for you.

Sturdiness is relative. The strongest fur you can buy is mouton, a lamb that is thick and heavy. It is water repellent, very warm, and will last forever. It's also often considered the least attractive, weighs a ton, and is often priced lower than other furs. With a mouton coat you are never going to look chic, just practical. Most of us prefer the prettier coats. Who cares if something lasts forever, if you never want to wear it? Realistically, if all you're after is to be warm and waterproof, you can buy one of those quilted coats with miracle padding. Fur is for the soul.

Fur coats were popular in the thirties, forties, and fifties, and widely available at affordable prices. It wasn't uncommon for a middle income woman to own a full length fur coat. In fact many did, which is why there are so many vintage coats around now. These coats are seldom of mink, mind you. The vintage furs we most often come across are squirrel, muskrat in various forms, lamb, Persian lamb, nutria, beaver, opossum, ermine, rabbit, fox, and marten. Raccoon, skunk, mole, mink, chinchilla, sable, seal, and monkey are less common but will pop up occasionally.

Muskrat is a lovely fur with an ugly name and an interesting history. It's probably the most common type of vintage fur. A soft, silky, long haired fur, it was often dyed in stripes to imitate mink. It was also used to make the most popular fur coats of the thirties and forties, the Hudson Bay seal. These coats were sold cheaply, because the muskrat was a common animal and serious pest throughout the United States. During the Depression boys would trap muskrats and sell them for 30 or 40 cents to wholesalers, who sold them to furriers for a couple of dollars. It takes about forty muskrat pelts to make a full length fur coat, so even with labor (which was also pretty cheap then), the coats could be sold for retail for considerably less than more exotic furs. However, they were seldom sold as "muskrat," because the name was such a turnoff. Take the Hudson Bay seal for example. Until 1948, when the federal government decreed that furs had to be labeled with the true name of the animal, the Hudson Bay seal was the most popular fur around. You've probably seen dozens of them, a black short haired fur, soft, and pretty, with a reddish cast to it. Part the fur and you'll see that the underhairs are red. When the labels were changed to read "sheared, dyed muskrat," which is what they really were made of, the bottom dropped out of the market. Unfortunately, the shearing and dying of muskrat to imitate seal is a craft that takes twenty years to learn. The fur is bleached, then dyed in a series of baths, starting with red and working up to black. With no one to buy them, there was no need to apprentice workers to learn the skill and it has virtually disappeared.

Those of you who worry about endangered species can wear vintage muskrat without worry. The muskrat is a vicious, dangerous pest that reproduces at an alarming rate. One pair will produce over eight-hundred descendants in a year, so they can overrun their territory in a short space of time. At one time muskrats were only found in the United States, but in the 1930's a furrier from Russia decided that it would be a good idea to import muskrats for the Russian fur trade. He took eight pair of muskrats, some of which escaped, and spread all over Europe. They have become such a menace that the Netherlands government began offering a bounty for them recently. You see, it's almost a public service to wear muskrat coats!

A muskrat coat has a life of forty to fifty years, depending on how it's been treated, which means that the coats and jackets we find from the forties are coming up on the end. You can expect to wear your vintage muskrat for one to five years, if you get one before the pelt begins to split and give it reasonable care. Once the skin starts to dry and come apart, its days are numbered, so check out muskrat before buying.

Persian lamb, or karakul, is another vintage fur that is found regularly. It has a tight, curly coat that is usually black but can be found in gray or brown. If you've looked at fur coats much, you've probably noticed that some Persian lambs are lightweight and others very heavy and coarse. Persian lambs are actually raised in Persia, because they thrive best on a certain variety of grass that grows only there. Attempts to raise Persian lambs elsewhere have been resounding failures, with the exception of South Africa and parts of Russia. By cross breeding both the sheep and grass varieties, a type of Persian lamb can be raised in these places, but it has a much heavier pelt and the finished coats differ in weight and silkiness. The Russian variety was known as "Astrakhan." Persian lamb coats were fairly inexpensive and aren't particularly long lasting. The prettier, lighter ones have less longevity, and that accounts for the number of vintage Persian lambs we find in less than perfect condition. The heavier weight Persian lambs will usually last longer, but even they are less durable than many other furs. Don't expect a long life from a vintage Persian lamb.

Squirrel, another fur that is not even close to being on the endangered species list, is beautiful, often inexpensive, and much underrated. A vintage squirrel coat, if it's in good condition when you get it, will give years of wear. I learned this by experience when I bought a jacket for $35 from a thrift store. It was pretty and in good condition, but I thought, "Heck, how long can a *squirrel* skin last?" So for the last three years I've been wearing it as an everyday coat, to the grocery store, walking the dog, running errands. I shudder to admit that I toss it on a coat rack, using no strong padded hangers to give it good support. I've made no attempt to keep it well covered, didn't bother to put moth repellent with it, and even left the darned thing hanging out all through the summer when the temperature got high. To my amazement, it still looks great! The skins are still soft and flexible; the fur is in unusually good condition. The only repairs I've had to do are to sew up the pocket where I pulled on it and replace a hook and eye closing that I was rough with. What goes on here? I checked all this out with my friendly furrier, and he told me that squirrel is, indeed, a long lasting fur. Since vintage squirrel coats and jackets are often comparatively cheap, they are well worth considering.

Of the other inexpensive furs available, beaver, nutria, opossum, and marten will give a respectable amount of wear, taking into consideration the shape they're in when found. Rabbit is not a particularly good investment. You'll rarely see vintage rabbit coats or jackets, although they were common. That's because if they were worn at all, they disintegrated long ago. Every once in a while you'll find one in spectacular condition, but that's because it was seldom worn. Once you start using it, you'll find that it quickly begins to fall apart. Mole was another cheap fur that does not stand up. There is a collecting interest in mole fur coats because of the novelty, but the pelts are usually in terrible condition and won't give reasonable wear.

Fox and ermine have each moved in and out of style over the years. They were more costly than the furs in the muskrat, squirrel category but still within reach of regular folks. Ermine is a very beautiful, lustrous fur, most often in shades of brown, and can be expected to wear for a reasonable amount of time. Fox is in the throes of being popular in the new fur market. Most often used for jackets (vintage and modern), it has a long, dense hair and can be white, gray, or a mixture of brown tones. Regretfully, because the fur is so thick, it adds pounds to the figure. Since we aim to looking elegant, rather than like fuzzy beer kegs in our furs, make sure you stand way back from the mirror when trying on a fox jacket. A short woman, even if she's thin, can look decidedly chunky in fox. At one time this was a desirable look—fox was used for a type of jacket called a "chubby" during the thirties and forties. A chubby is a very short (usually waist length) thick fur jacket with large padded shoulders. Everyone looked short and squatty in them, but that was deemed fashionable. I have a silver fox chubby, and while I love it on its hanger, I don't dare look in the mirror when I wear it or I never would. Fox is about medium in terms of longevity, but I've noticed that I wear my fox much less than my other furs, so that it will likely last a long time.

I say with deep regret that there is no such thing as a "cheap mink coat." Mink is . . . well, it's mink, for goodness sake! It's beautiful and warm, and it will last for years. If you're going to spring for several hundred dollars for a vintage fur, a mink is probably a best buy. Those who have lower fur budgets to work with may have to settle for mink hats, muffs, stoles, or collars, although this is not a hardship. Mink is beautiful in any form. Every once in a while you hear about a bargain vintage mink coat, it's one of the perpetual dreams of those who pursue vintage clothing. Who knows, it could happen to you!

Chinchilla and sable are even more expensive than mink and not particularly easy to find in the vintage world because of that. Few ladies dropped their old chinchillas in thrift store bins. (Of course, we all know that this *could* happen, being devoted believers in such things. Isn't that why we're such dedicated scroungers?) Both are, as you might expect, gorgeous and very long lasting. Unless you are extremely lucky or dripping with money (both desirable conditions!), don't hold your breath until you find one.

Raccoon, skunk, and monkey were popular at various times as novelty furs. Monkey usually dates from the 1920's, when it was the "fun" fur of its era. Coats, jackets, and muffs turn up periodically, and you'll occasionally find garments trimmed with it. It is a very long, spikey sort of fur, nearly always black, and fairly sturdy. I must confess that I've never been able to bring myself to wear monkey fur. Partly because I don't find it attractive, but mostly because the idea bothers me. I simply can't get into wearing Bonzo on my back. Some very sophisticated ladies, however, find it very classy, and certainly it's unusual! Skunk fur is usually black but occasionally brown. It's a thick, coarse, long haired fur and very long lasting. It isn't a particularly appealing fur, because it isn't glossy or soft and is too bulky to be flattering. Again, some find it interesting for a novelty look. Raccoon, on the other hand, is also a long lasting, sturdy fur but is very pretty. (My prejudices are showing!) Whether sheared or left long, it is thick, soft, and appropriately cozy. Raccoon is multi-colored, usually in shades of gray, white, black and brown, and is more often found in collars and hats than coats. It can be as thick as fox and was frequently used in chubbies. Raccoon wasn't, and isn't, a particularly expensive fur and was never considered luxurious. During the 1920's it was a popular fur for dashing college boys, and full length men's coats are becoming collectible.

Some cats were used for fur coats and accessories, mostly the lynx and leopard. The leopard, before it was put on the endangered species list and became unobtainable, was one of the most expensive, if not *the* most expensive, furs. It is a beautiful fur, but one you seldom see. Occasionally you bump into one, but it can be risky to wear it. There are dedicated conservationists who will approach you with anger; and explaining that the fur is older than you are and predates the banning of its use for clothing will not alleviate the situation noticeably. Despite this, there are women who adore these coats, so they do find loving homes. Fake leopard coats and hats were a big item in the fifties, so it's wiser to stick to them if your heart cries out for fuzz and spots on your coat.

I used to buy everything made of fur that I could afford. I mean, I'm really addicted to the stuff, but I've started being more selective. Fur stoles are often beautiful, and even more often, they cost less than coats and jackets. However, they are hard to wear. During the years when furs were everyday garments, women routinely wore them not only with evening clothes but even with suits for fairly informal occasions. Now I find that a stole seems more pretentious than a jacket or coat. After all, it doesn't really *do* anything. At least a fur coat can be justified as keeping you warm. Don't take this as a signal to start chopping up any vintage fur stoles you've got around. Be patient for a year or so and see what happens. Several years ago, when fur coats were out of style, lots of people cut their old ones up to make rugs and chair covers. Think how they must feel now! Short capes, on the other hand, can be worn over full length wool coats with a attractive and charming results, even as we speak. I've begun to wear short fur capes with vintage velvet dresses, and I think the world may be just about ready for them. We progress, we progress.

Fur collars come in handy all the time. For instance, I once found a 1940's cashmere coat lined with silk, in perfect condition. That's the good news. The bad news is that this coat was remarkably dull. The color (slate blue) and the style (plain as a pikestaff) left a lot to be desired in general, and on me—let's just say I never seemed to find a reason to wear it. Then I found a huge white fox collar, put it on the coat, and voila—spectacular! I've done this miraculous transformation more than once, so I'm an advocate of the fur collar as a good investment. However, this only works if the collar is particularly special. Put a dull fur collar on a dull cloth coat and you've still got dull. Classier, maybe, but classy dull is still dull.

Some people really enjoy the fur neckpieces that feature the complete animal, head, tail, and paws. Personally I just can't get into it. There's something about those beady eyes, even though I know they're really only glass, that makes me hesitate; but the worst part is the paws. I simply cannot go around wearing paws on my person! I don't want to make you feel bad if you're into draping full size fur corpses all over your shoulders, we are all entitled to our various enthusiasms.

If you bump into a fur that you can't identify and don't have any furriers lying around loose, take it to a taxidermist. Often he can tell you what type of fur it is. During the period that women's fur coats were popular (1930's through 1950's), an unbelievable variety of animals were used for them. It's possible to become familiar with the more common ones, but there will always be one more type that pops up that completely throws you.

When you have your fur at home in your loving care, there are some things that will help contribute to its longevity. You've probably found vintage fur coats with all the fur rubbed off one shoulder. This happened because its first owner wore a shoulder bag with it, and it can be painful to see an otherwise good fur with such a blemish. Don't make the same mistake yourself. You can avoid ruining the back of a fur coat by slipping it off when you drive. Just pop it back on when you get out. That way your grand entrance won't be marred by a furless behind! Don't worry if you are caught in some rain while wearing a fur. It should survive quite nicely. Just give it a good shake when you get inside and hang it over the back of a chair so the air can circulate inside and out while it dries. Don't hang it in the closet wet, as this can encourage mildew. Get your fur cleaned and glazed every year, preferably just before tucking it away in the spring. This is probably the single most positive fur care step you can take. Use a storage bag and lots of moth repellent during the off season, and try to keep the temperature at an even keel with some air flow around it.

Now comes the most important message of all: *Wear those furs!* Don't buy a vintage fur, then tuck it away, and only bring it out for state ceremonies. For one thing the little darling is just sitting around deteriorating, whether you wear it or not. Do you want to lay it to rest without having established a meaningful relationship with it? How will you feel on the fateful day that you find the first split in the skin or when the left sleeve falls off, knowing that you barely got to know it when you had the chance? Worse yet is the waste of a good, warm, glamorous garment. Did those minks die in vain, just to have their gorgeous skins hang around in someone's dark closet? NO! Put on those furs and march!

CHAPTER FIVE

THE CARE AND FEEDING OF VINTAGE CLOTHING OR HOW TO PROVIDE A LOVING HOME

Bringing home a sackful of vintage clothing from a shopping trip can be something like bringing home a new baby from the hospital. You had a lot of fun getting in this condition, but it appears there's a little more to the follow through than you originally intended! After all the fun and excitement of tracking down elusive treasures and the euphoria of finding at least one long sought "meant to be" comes the "What do I do next?" Of course you're going to wear them, wearable clothes are what this is all about, but what do you do when you take them out of the sack?

I'll say right up front that taking care of vintage clothing properly can appear to be downright daunting. When I first realized that I was developing an interest in vintage clothing, I took a class from a museum textile expert on caring for textiles in the home environment. At the end of the class I staggered to my car thinking "I'm going to go straight home and get rid of the lot. This is impossible!" It turns out that all those garments I love are just sitting there being damaged by air, light, humidity, abrasion, body oils, and acids.

Everything that I do or don't do damages them. If they're dirty, they're deteriorating. If I clean them, I'm stressing them. If I mend them, I'm causing strain. If I leave holes, the cloth will crumble. Egad, I'd stumbled into a morass!

Once home among my beloved clothes, I realized that (a) I like my clothes too much to get rid of them; (b) I am not prepared to be ruled by things, even things I really enjoy; (c) as long as I have to do something with the clothes anyway, I can use some of the safer ways of caring for them without too much pain; (d) I can continue to have fun with my clothes; and (e) I am not a museum.

Basically, my aim is to minimize exposure to the things that contribute to deterioration, within the framework of wearing and enjoying the clothes. Extra protection from light and dust, a bit more concern about support for heavy or fragile clothing, and regular cleaning and inspection will help keep vintage clothing usable a bit longer. All the suggestions that follow can certainly be used on new clothing as well, particularly garments that you might want to save to become vintage someday.

SUPPLIES

You'll get sick unto death hearing about *acid-free tissue paper*, which I consider essential in storing old clothing. Do spend some of your precious shopping money on a supply. It isn't available just anywhere. Sometimes a local museum will sell it to you by the sheet, although for a premium price. If you're dealing with one beloved vintage dress, this is a quick and easy way to get hold of it. If you've been bitten by the vintage bug and have more vintage clothing than common sense, buy it in quantity by mail order, which is much cheaper. I like to have it always on hand, and don't want to be skimpy with it. Regular tissue paper *will not do*! Paper is manufactured with acid, and that acid will work away at the cloth fibers. This includes cardboard boxes, news print, and regular tissue paper. A list of mail order sources for acid-free tissue paper is in the Appendix.

Use acid-free tissue paper to wrap clothes, pad hangers, line boxes, stuff and wrap shoes, cover clothes on hangers, cover and stuff hats in boxes. If the insides of drawers are unvarnished wood, line them with the paper too. Wood is also acidic and can cause stains on clothing. You don't really have to eat the stuff, just use it for clothes!

Sturdy hangers and *padded hangers* are high on the list of necessities. Your old clothes need good support, just like you will when you're getting on in years, and those thin wire hangers just don't have it. The tubular plastic hangers that are sold in many stores now are really not much better than the wire ones. I find good wooden hangers in thrift stores, and occasionally some that are padded. They are also available new at many retail stores. Often chain clothing stores or discount department stores will sell their heavy plastic hangers for a few cents each when they begin to turn yellow. It's also possible to get skirt hangers from the same sources. These tend to be thick and sturdy, and work well.

Always cover wooden and plastic hangers with either padding and crochet or fabric, or acid-free tissue. Wood and plastic both emit acids that can damage and/or weaken fabrics over time, and the more padding the better when hanging clothes.

Boxes with lids are another thing to scrounge for. Acid-free boxes are available from the same sources as the tissue and are really the safest bet. However, they are very expensive. So unless you have only one or two pieces to keep in boxes, or have a pleasantly bottomless pocket book, I suggest establishing a meaningful relationship with a copy or print shop. Then you can cadge the wonderful boxes with lids that copy paper comes in. Do line these boxes with acid-free tissue, as they are made of cardboard, which is even more acidic than regular paper.

I use stacks of *old sheets* (as in bed), minus holes, for covering clothes on racks, in closets, and when I'm transporting them. Purists would say to use only white cotton sheets. However, if they're sufficiently faded from many washings, even colored sheets are fine. Light, artificial or indirect sunlight as well as direct sun, is very damaging. Keep all clothing that is out well covered, and it couldn't hurt to toss sheets over clothes that are hanging in closets.

Never, and I do mean never, use plastic to cover or wrap clothing. I include hats and shoes in this sweeping statement. Regular plastic emits a gas that is harmful to both cloth and paper products. There are some inert plastics around, available in conservation supply catalogs and where old comic books are sold. However, plastic also keeps moisture in, and prevents air from circulating. Do you love mildew? If not, use cloth. When you bring clothing home from the dry cleaners tear off the plastic wrap cover and toss it out immediately. That particular plastic is just about the worst type for long term storage of clothing. When you're storing vintage paper products like old sewing patterns or magazines, invest in inert plastic envelopes, which come in a variety of sizes.

Clothing bags are really wonderful, and if you're only dealing with a few pieces it should be a priority to make sure you've got some for your vintage clothing. Since we only find cotton clothing bags acceptable (please refer to the preceding paragraph; go get yourself a cup of coffee and do some stretching exercises if you've already forgotten), you'll either have to make your own or do some heavy duty searching through better department stores or closet shops. A mail order source for a large cotton clothing bag, which holds over twenty garments and is a boon to those of us who have more clothes than sense, is in the Appendix at the end of the book. When making your own, use a tightly woven cotton, chintz for example, which will allow the air to circulate, yet keep out dust, light, and bugs. Homemade bags can be rough-looking, but as long as there are no holes, they should do the job.

Wrinkles Away is a hand steamer that does a decent job, which is more than I can say for others I've tried. It is available through shop supply houses, and sometimes a major department store will carry it. I've found one or two in thrift stores, as well. While this might appear to be a Cleaning and Pressing item, I'm including it in storage because I'm more likely to fold things in boxes if I know I can steam them up quickly when I want them. Some clothing really should not be hung, but it's awfully hard to fold it up when you know it'll come out looking wrinkled when you want to wear it. Those of us with other things to think about on occasion, like making dinner and fostering world peace, get tempted to pass over clothing care activities that we know will take time and effort. This is reasonable and understandable; but with your nice little steamer close at hand, it's only a matter of a few minutes and the garment will look quite tidy.

PRACTICAL CARE IDEAS

When you get home from the store and start pulling out your pretty things to play, take a minute to examine each one and see if it needs mending. You can count on finding various blips at this time, no matter how perfect it looked in the store. Old clothes nearly always need something, that's just the way it is. Mending is a royal pain, you should excuse me, but it's got to be done if you're going to wear the garment, and it's also important to prevent the problem from getting worse. The wisest thing is to get any necessary mending done right now, before you put it away thinking "I'll get around to it soon." Hoo ha! You'll get around to it about the turn of the next century, if you're lucky! If I had a nickel for every time I've done this and then grabbed the garment to wear realizing that the hooks were still missing or the hem still needed repair, I could invest in muncipal bonds. On the other hand, if I were smart I'd already be doing that instead of investing in becoming the best dressed lady in the poor house! These things are relative.

Decide if you should hang the garment or if it would be happier folded in a box. A dress or blouse that is heavily beaded will pull if it's hung, causing problems in the shoulders as well as stretching the dress out of shape. Most of the chiffon velvets, particularly long ones, will stay in good shape longer if they're kept folded instead of on hangers. Check shoulders carefully, especially on very old garments, for any signs of fraying or damage. If you find damage, don't hang the garment up. Lay it flat and put one or more sheets of acid free tissue on top. Then fold the garment over the tissue making sure there are no sharp creases in the tissue. Wrap the whole thing in more tissue paper, and store in a box or drawer. It doesn't hurt to label the boxes after doing this. I'm always pulling out boxes full of unidentified bundles of tissue, unwrapping them, and saying, "Omigosh, I forgot all about this." Of course, it does result in pleasant, unexpected treasure troves, but doesn't help one bit when you're looking for a certain blue chiffon velvet dress that you just know is in one of the boxes in the hall closet.

If you've been out scrounging among thrift stores or garage sales, you very likely will need to do some cleaning. The sooner the better, as the dirt not only is a deteriorating factor itself, but also will attract bugs. I try to get the dry cleanables to their appointed place within a week of bringing things home and aim for getting washables clean within the same time frame. I will not even try to pretend that I accomplish this every time, but it's a good plan to work toward. One thing that happens when you let this go is that you delay longer and longer getting around to it. When you only have to dry-clean a couple of items, it's a reasonable thing. Once you build up a huge stack, you start to see big bucks going for cleaning rather than hats. Then you put it off some more. Better to do it a few pieces at a time as they arrive. Washing is the same problem. Washing vintage clothing is not a matter of dumping a load in a machine and pushing buttons. It's a project; and the larger that the project gets, the more a person's avoidance mechanism goes into action. As you can probably tell, this comes from much experience, and from one of the best avoiders of all time.

Speakng of bugs, and I devoutly wish I weren't, be cautious about bringing them in on new old clothes. Look the clothes over carefully for any signs of moth or silver fish damage, such as holes or tracks in the fabric, white larva casings, or dead bodies. If you see anything suspicious, I'd leave the whole works in the garage, or somewhere away from the inside of the house. Usually this is not a problem with clothing from a vintage clothing shop; however, bugs can crop up anywhere. It's the larvae that do the damage, so by the time you've noticed the adult bugs, you've already got problems.

If you regularly bring home old books, magazines, photographs, or patterns, remember that silver fish may be along as passengers. Bring paper goods into the house only after close inspection. I recently had a silver fish invasion, which I traced to a box of vintage sewing patterns that had been living in someone's garage for decades. Silver fish are even harder to get rid of than moths. They love all kinds of fabrics, cottons as well as wools, and paper too.

The best bet, should you find evidence of nasty little critters, is to clean all your new treasures before bringing them into the house. Sit outside on the porch and put all the dry cleanables in one sack, and the washables in another. Then get them to their appointed places post haste. Some museums put all incoming textiles in an airtight chamber with insecticide for a week or two before moving them into the storage area. I know one that uses an old refrigerator with a name brand insecticide strip for this purpose. This is a good idea for someone who is serious about conserving textiles and could be done easily at home. It should be used with appropriate caution, however, because it's high risk for any home where small children or pets roam around. Even if you're like W. C. Fields, and don't much care for small kids and dogs, you'd feel pretty awful if you contributed to the injury or demise of one or the other. I try to use common sense on this subject, although some would say that anyone who has just spent the grocery money on a few sacks full of old clothes hasn't got much of that commodity! Be that as it may, take some precautions if you see signs of insects on any of your new and/or old purchases. It's foolhardy to bring them into a house, where they will multiply and infest everything made of cloth, vintage or new.

When you bring home leather goods—shoes, purses, or gloves—get into the habit of wiping them with a leather conditioner. Leather that's been stored in a garage or basement for a long time can use a little perking up, and most leather conditioners clean as well. Repeat the application occasionally, and you'll add to longevity and good appearance. When I saw how nicely my vintage shoes stayed when I did this, I began to do it with new shoes as well. The results are amazing, and the effort is small. Put on leather gloves and rub the leather conditioner into them as though you were putting on hand cream. Often old leather gloves are very dry, and while Lexol can't save leather that's completely over the hill, it can perk up those things that just need some love.

Shoe polish not only helps appearance, it also is a good protective measure. It's possible to get shoe polish in almost any color or shade thereof; so even if you're prone to bringing home kelly green ankle strap wedgies, it's possible to find a matching polish. Instead of using shoe trees in vintage shoes, stuff firmly with acid-free tissue, which will hold the shape, but has some give. Wrap shoes and gloves in acid free tissue paper.

SEASONAL STORAGE

This is one of those things that sounds easy, but can slip right by if you're not paying attention. There is seldom one day when winter comes to a screeching halt and spring begins, and the end of summer seems to drag over a couple of months. You find yourself gradually wearing the previous season's clothing less and the new one's more, and before you know it, it's time to get out all the things that never got put away. A person tries to pay attention to all these details, but I know that it's easy to miss things. However, your clothes will last longer with some seasonal storage.

First and foremost is getting the clothes clean. I don't mean clean them and wear them "just one more time"; I mean clean them and get them put away in one fell swoop. Dry cleaning is a good moth repellent, they just hate the fluid. When the days and nights get balmy, take every woolen you own to a dry cleaner. This can be an expensive proposition, obviously, so I take the sturdy items, and those that don't need special cleaning methods, to a bulk dry cleaner. The delicate and very old I take off to my beloved Richard, Prince of Dry Cleaners. Since they're being stored, I don't have them pressed. I'll do that when I'm ready to wear them next fall and save myself from bankruptcy right now. Make sure to include silks or rayons in this grand clean up, as the remains of perspiration from even one wearing can cause irreparable damage over a period of time.

Once clean, wrap each piece in acid-free tissue and store away in your nice boxes with lids. If you've got extra closet space, set up an "out of season" closet, and cover the whole works with some of your old sheets. Clothing bags, as I've said before, are ideal, especially for long term storage. I've opened up cotton clothing bags after several months of storage and gotten a whiff of drycleaning fluid. This makes me very happy, knowing that any stray bugs will get the same scent and go next door for after-dinner snacks.

Furs should be cleaned and glazed at the end of the season, then stored in individual bags made of either cotton or brown paper (which is the old-time way of storing furs). At the very least, wrap an old sheet around them. Cold storage is not so much a necessity now as it was before the days of central heating and air conditioning. It's abrupt changes in temperature and humidity that damage the pelts, rather than the need to keep them cold. If you keep your house comfortable for people in the summer, you should be able to store your furs at home safely. Make sure there is enough room for air flow around the fur piece; and put moth balls or herbal moth repellent sachets liberally in and around the fur. I put some in each pocket and hang a sachet from the neck of the hanger. Wrap moth balls, if that's your choice, in acid-free tissue so they don't touch the garment. If your furs are very valuable and you travel a lot without them, if you are really worried about moths, or the temperatures in your house will rise or drop abruptly, then cold storage is a good option. If you opt for cold storage, call around and do some comparison shopping. Cold storage fees vary widely and frequently they are cheaper at a furrier than through a large department store.

Clean and condition out-of-season shoes, then stuff and wrap with acid-free tissue. If your climate is damp, make sure your shoes and purses are off the floor and in a dry part of the house. Leather is very susceptible to mold and mildew, so extra protective measures are in order.

Incidentally, don't think I'm casting aspersions on anyone's housekeeping with all this talk of bugs and mold, and so forth. Believe me, I'm in no position to throw stones myself. Even the cleanest of houses can become infested with pests or mold as people come in and out. This is especially true if you're bringing home stuff from estate sales and thrift stores on a regular basis.

It's easy to forget that hats are seasonal as well as clothes. I like to keep my in-season hats close at hand so I can grab one on the way out the door; but I find little use for black wool felts with my summer cottons. Before storing hats away for a season, clean or brush them, then stuff with acid free tissue paper so they will not get crushed. Wrap with tissue and tuck away in boxes. By accident I stumbled on a great way to do this. My hat boxes are stacked all around the piano, next to the telephone. I found that I can clean, sort, and put away hats during a good long chat on the phone; because this is not a job that requires concentration. How long a chat depends on how many hats. Ideally, one has acquired one hat box per hat; but for some unknown reason antique stores have decided to charge an arm and a leg for old hat boxes, so it can be a painful experience to buy them. Large wig cases can be a workable substitute, and they are usually fairly cheap at thrift stores. If all else fails, it's possible to get by with those covered boxes from the copy shop. Don't forget to put moth repellent in with the hats, especially for wools, fur felts, and feathery trims.

Summer clothes should be thoroughly cleaned before storing, again because of possible deterioration from perspiration or body oils. I usually use starch on my whites while I'm wearing them, so have to be sure I've washed all the starch out when I put them away. Silver fish, mold, and mildew love starch. It's not necessary or even desirable to press them, you'll be relieved to hear. That's a chore you can save for next spring, when you're ready to sashay around in your pretty cottons and silks. Fold the clothes with acid free tissue inside and out, then tuck away until the sun shines and the buds come out.

MOTHS AND OTHER OTHER OBNOXIOUS BEASTS

I hate moths. I have a yellow plastic fly swatter shaped like a butterfly and can be seen with it and a killer commando expression, leaping around squashing members of any moth family that dares to move in with me. However, this activity is for my own benefit and revenge. Once you see the moth, the damage is already done, since it's the larvae that do the munching. There are many and various moth solutions, both old-wives' and new chemical, but the important thing is to do *something*. Unlike other problems, moths don't go away by themselves, and as long as they're around they eat wool, fur, feathers, and sometimes silk as well. Also, don't wait until you're storing clothes away to take action. My own resident moths tend to hold breakfast meetings over clothes hanging on racks in my room. They have absolutely no shame or discretion.

Moth balls and camphor flakes do work—however . . . The big however is the smell. Few people can stand the smell of moth balls, and to have to live with that odor all over the house is just too much. If you aren't bothered by the smell, or by various rumors that constant exposure to moth balls can cause depression (this is unscientific information that I picked up from a friend I was visiting with in the grocery store recently), then you'll have the easiest and best protection. To work, though, the clothing and moth balls have to be in a well sealed closet or trunk. Always make sure there is acid-free tissue in between the moth balls and the fabric, as the moth balls or crystals are not kind to fabric when they touch it directly.

Some folks are anxious to avoid chemicals, and what with the new federal and state laws on insecticides, they are not so easy to come by anyway. So I'll start with natural solutions. Industrious vacuuming is strongly recommended by most experts. This means the room and closet, in cracks and nooks and crannies, and the clothes themselves. A variable speed hand vacuum can be an invaluable aid in this activity. Do your best; however know thyself, and if you are not going to turn into a good housekeeper overnight, plan to do more.

Clothes that have been dry cleaned will have moth immunity for about six months if being stored, for a lesser time if being worn. No cleaner will promise this, but experience indicates that it's a safe assumption. If you store freshly dry cleaned clothes in tightly woven cotton bags, you should be able to count on protection for some time. However, moths move fast, so be ever vigilant! They will appear from nowhere, and multiply before you've even noticed that they're sharing your premises. Never store woolens dirty, even if they've only been worn once since the last cleaning. Strong sunlight will destroy larvae, according to old textile sources (remember the airing of clothes in the spring?), but it has to get everywhere, including inside pockets and along seam allowances to work. When you're moth proofing, don't neglect garments that have a fur or feather trim, even if the main garment is made of fabric less appealing to moths. The nasty little creatures have no scruples about jumping right in wherever you've forgotten to deal with them.

Some knowledgable people poo-poo the herbal moth repellent approach, but others swear by various home remedies. Cloves, cedar chips, rosemary, pennyroyal, wormwood, and southernwood are all herbs that have reputations as moth repellents. Tobacco is a time honored moth and bug deterrent. I know a woman who has a trunk full of old clothes that her family has preserved from the 1880's, which has plug tobacco tucked in every corner. The clothes aren't exactly sweet smelling, but no bug has dared stick a toe in that trunk!

I'm a herbal user myself and purchase a herbal moth mixture in bulk from a mail order herb company. I won't pretend that the scent is as attractive as some of the nice potpourri mixtures that are not specifically for moth control, but it is pleasant enough. I make up literally hundreds of little sachets, put them in pockets and drawers, hang them on hangers, and make sure there are one or two in each hat and storage box. These sachets are not of the lovely to look at variety. I'm working in quantity, with intent to do bodily harm to bugs, so I'm not worried about appearance. I take light weight cotton remnants or scraps and use pinking shears to cut circles approximately eight inches in diameter. Then I dump a good spoonful of herbal moth repellent in the middle and tie the whole works together with ribbon or yarn. I have also done this with cloves that I've purchased in bulk, and it seemed to work well enough. I must confess that out of pure fear I switched to a more official moth repeller. We had a moth invasion a couple of years ago, and I was doing everything but shooting at them with a machine gun before I got rid of them. The drawers with clove sachets did seem to evade moth attacks during this time, but I was too worried to risk it any longer. Cloves do smell nice with clothes, I must say. In the Appendix are some sources for herbal moth repellent. You can get made up sachets from all of them and bulk moth repellent from at least one of them.

Some authorities claim (so, okay, Coby Richardson told me this while we were looking through the bins at the Goodwill—you get your authorities, I'll get mine!) that any strong smelling concoction will repel moths. That should mean that any potpourri will give some degree of moth protection. However, I've seen too many garments destroyed by moths, and prefer to stick to those herbs that I know have a reputation in the field. The only good moth is a dead moth, and silver fish have even less excuse for getting free room and board!

When it comes to chemical treatments there are definitely some limits. The chemicals work, but many are no longer obtainable because of state and federal regulations. Those that are have long lists of cautions on the container. Official opinion seems to be that "if it'll kill bugs, it isn't so great for people either." Odorless sprays can still be found at various outlets, notably feed and seed stores, but most labels advise not making contact with the skin. This, obviously, knocks a hole in spraying clothes that you are wearing; however, they can be used for long-term, seasonal storage. Another preventive aid is the clear, odorless spray that is used for treating wool rugs and available at some carpet cleaning firms. All of these chemicals will also work on carpet beetles, which don't always stick to carpets. They will attack clothing with just as much gusto! *Don't ever use one of these sprays on fur,* and always follow direction on the can religiously.

I used to use chemical sprays on all my moth attracting clothes, whether I planned to wear them or not, because I had decided that I'd just as soon risk my health as risk losing some of my precious old clothes. However, pressure from friends and family, and impending age have changed my mind. I finally was convinced that being in close contact with heavy duty bug killing chemicals was probably not a good way to become vintage myself. Not to establish an undeserved reputation as a sensible person, I have to confess that finding successful alternative solutions had a lot to do with this.

Silverfish are more troublesome to get rid of than moths and have an indiscriminate appetite for any fabric. If we ever were to have a nuclear holocaust, God forbid, I swear the world would be left populated with silverfish and cockroaches, which also are hard to eliminate. Not enough that they like to hold award banquets on your clothes, silverfish also make inroads on old books, magazines, and sewing patterns when they get the chance.

Feed and seed stores are good sources of sprays that kill silverfish. Usually a spray that is specifically for around baseboards is what you're looking for. It may take more than one application and some time for all of them to die, because silverfish have a strong lease on life. But perseverance will pay off. Make sure when spraying to get into every nook and cranny, including inside closets. Flea bombs, available from veterinarians, will also make a dent in the silverfish and moth population. Again always follow directions, since what you're after are the bug members of your household, not the people and pets on the premises.

If all else fails and you're about to lose your mind, and more importantly, your clothes, don't hesitate to call an exterminator. The cost of hiring professional bug killers is nothing compared to the comparable loss of valuable clothing, not to mention your sanity.

MOLD AND MILDEW

Mold and mildew are always present in the air around you, which is not the most pleasant thought, but there it is. All it takes is the right set of conditions, and mold and mildew are happy to start taking on more substantial form. Any type of clothing is susceptible, as are shoes, purses, and other accessories.

A combination of heat and damp is the most congenial atmosphere for these nasty spores; but even a cold damp can be inviting, so keeping things dry is critical. This is the best reason for *not* storing cloth in plastic, even inert plastic. If there's even a touch of dampness inside the plastic when you put things away, it will remain and provide a pleasant atmosphere for unwanted guests. Dirt and starch feed the spores, so never, ever store anything dirty; and always wash out all starch from summer cottons before storing.

If you keep things in sealed closets or trunks (which helps with moths) then periodically air the enclosed space. Pick a time when it is cool, and the air is dry. Don't pack clothing too tightly in closets, boxes, or drawers, so that air can flow around the pieces. A small light bulb kept burning in a closet may help prevent mold and mildew from developing.

Keep leather items like purses and shoes on shelves instead of on the floor; you want some air flow around them. Here's a tip that will help protect leather, which is highly susceptible to mold and mildew: after testing to make sure the color is not affected, wipe with a 1 percent solution of dichlorophene in rubbing alcohol, inside and outside the shoe followed by a rub down with leather conditioner before storing. This can also be used on the leather portions of purses. Get dichlorophene at hardware stores, and some pharmacies carry it.

Mildew usually announces its presence by a strong odor. If you smell any mustiness around your clothes and accessories, investigate immediately. The spores can develop very rapidly, virtually overnight; so don't think just because you were looking in that box last week and nothing was wrong that it isn't now. This can happen to the best of us, and doing good deeds and having kind thoughts are no protection. The protective measures I've suggested will lessen the possibility of an invasion, but don't be too hard on yourself if you find yourself in the midst of a mold or mildew outbreak. The cleanest and tidiest of people can be hit when the right combination of spores, air, humidity, and temperature happen to coincide.

When you find mold and mildew on clothes and accessories, take them outside and brush them immediately. Even if it's winter and too cold for this, you don't need to spread the stuff around the house any more than it already is. Those nasty little spores that you brush off will just float along until they hit more of your precious belongings, if you give them a chance. Once you've brushed everything thoroughly, clean washables in warm sudsy water and take the nonwashables to the dry cleaners. Do it right now, not in a day or two, because you may be able to prevent stains if you act quickly. If stains persist on washables, try either lemon juice or a mild solution of chlorine bleach, then dry directly in the sun, if you've got any at hand. How tough you are will depend on the sturdiness of the cloth. You may be faced with making a difficult decision: Should you risk losing the garment by using methods that will remove the stains but damage the fabric or risk having the garment permanently stained? Did Solomon collect vintage clothing? It may be that's where he got in his practice at tough decision making!

You can wipe shoes and other leather things that have been invaded by mold with a solution of 50 percent water, 50 percent rubbing alcohol, then air-dry. Be as thorough as possible and get into every nook and cranny. It only takes one little spore to survive for a repeat performance. Touch up any color loss with dyes and/or shoe polishes.

I realize that all this information may sound terribly off-putting; after all, you're already busy running General Motors, being a scout master, and taking piano lessons. So who needs to take on becoming nursemaid to a bunch of old clothes, especially when it involves so much hassle? Isn't it easier to take up raising pigeons or even ostriches? Let Mother McCormick give you a word of assurance: No one expects you to be practically perfect in every way. Of course you're going to find yourself throwing a pair of shoes into a corner and forgetting them on occasion. Sure you're going to forget to go to the cleaner and find yourself with enough dry cleaning stacked up to send your dry cleaner's son to Harvard. Relax. The real secret is to enjoy your clothes, because if you do, you'll find yourself wanting to do the little extras. When you love your fur coat and want it to last, you'll take extra care of it automatically. If you feel resentful about all this stuff causing you extra work, you simply won't take these precautions and you'll pay the price.

You'll probably find yourself reacting first to things that are immediately apparent. For example, I used to be fairly haphazard about moths until I found some holes, then I got militant. I was not as religious about using heavy or padded hangers until I noticed a beaded dress pulling out of shape, and showing "pook" marks on the shoulders. A dusty hat that has to be brushed and pulled into shape every time it's worn is obviously more trouble to keep up than one that's been tucked away in a box, stuffed with paper to maintain the shape. Harder to get into is taking the steps to prevent invisible deterioration. It isn't that you don't believe that acid free tissue paper is a good idea, it's that you can't just pick it up at the grocery store during a routine trip. So you say "Someday I'll get around to it."

Speaking as someone who finds housework of any kind a misery and would prefer to be followed around by a variety of minions who take care of such mundane items as vacuuming, I understand the problem. A key to all of this is getting together a stockpile of supplies, so that it's so easy to do the right thing, that you never think about it. Make it a practice to look for heavy wooden or padded hangers everytime you go to a sale or thrift store, so you've always got a good supply of them. Order a large supply of acid free tissue to have on hand and then you'll automatically grab some when you're putting clothes away. Make up a bunch of moth repellent sachets while you're watching television or visiting with a friend, then all you've got to do is reach in the sack and pull out a couple when you need them. Make it so simple for yourself that you don't even think about it, you just do it. The thing is, prevention, when possible, is always preferable to a mopping up operation. I'm not going to promise that your vintage clothing will last forever, if you do all this. I will say that it will probably last longer and certainly look better while it's sharing your life.

CHAPTER SIX

CLEANLINESS IS NEXT TO UNREASONABLE

In all of the handling, storing, caring for, and wearing of vintage clothing, it's in the cleaning process that you are most likely to cause permanent grief to a garment. At the same time (I just love double binds) if you don't clean the garments they will suffer continuous damage from the dirt in the fibers. Dirt, grime, and stains create a chemical reaction with the fibers. To remove dirt, grime, and stains you have to cause another chemical reaction. Old fabrics are going to be stressed either way. However, since we're dealing here with wearable vintage clothing, not museum collections, we're going to have to take the position that dirty clothing is not wearable and approach the subject, albeit with appropriate cautions.

If you feel as though I'm piling on the cautions, it's for a good reason. You *should* be careful when cleaning old clothes. More important, I don't want someone to get all upset because she's dunked great grandma's two-hundred-year-old petticoat in a basin of chlorine bleach, watched it dissolve, and then said, "But you said . . . " What I'm saying is "Here are some things that have worked for me and others, but always use common sense and good judgment when dealing with old garments." I've successfully cleaned vintage garments for years. I've lost a few along the way, and others have worn out as they've been worn, cleaned, and stored, like any garment that's been used. Some vintage clothes, I swear are being held together only by the dirt in them, the threads having long given up. When you're making a decision about whether or not to use a particular cleaning method, ask yourself if you'll lose sleep over it. If you will, don't do it. If you're comfortable with it, proceed.

I think it bears repeating that faced with an irreplaceable, rare historic, or valuable garment, we have to make some decisions about whether to proceed with cleaning at all. There are products available (see Appendix) that are specifically for museum cleaning of textiles. These work well, and if you find yourself moving toward a conservation-oriented viewpoint, do use them. My own decision has always been that if I can't risk cleaning it myself with the washing methods herein or with my beloved dry cleaner then I have no business fussing with it. Since there is more than one opinion on this subject, I leave it up to the individual person. Now let's get on with it.

WASHING CLOTHES AT HOME: GENERAL GUIDELINES

To wash at home or use a dry cleaner, how does a person decide? There are some fabrics that I strongly suggest you make no attempt to wash. These are any velvet, satin, moire, crepe, wool, plush, silk net, or metallic. You're more likely to destroy them than clean them. This leaves cotton and linen, flat rayons and silks, and nylon. Cotton can be dry-cleaned but will not get as clean. If consistently dry-cleaned, it will turn grayish over time. I've made a practice of taking all silk and rayon outer garments (dresses, suits, skirts, etc.) to the dry cleaner, but washing the underwear and blouses myself. One reason for this is the pressing, which is very difficult to do successfully.

Don't use your washer and dryer for any vintage clothing. It's okay to use the washing machine as a basin, but don't turn it on as the agitation from the machines will cause damage to old fabrics. Unfortunately, this is a limitation in cleaning, as agitation of the cloth is important to getting clothes clean. Nonetheless, don't do it.

And after everything is said and done, some dirt and stains are simply not going to come out. The key to stain removal is to attack immediately; a forty-year-old stain—even a twenty-year-old stain (for that matter a one-year-old stain)—is more than likely a lost cause. This is specially true of rayon and silk, which don't like rough handling. It's possible to work miracles, sometimes, on white cotton and linen because in some cases they can be bleached with chlorine. Bleaching doesn't remove the stain, however. It bleaches the color out so the stain can't be seen. Luckily, overall dirt and grime are often removable.

The purpose of a presoak is to open up the fibers so they will release the soils more easily during the washing process. However if you leave fabrics in the presoak too long they will reabsorb the dirt, so a short presoak works best. Should you leave things in too long, and the dirt is reabsorbed, take them out and begin again. There are a number of presoak products on the market; spend a rainy afternoon in the supermarket reading the labels. Take a couple of different brands home and experiment with garments that you know are unsavable. Enzyme presoaks (Axion, Biz) are designed to dissolve protein, so will dissolve silk and wool as well. Rayon, while a vegetable fiber, can also be injured by enzyme presoaks. I prefer Clorox 2, a peroxys bleach, as a presoak, but know hard core advocates of both Biz and Axion.

Chlorine bleach is best saved for cottons and linens, and then only when necessary. I use chlorine bleach in a weak solution for some things but always test first on an inside seam or inconspicuous spot to make sure the garment is up for it. When something is really grungy and repeated washing is making only a slight dent and your next alternative is to toss the thing out, then a mild bleaching may well make it usable.

Other bleaches on the market that are gentler and can be used for various fabrics are peroxys bleaches (Clorox 2, Biz Bleach). These can also be used as presoaks. If you dry your cottons and linens outside in the sun, especially if you spread them directly on green grass, a natural chlorine bleach is created from the interaction of the grass with the sunlight and dampness of the clothes. Again this is gentler than liquid chlorine bleach but should be used sparingly, as too much sunlight can be harmful. Some people also swear by lemon juice as a bleaching agent, particularly with rust stains.

I wish I could spare you this, but I can't. If you're going to clean clothes at home, you've got to press them as well. Before the wonderful world of science provided us with permanent press, every female person learned how to iron. It went with the territory. Everything from bed sheets to undershorts had to be pressed before using. Now there are millions of people who have never wielded an iron. However, most vintage clothing dates back to those prehistoric times when a day a week was set aside for ironing. If you're absolutely in the dark about how to start, having only vague notions that you need a wedge shaped metal object that plugs into the wall and a funny shaped board, call your county extension service, listed in the phone book with other county offices. They have pamphlets (inexpensive or free) that give good basic information about how to press clothing and the various pieces of equipment required. This is also a good source for stain removal charts and other home laundry information. Remember, though, that the extension service pamphlets are designed for laundering new clothing, so make adjustments for the age of the garment you're dealing with.

Equipment basics: (1) A good iron, which is very hard to find. The last time I bought a new iron (a year ago), I had to return four, count 'em, four irons before I found one that was satisfactory. Considering that I paid $40 for the iron, and the one I finally kept has a slow water leak, this is a miserable comment on the quality of iron being turned out these days. (2) A crummy old iron from the thrift store. I use this for ironing starched clothes, so I don't risk my good iron. If you do this, and if you work with whites I suggest you do, make sure the bottom is in good condition, unscratched and smooth. It isn't necessary that the steam mechanism be in working order, because the clothes are pressed when damp. (3) An ironing board that is tall enough to be comfortable. Don't get a little one that forces you to bend over at an uncomfortable angle or your back will protest. (4) A Wrinkles Away hand steamer. I wouldn't consider working with vintage clothing at all without this wonderful item; it makes life downright bearable. I have two, just in case. Some major department stores carry them, and those that don't might be willing to order for you. They are a standard item in store supply catalogs, so try asking a local shop manager to order one for you. (5) Various sizes and shapes of pressing hams. These aren't absolutely necessary, unless you are going to be pressing suits and dresses, but will make life easier if you do. They are available in fabric stores.

Always handle old garments gently and kindly, and make sure

they're well supported, especially wet. Remember, you'll need some extra support yourself as you get a little older. Don't wring or twist the cloth; press the water out gently. I always work with a plastic collander (kitchen variety) putting the garments in it while rinsing and shaking them out to start drying. I know others who make themselves net bags of various sizes to put garments in for the cleaning process.

Hanging old clothes to dry can cause enormous stress, as the weight increases when wet. On the other hand it's hard to find someplace to lay them flat, most of our modern homes being designed for people who use the washer and dryer exclusively. A portable drying rack that will fit over the bathtub can help. You can make a simple one by buying an old window frame at a junkyard and some fiber glass screening at the hardware store. Clean off the window frame, and tack on the screening *underneath* the frame, leaving a metal-free surface to lay out the clothes. Then you can dry clothes flat and store the rack away when not in use. Always make it as easy for yourself as possible, because then you'll actually do it, rather than just think about it!

Woolite is a mild detergent that is designed to remove oils and dirt without damaging fabric. Ivory Snow is a pure soap, as it says on the package. When using Ivory Snow in lukewarm water, dissolve it before hand in very hot water, then add the soapy solution to your wash water. There are some detergents on the market for use on antique quilts that can also be used with old garments.

Vacuuming can be a big help in removing surface dust and dirt. Don't use a vacuum cleaner that is intended for the floor, as it will pull too hard on even the sturdiest fabrics; and never vacuum a fabric that is beginning to come apart or is fragile. There are some little, teeny, tiny vacuums on the market that are designed to clean computers and electronic calculators. One of these can be very useful with clothing. The suction is much lighter than with a large vacuum, and the little brushes will reach inside pockets, purses, and around trims on hats. Check office supply shops and stores that specialize in luggage and unusual gift items. Variable speed hand vacuums are also useful but should be used more sparingly than the little vacuums. Keep a piece of netting around, place it over the garment, then vacuum through the netting, when you feel the fabric might be damaged.

Having loaded you up with do's and don'ts, I feel obligated to say that when you're working with clothing of your own you may want to experiment without feeling guilty. I get letters from people who tell me that they've taken a badly stained satin (for example) to the dry cleaners without success. They brought it home, washed, pre-soaked, and bleached it, and it comes out looking great with no signs of falling apart. But you should be aware that, even though the fabric doesn't show signs of deterioration at first, at least some has taken place. If it's yours, and you can get some use out of the garment by using a tough cleaning method, it's your decision. I'd be leery, however, of doing this to a garment eventually intended for resale. As a customer, I'd rather purchase an "as is," play around with it, and take risks myself, than pay a high price and have the piece fall apart shortly thereafter.

WASHING SILK AND RAYON

There are few options for washing rayon and silks, just so you don't get all excited. You can do a brief (half hour to an hour max) presoak in a weak solution of peroxys bleach and warm water. Then wash by hand in lukewarm water with Woolite or Ivory Snow. (When using Ivory in lukewarm water, dissolve it first in very hot water, then add to wash water.) Rinse thoroughly, roll in a turkish towel until damp dry, then press. If the garment doesn't get clean, repeat the process a time or two. Sometimes it takes several washings to get out all the ingrained dirt. However, after two or three washings and no results, you may want to throw in the towel, literally. Rayon fiber is weaker when wet than it is dry, so the handle-carefully rule should be carefully followed. Both silk and rayon are easily damaged by sunlight. This includes new fabrics, but goes double for old ones. Always dry them away from direct sunlight.

Always wash colored rayons alone. During the development of rayon, there was much experimentation with dying methods, and some were more successful than others. While modern dyed rayon seldom, if ever, runs, vintage rayon is another thing. Some vintage rayon dresses have never been cleaned, and you can find yourself with a pot full of dye when you wash them.

Stain removal options are essentially nonexistent. There isn't anything that will remove old stains that will not irreversibly damage the fabric. Appliqué and embroidery cover-ups are your first line weapons. For new stains that you've created yourself, use a stain removal chart or get the garment to your beloved dry cleaner immediately.

Silk and rayon press out best when damp, hence the suggestion to roll in a towel and iron inside out while damp dry. I've seen a woman trying to press a rayon dress and getting more and more frustrated. No matter how hard she worked, there were tiny wrinkles all over it. Turned out she was pressing a dry dress with a dry iron. If she had rolled the dress in a damp towel, then pressed on a low setting with steam, she'd have had an easier time with a better result. Allow an hour or so between pressing and wearing, as often the fabric will remain slightly moist after pressing. Silk and rayon tend to water spot, so don't use a spray or you'll be sorry. To touch up, use your trusty steamer.

Pressing is something one has to learn about, and with silk and rayon it can be a tricky proposition. Goodness knows how our foremothers ever did it with those miserable flat irons that they had to use. We, however, are only slightly better off with our fancy irons that are supposed to do everything but cook dinner! Don't trust your temperature controls until you're absolutely sure that they work properly. Few do. Instead, start with a heat setting slightly below the recommended one on your iron and make sure the steam is on. If necessary, move the heat up slowly until you hit the point that the wrinkles are disappearing but before the iron drags on the fabric. Do this experimenting by pressing a facing or inconspicuous place on the garment. Too much heat can be curtains for a silk or rayon.

Even when the heat is correct, rayon tends to get shiny when pressed. I'll bet you've found more than one rayon garment that has been overpressed and looks terrible. That's why, as much as humanly possible, you should work on the inside of the piece while pressing. There are some corners where you've got no option but to press on the right side, so use a pressing cloth. I've been told that you can temporarily restore a low luster to black rayon by putting the shiny side down on a piece of newspaper and pressing it on low heat.

Be especially careful when pressing silk or rayon crepes, as they can pull up and shrink from the heat. Normally I let Richard, Prince of Dry Cleaners, deal with my rayon crepes, and I just steam them in between times. However, when working on hems (either raising or lowering) it can be easy to forget. If you find yourself with fabric that is shrinking up, try steaming the area and pulling the fabric gently back into shape while it's damp and warm.

WASHING COTTONS AND LINENS

Many old petticoats, corset covers, and other cotton whites have yellowed with age. Because the whites you see in museums are not deep cleaned, many people think that old cottons and linens were actually an ecru or off-white color naturally. Not so. White was white, then as now. How to restore them to their original prettiness is what we're about here. Since we are not museums we have fewer constraints to prepare the clothing for use.

There is often some confusion when talking about cottons and linens, as things like pillowcases, tablecloths, and runners are commonly referred to as linens, even when made of cotton. For our purposes the term refers to the fiber content, no matter what the article is. Cotton and linen are both stronger wet than dry, and have a bit more resistance to heat and sunlight than other fabrics. Linen is especially resistant to bacteria and tends to release dirt easily but doesn't stand up to heat as well as cotton.

Almost every vintage person I know has a cleaning method that she or he swears by for old cottons and linens. All are slightly different, which leads me to believe that there is room for some experimentation. Of course, mine is the absolute best of all! I should also tell you that taking a pile of yukky, yellowed cottons and turning them into sparkling white pretties is one of the all time highs. You feel like a magician! For colored cotton and linen, wash alone the first time to be absolutely sure the dye is set. It doesn't seem possible that a fifty-year-old dyed fabric will leak color but it is, and then you really have a mess on your hands!

Presoak in either peroxys bleach or one of the brand name presoaks, diluted in lukewarm water, about half cup to a wash tub full. This is a good time to use your washing machine as a wash basin. Keeps your sinks available for such frivolities as washing dishes and hands. You can leave things in as long as over night but longer will cause the fabric to begin to reabsorb the dirt. I try to presoak only as many clothes at one time as I'm able to wash in one session. You might try pretreating stains with a stain removal product. We'll save more heavy duty stain treatments for the next try, if needed.

Now to the wash method. My own method is to boil cottons just like great grandma used to do. Well, not quite like great grandma, since I'm working on top of an electric range, but otherwise the same. Linen doesn't like to be boiled and may suffer some damage from the high heat, so I use one of the other wash methods given below. Some experts claim that boiling doesn't clean any better than regular washing, but I differ with that opinion. I think that the boiling action creates a mild agitation and helps get things cleaner.

Boiling clothes, like boiling potatoes, requires some concentrated time and attention. One doesn't get started and then pop out to run errands. I save up enough garments to make it worthwhile and plan on spending a morning at it. Put the clothes in to presoak the night before, so their little fibers are all opened up and ready to release the dirt. I use a large pot and put in about one fourth cup of Ivory Snow, fill with hot water, and put in the clothes. Don't overfill the pot, as when the boiling starts you'll have water and soap suds all over the top of the stove. Make sure the garments are not overcrowded, because you want the water to circulate around and through the cloth. I bring this whole mess to a rolling boil then turn down the heat, making sure that the rolling boil is maintained. I hang around and keep an eye on the color of the garment, stirring occasionally with a wooden spoon if part of the cloth bubbles out of the water. If the water gets dirty, and the cloth is still not white, I pour out the old water, add new soap and water, and go again. How many times I repeat this process varies with the amount of dirt. For instance, I once had to change the water four times (and we're talking read mud!) for one small boudoir cap. On the bright side, when it got clean I found that it had a pink border which hadn't been visible when it was dirty. If you have more than one piece in the pot, some things might get whiter sooner than others. Remove the clean pieces as you go, lifting them out with a wooden spoon.

When it's apparent that the garment is as clean as it's going to get in this session, or the water is becoming too dirty, I pour the whole works out, using the collander to hold the garment. Remember, this is boiling water, so no touching with the hands! Then I rinse, using the hottest possible tap water. I learned that if you rinse cottons in a water temperature substantially different from the wash water, you seal in the soap instead of removing it. After rinsing all the soap out in hot water, I rinse again in cold water so I can touch the cloth.

Now I survey the situation and decide whether the piece is as white as I want it. Usually it's pretty close at this point. If it still needs some serious work, I go through the above process again, including the presoak. If it's almost there, and the fabric is in good shape, I dilute a small amount (less than one fourth cup) of chlorine bleach in a large basin of water and put the garment in for a few minutes. It's a good idea to dunk a Q-tip in the solution and test it on a seam or inconspicuous corner first, just to make sure the whole thing won't dissolve.

I admit boiling is a bit of a process, and not everyone is going to find it a pleasant occupation. I rather like doing it myself, but must allow for many tastes here. For those of you who want other options and for linens, here are alternatives. Start by presoaking, then put very hot water in a basin with Ivory Snow or Woolite. Make lots of suds, and put the cottons and linens in to soak. Check periodically to see how it's going. After an hour or so, if the clothes still aren't as clean as you want, change the soap and water and try again. It may take several washings to get the clothes clean. Another method is to use lukewarm water, and repeat as many times as necessary. One reason that I boil clothes is that I think it is actually faster and in the long run not any harder on the clothing than repeated washing. However, play around with these methods until you find one or a combination that works for you and that you're comfortable with.

I seldom have to use any more muscle than my trusty wash method to get cottons clean, but sometimes a stain will persist or the yellowing won't completely dissipate. Here are some last resorts for when you are about to toss the offending and uncooperative garment out. Shampoo can dig out some stains and ingrained soils. Automatic dishwashing soap also has its advocates but is really caustic. Color remover, sold by many dye companies, can work miracles when all else fails. I know a lady who uses a combination of color remover (which is boiled with the clothes) *and* chlorine bleach. She swears this will cure anything, although she admits she wouldn't use it on anything she really treasured. For rust stains, Whink, a product sold in hardware departments, can sometimes provide a solution. Many people use lemon juice, slightly diluted, on a rust spot then dry in the sun.

I recommend starching cottons and linens, as then they tend to wrinkle less. After you spend time ironing the darned things, it's nice to have them stay that way through a few wearings, if possible. If I'm going to starch, this is the place in the process, after washing and before drying, to do it. I prefer either liquid or powder starch, as I find spray-on starch messy and hard to keep even. Use a large basin or your washing machine and dissolve the starch following package directions. It only needs a few minutes for the clothes to absorb the starch, then you're ready to dry them. Other people think that spray-on starch is the only way to go, so try both and settle on the best method for yourself.

Now on to drying. When you lay cotton directly on the grass in the sun, it creates a natural chlorine bleach. You may want to substitute this method for the bleach itself, or combine them if you think more whitening is needed. Drying clothes in the sun is about as controversial a topic as there is in the vintage clothing world, with people lining up with poleaxes on both sides. I do it myself, particularly with clothing that I'm turning from yellow rags into white wearables, but you all know by now where I stand on wearable clothing. Drying in the sun shortens the life of the garment, I don't argue one bit, but I like the white, white look and clean, clean smell that results. Talk it over with your conscience and proceed accordingly. Once things are basically clean and I'm washing them in between wearings, I dry them inside on my portable rack.

Try to catch starched items when they are just damp dry, then roll them up in plastic bags, and put in the refrigerator for a couple of hours before ironing. If they get completely dry before you get to them, sprinkle, and then pop in the refrigerator. This may or may not be an old wives' tale, but it seems to make ironing easier. But don't leave in the refrigerator too long, as starch is a wonderful breeding ground for mold and mildew. A day or two is probably all right, but no longer. It's just too painful to pull something out and find it covered with mold. I speak here from experience.

I had made a dress out of vintage linens and laces, that was scheduled to be in an art exhibit. Since it is something I wear often, I washed and starched it, and tucked it away in the refrigerator so it would look nice for the occasion. Unfortunately, I did it a week in advance and forgot to take it out to press until the morning it was going to be hung. It was covered with mold and mildew, nasty red and black splotches! After much wailing and gnashing of teeth I did save it; but I had to bleach it so heavily, both with chlorine bleach and sun bleaching, that the fabric suffered badly. It looked okay on display, but for wearing apparel its days are sadly numbered.

If you're spray starching, follow directions on the can.

To iron, use the cotton or linen setting on the iron, depending on which fabric you're working with. Incidentally, while our modern irons have linen as the hottest setting, my textile references all claim that linen should be ironed with lower heat than cotton. Try a lower setting first, then increase the heat gradually until it's exactly hot enough to do the job. To iron with starch, use your thrift store iron and keep a tube of hot iron cleaner close by, cleaning the bottom as you go. The starch builds up remarkably fast on the bottom of the iron, and you'll find it dragging periodically. Always clean the iron after you've finished, and make sure all the starch is washed out of the container you used, if working with liquid or powdered starch.

When you are cleaning your whites to store away for the winter, don't starch them. Mold, mildew, and silverfish will just love you if you do, but you'll hate yourself. It's also unnecessary, not to mention downright silly, to iron things you're tucking away. When you take them out in the spring you can fix them up pretty and wearable again.

WASHING NYLON

Nylon is a synthetic fabric that is heat sensitive, meaning it should be hand washed in warm water with mild soap. Always wash white nylons separately, as they pick up dyes from other clothing easily. Nylon will drip dry and seldom needs ironing. In fact it doesn't really like to be ironed. If you must touch up, use your steamer; but move quickly as you work and don't put the steam in one place for too long, as that may stretch the fabric out of shape. Nylon garments date from 1945 to now and are usually extremely sturdy. However, old nylons should not be machine-washed or -dried. Dry inside, out of the sun.

DYEING

The value of dyeing clothing is to improve the appearance, change the look, or change the color. Unfortunately, it isn't a solution to faded spots or stains, as the spots will take the dye differently and your dyed garment will just be a different color with different colored spots in it.

Each vintage piece is individual, so treat it that way when planning to dye it. Remember that many old clothes are blends of fibers and that different fibers take dye differently. Linen, for example, doesn't take dye as well as cotton, and while rayon will dye quite nicely, it requires a different type of dye than silk.

There are plenty of brands of dyes on the market, from the variety that you find in the grocery store to imports from Germany and Switzerland. The important thing is to find a dye that works well with the fiber. Visit a local shop that caters to spinners and weavers, and see if they have some suggestions. Some dry cleaners will dye garments for you, and if you're considering doing a special fabric or garment, that may be the best way to go.

Here's a common situation that is easy to deal with: I found a wonderful black chiffon velvet dress with an ecru lace collar that was filthy. I mean it was the color of old oak around the neck; ring around the collar times five. I removed and washed it, and it turned sheet white. Often ecru colored cotton lace will do this, because the dye fades during washing. I preferred the ecru color on that particular dress, so I made a strong bowl of tea (regular grocery store variety), and put the collar in it until it turned the shade I wanted, then dried, ironed, and reattached it. A combination of one half tea, one half coffee is preferred by some people, as they think the tea tends to have a reddish tinge, and there are advocates of 100 percent coffee as well. Others use either ecru or tan commercial dye, following the directions on the label. Each of the above gives a slightly different shade, so try them until you find one that appeals to you.

PROFESSIONAL HELP

Before I found a good dry cleaner, I used to say, "I'd rather ruin it at home for free, than pay someone else to mess it up." I could tell you stories about clothing ruined by cleaners that would give you nightmares. They do me. Now I feel comfortable sending almost anything to be cleaned and pressed, because I have found a darned good cleaner. And the good news is that while he charges a little more it's very little more. A pittance compared to the loss of a much loved vintage piece.

Finding a dry cleaner who can deal kindly with vintage clothing takes some work; but it's so important to your clothes, not to mention your mental health, that I urge you to take some time to do it. How did I find Richard, Prince of Dry Cleaners? I asked everyone I bumped into and someone told me about him. Do the same, and maybe your dry cleaning prince will appear too.

Failing this, get out the yellow pages and prepare to spend a morning doing some serious phone canvassing. Don't restrict yourself to your own town or city. A good dry cleaner is worth a monthly drive, or even mailing, so prepare to range far afield. Good dry cleaners are where you find them, and that includes tiny hamlets, as well as big cities.

What's the difference between a good dry cleaner and a clothes mangler? Glad you asked that. The obvious one is that when I take vintage clothes to someone else they say, "It's at your own risk; I don't guarantee anything about those beads"; while at Richard's they say, "It'll be ready on Tuesday." Not so obvious is what happens to the clothes once they're left behind. Most cleaners nowadays have huge machines into which they toss piles of clothes and push a button. Once "cleaned" (a term loosely used in this context) the clothes are pressed on forms with machines that use a standard amount of steam and pressure, regardless. Often no attempt is made to spot clean, and certainly no one even considers removing buttons or testing beads and sequins with the cleaning solution.

Now, a good dry cleaner doesn't take clothes so lightly, and there are others like him around and about. When you call you want to know: What do they do with unusual buttons? Do they test trims, beads, sequins, and buttons before dunking in the solution? Will they clean a special garment separately, or does everything that comes through the door get the same routine? Do they spot-clean? Do they have a person on staff who is an experienced silk presser? (This is a critical question as it will save you hours of pressing and fretting.) How long has the person doing the cleaning been a dry cleaner? (Some firms have been in business a long time, but someone new has bought it in the last few years and might not be as knowledgeable or careful as the original people.) My friend Karen insists that you should ask, "How long have you been destroying clothes?" but she's become cynical over the years and should be excused.

You also might want to know something about the training of the cleaner and whether there has been any apprenticeship served. At one time the training for becoming a dry cleaner took two full years of study. Frequently someone served an apprenticeship in addition to or instead of this training. Now you can attend a six week course and become a certified dry cleaner. You can also buy a dry cleaning shop and set up without any of the above. Many cleaners hire people at minimum wage to do the cleaning and pressing with or without supervision. Before trusting your hard won vintage treasures to someone, you should investigate their expertise.

There are two kinds of dry cleaning solvent in use. Perc, currently the most commonly used, is a synthetic solvent that has been developed in recent years. A good dry cleaner who uses Perc will do fine with your clothes, other requirements being met. The other is Stoddard, a petroleum based solvent that was the most common cleaning solution for many years and still is employed by some cleaners. It is a more flammable solution than the Perc, so is not as widely used. If you find a cleaner who does use it, it will likely be a long time professional cleaner. Stoddard is reputed to be gentler on clothing and is worth seeking out if you are allergic to dry cleaning fluid.

Once you've found your wonderful dry cleaner, tell everyone about him or her. Make sure all the shops in town have the name, so they can pass it along to customers. Turn into a one-person fan club and keep that firm in business as long as you can.

Until you find your dry cleaning expert, you should take some precautions before sending clothes to be cleaned. Remove any buttons that might be damaged by rough handling or the cleaning solution, including those made of plastic, glass, or soft metal. Take off lace and fur collars. Provide yourself with mesh bags large enough to hold beaded sweaters and beaded dresses and put such garments in them when you take them to be cleaned. Do all pressing and steaming at home. Get some old clothes that are in an advanced state of decay and practice on them and invest in the whole range of pressing paraphernalia. Some garments will come back from the cleaners minus wrinkles, because the process will relax the fabric and loosen any creases or folds. Whenever you take something very fragile to a cleaner and she or he expresses serious doubt about its survival, take it right back home and wait until you find a cleaner who feels able to tackle the job.

FURS

Furs need to be cleaned and glazed by a fur cleaner. Don't ever send one to a dry cleaner, even if he or she says it's possible. It isn't. The skin will dry out in the process and you'll have a stiff, crumbling mess on your hands. Furriers usually do cleaning themselves, in house, and it is not an inexpensive process. Depending on what needs to be done, the size of the coat, and whether the lining has to be removed, it usually costs from $45 on up. This can be quite a shock to the old system, particularly when you only spent $45 for the fur in the first place! However, regular cleaning and glazing will keep an old fur going for much longer, and it will certainly look spectacular.

For in between touch-ups, you can get something called "lining cleaner" from the furrier supply places in the Appendix. This is used to clean linings, but can be applied to the collar, cuffs, and edges of the fur to freshen them up. A fur coat with a musty odor can be helped by wiping inside and out with a cloth dipped in lining cleaner, then hung outside to air. Since my container of lining cleaner didn't include instructions, I'll provide some here: Use only in a well ventilated area; keep container away from intense heat or flame (don't store by a radiator or woodstove); use rubber gloves, and minimize skin contact. Wash hands immediately if solution gets on them; at all times keep well away from small children and pets. This stuff does work, but it smells absolutely lethal and is available only in large (minimum of one gallon) containers. Treat it with caution and respect.

HATTERS, MAD OR OTHERWISE

Surprising as it may seem, there are still businesses around that will clean and block hats. You find them by looking in the Yellow Pages under "Hats." They will put your old hats into nice shape, straws too, and will usually include waterproofing at the same time. The price varies from place to place and business to business, but usually starts at about $15.

You can do some things at home, but anything serious requires a hat block. Lacking this, you can breathe a little life into an old felt by steaming it with your steamer, then brushing it. A variable speed vacuum can help with surface dust and loose dirt on a sturdy hat, but tread carefully around trims. Straw hats can be lightly wiped with warm suds, but don't get them too wet; they tend to shrink. A limp straw can be stiffened with a light coat of shellac, diluted with equal parts of alcohol.

Fabric trims, particularly flowers, will perk right up if you give them a steaming. I've put many a hat back into circulation by doing this; it's another little miracle you can perform easily. I once found a wonderful velvet cloche with pink roses and bunches of lemons, that looked like it was on it's last legs. A steaming gave it a whole new lease on life, and those roses looked like new.

Preceding were a number of ideas and procedures for getting vintage clothing clean. Try some of them out and develop methods that work for you, your clothes, and your peace of mind. I know I've had to go heavy on the warnings in this section. The cautions are real, but don't let them get you down. Unless you are dealing with rare and valuable vintage clothing, in which case you should be working only with approved conservation methods, you want to get your clothes clean and pretty. It's perfectly reasonable to do that.

CHAPTER SEVEN

A LITTLE MENDING A LITTLE ALTERING

In the otherwise blissful world of vintage clothing, mending and altering loom as thorny patches. It's a little like being married to someone who is almost perfect, but has one or two tiny flaws that drive you crazy. If you deal with them kindly and firmly early on, the problem might be solved in a few minutes with minimal fuss. If you let them go too long, they may grow into big flaws that require drastic solutions. In mending, as in correcting marriage partners, the approach is everything, and getting started is usually the hardest part.

Needless to say, faced with a choice between doing almost anything else and mending, mending always loses. And alterations! I know some experienced sewers who turn green at the thought. On the other hand, most vintage clothes need something done to them, so I've tried various tactics. First I piled the mending in the middle of the floor so I couldn't ignore it; I jumped over it. Then I put the offending garments on top of my sewing machine, so I couldn't sew without mending first; I stopped sewing. I threw up my hands and tried wearing clothes without mending them; I lost critical pins at inopportune moments. There's nothing like feeling elegant and well-dressed, only to look down and see your petticoat nestling around your ankles!

I have finally found three things that work. (1) I try to mend or alter each thing as soon as I bring it home. The same day if possible, or the next at the latest. When I stick to this, I'm always happiest. If not (2) when I plan to go somewhere, I make a promise to myself that I'll wear a certain garment and force myself to make sure it's wearable. If it isn't, I can't go. (While I sometimes hedge on this one, it does work.) And recently, (3) I listen for two hours every weekend to a favorite radio program and mend. This latest solution has been a godsend, as I've cleaned up a lot of odds and ends, which is what most vintage clothes mending really consists of. With all of the above I only have thirty or so mending and alteration projects stacked up waiting for me. Life is terribly unfair.

Some of you probably break out in hives at the sight of a needle and thread, while others are given to picking up darling silk 1920's dresses that only need their entire tops renovated. These things do vary. Because of that, I'm going to focus on what I call "meatball mending and alterations." That means that we'll try to make things wearable but not aim for first prize at the state fair.

By now you have gathered that I have personal prejudices and opinions on all subjects related to vintage clothing (no shrinking violet here!), but when it comes to mending and alterations I get downright hostile. That's because I've found a number of vintage pieces that would have been fixable and decently wearable if someone *hadn't* done something to them. Sewing is something you should have a bit of background in before plunging in, particularly when working with a vintage garment.

While many of the ideas and projects I'm going to talk about are simple enough for a novice, if you are a novice—*get help!* Ask a friend or relative (I never assume they're the same!) who sews to come advise you and to loan you some equipment if necessary. This will pay off, because you will learn a skill each time and eventually feel secure working on your own. Failing that, pay for the work to be done or trade for it. Take someone's children off his or her hands for the day in exchange for some mending projects or balance a friend's checkbook while he or she puts up your hems.

There is absolutely no dishonor in this, contrary to popular belief. Sewing is a specialty too, and while simple sewing (like simple skiing) is within most people's reach, you gotta learn how before you tackle the slopes.

EQUIPMENT AND SUPPLIES

Seam ripper—available in most sewing departments. Please, please, don't use a razor on a vintage garment. If you think you've got troubles now, just wait until you try to repair a razor tear!

Sharp scissors—large shears and small embroidery type. Don't try to make do with the kitchen shears! This item can run into some expense, so you might want to see if you can borrow a good pair or two until you're sure you're going to use them regularly.

Universal point sewing machine needles—various sizes from very small (9) to large (16). Using the right size needle for the fabric will make your work easier and make it look better.

Hand sewing needles of various sizes—both sharps and ballpoint. Pick up a needle threader as well, it's wonderful for threading needles with tiny eyes.

Small (6 inch) metal ruler with slide tab—available in fabric stores. This is an invaluable piece of sewing equipment for situations ranging from replacing zippers to taking up hems.

Seams Great (brand name) or clone—available in most fabric stores. This is a lightweight mesh (not iron-on) that comes in rolls 1 or 2 inches wide at fabric stores. Use it to enclose frayed seams, as reinforcement for buttons on lightweight fabric, under darns on lightweight fabrics, and in any tricky spot where an invisible backing will help. While it only comes in limited colors (black, white, ecru), it will not show when used under most fabrics.

Bias tape maker—available from most fabric stores in a variety of widths. With these you can make your own bias tape in matching or contrasting fabrics to cover worn edges. Bias tape can save an otherwise too shabby coat, including furs, and help disguise obvious mends and alterations.

Silk crepeline—a super lightweight, flexible silk netting sold by the yard in museum supply catalogs. Use it when you have large areas that need backing or to reinforce the underside of bead repairs on shoulders and when doing serious fur repairs.

Fray Check (brand name)—sold in most fabric and craft stores. Do try this out on an inconspicuous spot before using, as it will spread on some fabrics. However, it will do a good job of stopping fraying, which can be a serious problem with chiffon velvets and some rayons. With a little practice you should be able to use it without injuring the fabric.

Silk thread, or if unable to find, machine embroidery thread—great for silk and rayon garments.

Water soluble wafer paper—available from Aarvark Adventures, P.O. Box 2449, Livermore, CA 94550, fifty cents a sheet. Use this between the fabric and the sewing plate while machine darning cottons. The fabric has to be held flat in this process, but most old fabrics will be damaged by stretching on a hoop.

Old buttons, pieces of lace, fabrics, collars, etc.—You'll stumble on these in your travels. I keep a couple of boxes of old buttons, various sizes of common ones (small whites, mother of pearl, etc.), and some sets of especially nice buttons for replacements. New buttons usually look out of place, and I've found myself thanking my lucky stars I have some old ones around when necessary. Look for garments that might have lots of problems of their own (big stains, for example) but do have some good fabric that can be used for patching and repairs. For old cotton whites, doilies, lengths of lace, etc., can be wonderful patching materials. Lace collars can hide many a neckline problem that would be miserable to try to fix; and fur collars are wonderful for repairing fur coats. Many beaded garments use similar types of beads, so keep an eye out for beaded things that are beyond salvaging themselves but whose beads might come in handy.

Mend It!, Maureen Goldworthy, published by Stein & Day, $5.95—This book is my mending Bible, it has answers to almost all mending dilemmas.

GENERAL TIPS AND CAUTIONS

There is a golden rule of vintage mending that I'd like you to engrave on your hearts (and even on your toes): *Never use an iron-on product on a vintage garment!* On this subject I'm fairly stiff necked, and I'll tell you why. First, many vintage fabrics can't handle the amount of heat that is required for a good bond. You'll find yourself with either an iron-on patch that falls off all the time or a shiny place that looks almost as bad as the original hole. Second, iron-on products stiffen up when they are bonded, so the surrounding fabric is constantly pulling at the patch and will begin to come apart even more quickly. This is the case particularly at stress points, for example around the sleeves and shoulders. Iron-on patches will destroy velvets, and this is not reversible. And, unlike sewing, once you've got that patch on, it's almost impossible to get it off without causing even more damage. If it's sewn, it can usually be unpicked if necessary.

Are there any exceptions to this rule? Darned few. A tiny hole in a rayon or silk dress is almost impossible to fix otherwise. Just be sure to use the lightest weight, most flexible iron-on product you can find so as not to create a stiff spot.

Avoid wearing a garment that needs mending, as usually it'll get worse and you might find yourself dealing with more problems than you would have otherwise. Before sticking in a safety pin or adding a piece of scotch tape, make sure the temporary measure won't cause permanent damage. Having found staples in hems, I know that, while you may not consider such a thing, there are those who do.

Use the sewing machine for most mends; it looks better and holds more securely.

Keep pieces that need bead repairs in the sack until the minute you're going to work on them, else you'll lose more beads.

Darned spots and patches are very authentic in vintage garments. In our throw away society, we've lost the concept of repairing things; but many old pieces that we find have already had a patch or two fixed up, and this doesn't necessarily detract from the garment.

It's also not uncommon to find clothing that has been altered, another concept that we've lost touch with.

Old sewing books will often have entire sections devoted to mending and alterations, and these can be immensely helpful to modern people who've never replaced a button, let alone replaced a collar. For the best information look for copyright dates from the 1940's and before.

PATCHES, REWEAVING, AND HOLES IN GENERAL

Anyone who buys vintage clothing, whether it's an occasional piece or truckloads, should find and cultivate a good reweaver. After the reweaver has finished working on a wool coat, jacket, dress, or sweater, you'll find it hard to believe a hole ever sullied the garment. This is one of those times you can say, "Aha! It really looks as good as new." Reweavers can sometimes work on other fabrics as well but will decide on a garment to garment basis. Once upon a time there were reweavers everywhere, and they tackled almost everything—if you're over forty you might remember the booths in Woolworths and Kresses where ladies rewove stockings. In the age of polyester, reweavers were not in demand, and it's almost become a lost art. But as we've returned to wearing wool suits and coats, reweavers are starting to set up shop again. Look in your trusty yellow pages for one, or ask your local dry cleaner.

Reweavers charge by the hole and consider the difficulty of the weave itself when pricing. Get an estimate, and then keep the price range in your head while shopping, as some things will have several holes and may add up to quite an investment. An investment, I might add, that is often worthwhile if the garment is generally in good condition.

If you're faced with a darning or patch job that is not appropriate for a reweaver, such as on cottons, velvets, rayon or silk crepes, then you've got to make some assessment. Is the fabric surrounding the hole in good condition? A patch or a darn has to be anchored firmly to the surrounding fabric in order to hold, and if that fabric shows signs of deterioration, then it may be time to hold a wake over for the garment.

A darn is basically reweaving, but it is generally rougher

and more visible. It is useful for very small holes or slits. Most of us think of darns in terms of socks, but darns can be made in any garment. Most will look better if done on the sewing machine. Your sewing machine manual should give instructions for darning with a darning foot, but it is possible to use one of the zigzag stitches, switching from forward to reverse. The key is keeping the fabric firm while working. Your sewing machine manual will suggest a hoop, which is fine for new fabrics but too rough for vintage garments. I pin the fabric to water soluble wafer paper (mentioned on the supply list) and hold it firmly while working. Typing paper will also work, but little bits of paper will stick in the stitches, hence the value of the water soluble paper. Work with thread as close in color as possible to the threads in the fabric. Machine embroidery thread, available in most fabric stores, is lighter weight than regular thread and comes in several colors. Always make sure the garment is clean first, especially in the case of whites that might have a yellowish cast before washing. If you match your thread to this color, then clean the piece and find that it comes out sheet white, your off-white darn will stick out like a sore thumb!

Creative patching can rescue a garment from the rag bag. Say you have a white cotton blouse that has a hole on one side, but is otherwise in good condition. Find a piece of lace that looks good on it and design a pattern over the hole. Then put an identical lace patch on the other side, so it looks as though the patches are part of the garment design. Repairs like this are often undetectable. Use braid, beaded pieces, a little embroidery, and sometimes contrasting fabric to achieve the same effect. I know a lady who had a wonderful big, purple vintage coat with a moth hole right on the front. She embroidered a design in purple, pink, orange and red over it, and turned a so-so coat into a piece of wearable art. If you're using the same or similar fabric for a patch, experiment with cutting shapes that might conveivably have been planned (like a wedge-shaped insert), and then repeat the shape elsewhere.

Sometimes you're reduced to simply putting on a plain, garden variety patch. One hates to be too common, but there it is. Always look inside the garment first and see if there isn't some extra fabric in a facing, seamline, or hem that you can use. Often dresses and blouses from the 1940's will have self-covered shoulder pads, and you can use this fabric for repairs and recover the shoulder pads with another fabric.

To do a simple patch, make sure the garment is clean and that the area you're working on is pressed and flat. Cut the patch enough bigger than the hole or worn spot, so that you'll be able to sew it to sturdy fabric, plus ¼ inch for a turn under hem. Press the ¼ inch edges of the patch under and sew the patch over the hole. Put water-soluble wafer paper between the fabric and sewing machine feed when patching, and the work will go more smoothly. More complicated patching techniques can be found in old sewing books or mending references, but this will do for most things.

We find so many silk and rayon garments that are in good condition except for the underarm area! Whether stained and ugly or completely shredded, this one hurts. I feel I at least have to take a stab at helping you out with this problem. An underarm patch is very difficult, I'm not going to pretend it's easy, but here goes.

If your problem is only the fabric on the bodice below the sleeve, put tracing paper over the deteriorated area and draw a pattern the size of the problem area, making sure you're one-quarter inch into the good fabric. Even out the bottom of your pattern so that it makes a symmetrical curve and be sure it fits around the bottom of the sleeve. Then add ¼ inch all around and cut a patch of matching fabric. Press the edges under ¼ inch, and sew over the problem area.

If the deterioration is up into the under part of the sleeve (most times it is), cut the ruined part of the garment out, making sure that you've only left sturdy fabric surrounding the hole. Use Fray Check, or a similar product on the raw edges of the garment to prevent fraying. Then take apart the piece you've cut out, unpick the seams, and press the pieces flat. For each underarm you should have four pieces, one from each side of the underarm sleeve seam and one from each side of the bodice side seam. Keep them separate, as there may be a variation in size between sides. Use these pieces as patterns, and cut out new fabric, adding ½ inch to the outside edges. Then sew the seams together, and press under ¼ inch on the outside edges. Sew the patches into the garment, overlapping ¼ inch.

It's common to find the lovely white cotton batiste blouses and dresses with missing buttons or hooks and eyes. The fabric is so light and fragile that it seems futile to sew on buttons that will likely pull out from the fabric immediately. If I have to replace one button or snap, I routinely take off *all* the buttons and snaps, and sew a strip of Seams Great, or a similar product underneath the placket, then replace them. This takes much less time than you'd think and saves a lot of exasperation later when you put something on and find another button has come loose. As a general rule, if you've got to replace a button on any garment, go ahead and sew all of them down while you're at it. Do this even if the rest don't seem loose at the time. Two thirds of the effort of sewing on buttons and snaps is getting out matching thread, needle, and scissors, and getting started. With a little extra effort you can prevent a future problem and save yourself some frustration.

BEFORE WE GET TO ALTERATIONS, SOME ODDS AND ENDS

For some reason people have a mental block about replacing zippers, but they shouldn't. I think it's because most vintage dresses before the fifties had side zippers, and since we're not used to working with them there, it seems more difficult. Actually, the matter is quite approachable. You simply *carefully* unpick the zipper and sew the new one in, exactly the way it came out. I do agree that the zippers in men's slacks can present a problem, but if you follow the method above, they'll come out fine.

Sometimes the fabric the zipper was attached to is frayed or torn. After removing the old zipper, apply Fray Check along the edges where the fabric is frayed, then back the overlap with Seams Great before sewing the new zipper in. Another zipper consideration: always make sure the zipper is the right weight for the fabric. I've got a lovely chiffon velvet dress that someone sewed a heavy zipper into, and it looks like the dickens. Some folks are into purity, and will only use metal zippers on vintage garments, but there are times when result is worth a little modernism. A lightweight plastic zipper is often the best choice for a vintage piece.

Relining a coat is another chore that some find off-putting but which can be a reasonable project. Unpick the old lining, paying attention to how it was attached. Use it for a pattern; then replace the new lining the same way the old one came out. A cape relining job is even simpler, since there are no sleeves. Just use the same procedure as for coats.

If the old lining has disappeared (which can happen with linings made of weighted silk), then you've got something to think on. Turn the coat inside out, and using pattern paper available in interfacing sections of most fabric stores, trace a front, back, and sleeves from the coat itself. Make the pattern a little higher on the underarm seams, so the lining won't pull on the sleeve hem and cause an ugly wrinkle. Allow a couple of extra inches at the center back and 1 ½ inches on each front. Make a pleat at the center back and on each front to allow for shoulder movement. Cut the new lining with a generous hem allowance, as you can trim later if necessary. A common problem with coat and jacket linings is that they pull up at the sleeve or hem, and this is easily solved by having the lining plenty long enough. Sew the new lining seams together, and attach to the facings by machine, right sides together. Then hang the coat or jacket over night, and sew the lining to the sleeves and hem the bottom by hand. Attach the lining hem to the coat hem by making long tacking stitches at the seams. Fur coats should have their linings completely sewn to the coat, including at the hem. This usually needs to be done completely by hand.

Frayed seams are a bugaboo of no mean proportions, particularly on the chiffon velvets. Sometimes I think I spend as much time repairing these pretties as I do wearing them (more!), but they are *sooo* nice. However, I have much less trouble if I take the time to run a line of Fray Check along all the seams and then overcast them. When overcasting, either use the sewing machine overcast stitch or enclose the seams in Seams Great, depending on how much fabric is left in the seams. Sometimes you find one that has only the very edge of the fabric remaining in the seam, precariously held together with machine stitching. In this case make sure it's a roomy fit, then move the seams over and overcast the entire seam. I'll repeat: when using Fray Check do test for spreading. I can guarantee it'll spread on chiffon velvet. However, if you practice, you can get the system down so that you're running a bead of the stuff along the edge of the seam, and it won't spread into the fabric itself. Sometimes applying Fray Check with a small paint brush will give you more control over the situation than using the applicator top.

For shabby looking edges on the outside, particularly in coats or jackets, take a look at the design and see whether a bias binding might do the trick. Velvet and velveteen work especially well with plain colored wools and furs. Buy some yardage in the same or a contrasting color and make your own bias tape with a tape maker. This can add years to the life of a vintage coat and is well worth the effort.

If you think I'm avoiding lace, you're absolutely right. Lace repair is a whole subject of its own and best left to experts. I never buy anything that needs major lace repair, as I know it'll sit forever. But some lace needs only a little bit of work, so it's easy to give in to temptation. For small holes work by hand, as you need a lot of control on the needle, and use thread as close to the same size as possible. For larger holes appliqué pieces of lace or doilies over the spot by machine, working over the water soluble wafer paper.

Beading is another complete category, and again, major repairs are for experts. However by using a back stitch or couching stitch, it's possible to do minor repairs. Sometimes there's just a little place that can use some help, and it's well worth trying. If the fabric is looking a little shaky, reinforce under the beading with silk crepeline, particularly in the shoulder area.

Shoe repairs belong in shoe repair shops. Lest you worry that a shoe repair person will refuse to touch sixty-year-old shoes, rest easy. My shoe repair people say they'd rather work on older shoes, as they are better made. They are usually nailed and glued rather than stapled and were intended to be repaired. Replacing a heel or sole is very possible, and often other problems can be fixed up as well.

Shoes can even be altered, to some extent. You can have them stretched or do it yourself. Buy shoe stretcher at the shoe repair shop (it's the same product the shop uses itself) and squirt it inside and outside the too tight area. Then put on an extra heavy pair of socks and walk around for about fifteen minutes. Repeat a time or two before you give up. After several applications, however, you may have to throw in the towel and pass them along. Heels can be lowered, sometimes as much as ¾ inch. It is possible to have them made smaller, but not all shops will tackle resizing shoes. Shoes that are too large can be a safety hazard, so I don't advise risking your neck in them. But there are shoe repair speciality shops that will work with padding and sleeves to make shoes a size or two smaller. It is worth taking the time to find a repair shop that will tackle difficult and unusual projects if you're going to indulge yourself in vintage shoes.

FUR REPAIR, IT'S EASIER THAN IT LOOKS

With the right supplies fur mending is one of the easiest types of repair. Little sewing expertise is needed, so those of you who wouldn't consider replacing a zipper in a skirt might find fur repair well within your abilities.

I do all my own fur repair since my closet contains several fur coats that are beloved, furry, warm and wonderful, but it doesn't harbor even one $16,000 mink. If you are fortunate enough to possess an expensive fur, have all repairs done by an experienced furrier. Do spend some time looking for one (a furrier, I mean, although you might find the mink of your dreams in the process!), because not all are the same in terms of expertise. On a trip one time my fur coat ripped, so I called around to try to get some advice and supplies. One furrier listed in the yellow pages suggested I use duct tape! Philistines! I wouldn't let this firm near any fur, even my $35 beauties. Incidentally, most large department stores that deal in furs pass on fur repairs and cleaning to furriers, adding a charge of their own to the furrier's price. Always call and compare prices before sending your fur for cleaning or repair, and always check with the furriers themselves first.

Now on to reasonable home repairs for reasonable down-home furs. Fur repair supplies are available from fur supply firms (imagine your surprise). They make fur mending so simple and easy to do, yet are so reasonably priced, that I strongly recommend investing in a supply to keep on hand. When repairing fur garments, always work on the inside. Unpick enough of the lining so you have easy access to the area you're working on, then lay the garment flat and proceed. See Appendix for fur supply sources.

Sticky-flannel is a lightweight cloth that has an adhesive backing. When you have a tear, unpick the lining, make sure the area is clean (use some lining cleaner), line up the edges so they match, and press a piece of the sticky flannel over the tear on the *inside*. Make sure the piece of flannel is large enough to press into the surrounding, undamaged skin. Then restitch the lining.

This is about as easy as fur repair gets, and many of my coats wouldn't see the light of day without it, but it does have a couple of drawbacks. One is that you must work very carefully. If you have to pull up the flannel and reposition it, you'll pull off a bit of the skin. Since it's weakened to begin with (that's why there's a tear), you don't want to make too many mistakes. The other drawback is longevity of the coat itself, as all adhesives have acid content which will eventually damage the skin of the coat. When I'm working on a forty-year-old coat that will likely give only a few more years of service, that isn't a problem. If I were dealing with a new, valuable coat I might feel differently.

Sticky-cloth is a heavier version of Sticky-flannel and is applied the same way. It can be used on heavier furs and some people simply prefer it to the flannel. Sticky-flannel and Sticky-cloth sell for about $5 a yard. One yard will take care of many repairs.

Cold tape is a narrow adhesive tape that is used along the edges of a tear if you're going to sew it. Often the skin becomes thin and weakened, and the thread will pull right out as soon as you've stitched it. The cold tape reinforces the skin so the stitching will hold firm. If you don't have cold tape on hand, the same effect can be achieved, although with more trouble, by cutting narrow strips of interfacing and attaching them to the edges of the tear with rubber cement. Always reinforce the torn edges before sewing tears in fur. Just about 100 percent of the time your stitches will pull right out the first time you put the garment on unless you do. For repairs in high stress areas, like shoulders, upper back, or near the armhole, sew and then cover the stitched area with sticky-flannel for extra reinforcement.

An important note: if you've got a fur with a rip and a piece of the fur itself is missing, don't under any circumstances try to get by with pulling the edges together. You'll come unstuck in an awkward moment, I promise. This is where those old fur collars you've been wisely hoarding come to the rescue. Make a pattern of your hole (just to the edges, no seam or turn under necessary) and cut it out of a matching collar. Then proceed with patching with either Sticky-flannel, or sewing, or a combination.

For a more professional repair, cut a piece of silk crepeline large enough to cover several inches around the torn area. Working from the inside, tack it down completely, then sew the torn edges to the crepeline and each other, keeping the fur hairs out of the stitching line.

Wedge point needles are used for sewing leathers and furs. However, don't use one in fabric as it will chew up the cloth. Fine sewing needles will also work, and I prefer them because they make a smaller hole in the pelt. I've found that wedge point needles work best on thick, heavy furs; fine point needles on lighterweight ones. Use silk thread if possible. If not, use regular poly/cotton sewing thread and strengthen it by pulling through beeswax (you'll find beeswax in fabric stores expressly for this purpose). A common fur mending mistake is to use heavy duty thread for mending. This is unnecessary and undesirable, as the thick thread will pull at the holes and cause more damage.

If you find a fur that looks good but smells musty, try removing the lining and see if that doesn't help. A musty smell usually means that the coat was put away damp (you might make this mistake yourself) or was exposed to damp and mildewed while it was stored. Often the lining is the part affected, and the fur can be cleaned and restored nicely. Relining a fur is more difficult than a regular coat, as it has to be done by hand, but if the fur is in good condition and the price is right, it's worthwhile.

Frequently an old fur will look good everywhere but around the edges. When the edges are worn (pockets, front edges, neckline) and the skin shows through, buy some matching velvet or velveteen and use your bias tape maker to make strips for a cover-up. Again the strips have to be attached by hand, but if the coat is otherwise in good condition, you'll extend its wearability years by doing this. If you use a contrast velvet, think creatively. Make enough extra bias tape to cover the seamlines along the shoulders and on the sleeves, or construct a frog closing. This will give your repair a more planned appearance and make it look like it's part of the coat.

How much time, money, and energy should you devote to repairing a fur coat? It all depends. If the coat is generally deteriorating, probably little or none. Use the good pieces, if any, for repairing other furs; or make a nice hat and muff. Sometimes you find a fur that you like so much that you are willing to fuss around more than is sensible. For example, I found a nice, lightweight, Hudson Bay seal at a thrift store for $3 one year. I liked it enormously, so while it was not in mint condition, to put it mildly, I nursed it along through two winters. I enjoyed it enough that it was well worth the effort.

The question when working with an old fur is, Is the fur so far gone that it will come apart at some point when you are not expecting it? There's nothing like sashaying around feeling elegant, only to find the back of one's coat has come apart at some point during the proceedings. We're talking embarrassing. If you're suspicious that this might happen, unpick some of the lining and do a serious survey of the inside of the coat. If you find that the skins are coming apart all over, then best to say a sad farewell, and remember that we've all got to go sometime.

MEATBALL ALTERATIONS

Don't stop reading, even if you don't sew! You need to know some of this stuff anyway. Even experienced seamstresses get uptight at the word "alterations," it conjures up pictures of taking garments completely apart and doing mysterious and difficult things to them. This ain't necessarily so. Altering really means changing, and for our purposes it most often means changing the fit. Everything from raising the hem to adding a belt comes under this category. One of the simplest alterations for a too large dress or blouse is a belt. You'd be surprised how many dresses work just fine this way.

Some alterations are easier than they appear, and others are surprisingly harder. For example, it's much simpler to take in or let out men's pants than women's skirts. This is because of the way they're made. Men's pants were designed to be altered easily. Why this discrimination against women I don't know, but there it is. Depending on how much too big, taking in a suit jacket (man's or woman's) can be a fairly approachable project, while a blouse may turn into a hand wringer.

Fit is something we have to be a little loose about with vintage clothing. Fortunately, the different look of the lines of old clothing allows a certain amount of flexibility in this area. However, there are some things that can be done without much effort and with little damage to the clothing, which can improve their look tremendously. I'm thinking, however, of making clothes smaller not making them larger. There are very few options for enlarging clothing, I regret to say, with the notable exception of men's suits. I'm aware that some people have successfully enlarged some clothes, including the boned bodices and tiny waists of early century pieces, and I'm going to discuss this a bit later; however, this doesn't exactly come under meatball alterations and is always a high risk operation for the garment.

Clothes that are enormously too big are really not meatball projects. Fixing up a size 14 dress to fit a size 10 body is a reasonable project, we can usually do something about that. Changing a size 22 to a size 8 involves taking the garment completely apart and recutting it completely. This is not impossible to do, but it isn't an afternoon project either. As for too large garments, remember that there are plenty of stylish ladies and gentlemen who are larger than you and who would love to find something that fits. Let them enjoy this particular piece, and keep on looking for the one that's meant to be for you.

Always keep in mind the following before tackling a serious alteration project, particularly with a very old garment: Don't risk destroying a beautiful old vintage piece just to make it fit. Remember the Laws of Vintage clothing. You will find what you're looking for eventually. There is always someone who will fit into that garment and enjoy it, and you'll get yours if you're patient.

Rule number one in altering vintage clothing: before proceeding always check the condition of the fabric. Old silks (pre-1940's), pre-1920's cottons, and most chiffon velvets are high risk propositions for much taking apart and resewing. If it's obvious that the garment will never be used without the work, and your choice is toss it or alter it, then you may decide to work with an iffy garment. I just hate to see anyone take the time and effort to work on something, only to have it crumble. It's not only discouraging; you might have been working on something else that would have repaid your effort.

Another critical thing when doing alterations is to keep within the context of the original design while you're working. It's one thing to shorten a dress to fit you, it's another to tamper with the basic line itself. Look at the lines of the garment and the detailing before shortening it. If there is shaping and cutting detail on the skirt (as in clothing from the thirties), you'll destroy the entire line by shortening the skirt. A dress designed with a small waist (late forties, early fifties) and full skirt will look downright bizarre with a short skirt. Dresses that have side drapes, gores, peplums, or flounces need length to allow the eye to follow the flow and are designed with that in mind.

The same is true with exaggerated details on the bodice. There are lines that are not pleasing to the eye, and a foreshortened silhouette will appear grossly out of whack.

When short skirts are in style, it's better either to tuck the piece away until that changes (as we all know it will) or wear the dress as is with low heel boots and simply brazen it out. Often a dress that's been ruthlessly shortened will be in perfect condition otherwise. The person who did the deed didn't want to wear it after she got a look at the results. I'm going to start the alterations section with hems, so you won't make this mistake yourself, and include how to undo someone else's bad decision making.

HEMS

When you think you've got to put the hem up, put on the dress or skirt, stand in front of a mirror, and take a good look at yourself in the dress. Make a point of looking from a distance, as well as close up, to get a true perspective. Try boots on with the dress before doing anything more drastic. If you *must* proceed and the hem is already even, pin it up and look again. You shouldn't be considering shortening anything more than two to three inches. More than that is tampering with design, not length. If at all possible, don't cut off the excess fabric. I know this is antithetical to everything you've been taught about hemming, but if you cut it the next person who owns the dress will be stuck. You can unpick the original hem and turn it up to the new length, then press lightly (no permanent marks if possible). With lightweight fabrics try doubling over the original hem without unpicking, if it's not too bulky. Use long stiches, barely catching in the underside of the outer garment fabric.

When you find something that someone else has butchered—I mean shortened—and want to restore it, make sure that it hasn't been cut too much to lengthen. If so, you may have to reject the whole thing or try to make a (groan) blouse out of the top. When the original hem has been folded up, you've got a shot at it. Remove the stitches with your seam ripper (people who commit these murders tend to use teeny, tiny little stitches that are wicked to get out), then with your steamer steam from the inside in the hope you can relax the fabric. If working with cotton, you can use a solution of 50 percent white vinegar and 50 percent water on a press cloth, which will sometimes remove the pressing line. Rayons and silks don't survive contact with acids very well, so don't use vinegar on them. Instead, after steaming, press on low heat with your iron on the inside of the garment. Often a line remains, but if you can get it faint enough, keep in mind that few people will stick their noses against your hemline. Before deciding that the lowered hem doesn't look good, put the garment away for a day or two, then put it on and look at it again. Often something glares at you when you're working on it, but is hardly noticeable later.

Wools vary in how well you can remove the pressing line. If the hem's been up long enough the nap may have worn down or faded along the line. Try steaming the mark with your steamer first. Then place right side down over a towel, put a damp press cloth on the inside, and press with your iron on wool setting.

Sometimes the design of the garment will allow you to tack a line of braid along the press line, especially if you have some detailing on the bodice that you can outline as well. With velvets you can forget removing the line; there's no way except covering up. While you're at it, you might want to replace the hem tape, as that old rayon stuff is not very sturdy. Instead of spending hours unpicking it, cut it off and apply new tape to the edge.

Well, now that's off my mind. I recently spent three afternoons trying to rescue some gorgeous black cocktail dresses from "hemitis destructosa," so I'm feeling particularly militant on this subject right now. But let's move on to some other things.

BODICES AND JACKETS

Shoulder pads are a wonderful solution to innumerable vintage fit and appearance problems. The change in how a dress or jacket looks when shoulder pads are added can sometimes be miraculous. As you become more involved with vintage clothing, you may find yourself needing lots of them. I solved this problem for myself by making detachable shoulder pads that can be moved from one garment to another as needed. Because I wanted a choice of color and size (sometimes a thick pair of pads looks good, other times less padding is more appropriate), I purchased four pairs of shoulder pads at a fabric store.

I bought two thick pairs and two medium pairs, and two yards each of white and black Velcro. I covered one large and one medium pair with dark fabric, and the others with white. Then I cut strips of Velcro to match each pair and sewed the loopy side of the Velcro to the pads. Whenever I find a garment that needs shoulder pads, I can sew a strip of the velvety side of the Velcro along the seam line. Then I simple attach shoulder pads of the right size and color whenever I wear it. Easier than trying to make or find a separate pair of pads for each jacket, dress, or blouse that needs one.

When shoulder pads aren't appropriate to the design, as on a 1920's dress, an easy solution to make the shoulder line narrower is to construct one or more pleats along the shoulder seam. Another option is to run a line of long machine stitches on either side of the shoulder seam, pull them up until they are the right length, then stitch them down with a regular machine stitch. The garment style will help decide which of the above is best. Personally, I nearly always prefer the look of pleats, but others will like the gathered look better.

The key to fit in a dress or blouse is the neckline. Sometimes this is not very apparent, and something else will look off kilter, the shoulders for example, but always try working on the neckline first. Very often everything else will fall into place once that's been fixed up.

Here's a good place to shove in a tip that will often help with fitting clothing, whether altering or sewing from scratch. Try the garment on and look at the creases. A crease will point in the direction of the fitting problem. Follow the crease along and make your alterations where it points. With a too big bodice often the creases will show along the front and back, but the point of the crease will be toward the neckline. If the point is toward the bustline, that's where your problem is, and so on and so forth.

If your garment has a simple round neckline, with no collar, put it on and pinch the excess fabric into two equal darts in the back neckline. Pin this in (it takes a bit of contortionist activity if you're working alone, admittedly), remove the dress, and turn it inside out. Mark along the dartline with chalk, then remove the pins. Fold the dart toward the inside and sew along your chalk marks. Don't be alarmed if the darts are a bit uneven, most of us have uneven shoulders, so one dart will frequently be a different size than the other. Most often the darts look best angled toward the outside, although it's possible to make them straight down if necessary. This alteration can make a dramatic change in the fit and appearance of a dress. It doesn't, admittedly, address the armhole–side seam issue. But try adding a belt at this point, and you may feel it looks good enough to make do with just the neckline alteration.

Now, dare I admit to how meatbally I really make this alteration? Just between you and me and the lamppost, if the fabric is not too bulky, I don't even take the facing off to do this. I just fold it over as is and press in the dart, tacking the loose end down with a stitch or two. You can remove several inches from the neckline with this method, without creating too much damage to the garment or your nerves.

When a collar is present, try running a line of basting stitches around the neckline seam and pulling them up about 1 inch to 1½ inches. Usually this much ease can be steamed out and won't look lumpy. Combine this step with the shoulder measures we've discussed, for a nice fit.

At first glance it seems like an easy solution to a big top would be to turn it inside out and stitch in a new side seam a couple of inches from the old one. If you do this and include the bottom of the armhole seam, you'll have a small enough garment but won't be able to raise your arms when you wear it. This can be a decided disadvantage. An armhole has a specific shape for a good reason: making arm movements possible; and when you take in the underarm and side seam without allowing for this, you'll end up with an oval shape that has no flexibility. You can take in the sleeve seam and/or side seams by sewing from the hem up to the underarm, tapering to a point at the underarm seam. Pin the new seam in first to see if you can get out enough of the fullness without cutting into the underarm seam.

With all of this you should have a wearable garment. If not, it may be so oversized that you have to look at completely taking it apart and recutting it, which moves us out of the meatball league and into serious, professional style alterations.

What about too much fabric in the bustline? Usually there is no solution without taking the whole thing apart and recutting from scratch. The excess material in the bustline is cut into the middle of the front, not the sides, so taking in the sides doesn't help much. It can actually make it worse, because as the darts disappear, so does any shaping at all. If you must play around with this, try making lengthwise or crosswise pleats across the front, if that's consistent with the design.

If you absolutely have to have that particular dress or blouse, and none of this has helped, then you're in for a project of some proportion. Unpick all the seams and press the pieces flat. Find a pattern that you know fits you and is similar in design. Lay out the pattern pieces on the fabric pieces, which will take some planning as you may want to keep some parts of the original intact, and cut. Then assemble per pattern instructions. In some places you may find that there isn't enough fabric, so you'll have to piece in with excess fabric left over when you recut the pieces. Don't waste your time doing this with old silk, as it will almost certainly bite the dust during the project or shortly thereafter.

I have to admit I think a major recutting is really silly, better to find something that fits. I also have to admit that I've done this myself for the sake of a wonderful linen dress with embroidery on the front. The dress, I should mention, was a very loose, simply styled, early twenties, and didn't require too much detail work. I still berated myself all the while I was working on it. "You idiot," I moaned. "Don't you know any better?" Apparently not.

Rounding in on jackets, both men's and women's, I find that fussing with lapels and collars calls for a lot more effort than I'm prepared to give. However, it's often possible to do a fair amount of adjustment in the back seam, including sometimes adding a little width. You'll need some assistance with the pinning, as I can't quite figure out how to pin a seam up your own back while wearing a jacket. Put on the jacket, and have your assistant pin a new seam, tapering to the neckline. Once pinned, you'll be able to see very quickly if this adjustment is going to work for you or not. If not, pass the jacket on to another person. If yes, remove the jacket, mark the seam as pinned on the inside with chalk, then unpick the seam. (Some jackets are lined, so unpick the bottom hem and make the adjustment in both the lining and the outer jacket.) Sew up your new seam, and try on. If it looks good, press and sew the lining back down. If not, and you realize the jacket will need major recutting, you might consider a professional tailor. Otherwise, move the garment along to someone whom it fits.

If you've taken in the back seam and the jacket still looks a little roomy but is close to fitting, try pinning in the sleeve seams. Often a baggy looking sleeve has an enormous effect on the overall appearance of a jacket. Taper the seam from the armhole (remember, we don't mess with this area without recutting) to the sleeve hem. If lined, unpick the lining from the sleeve at the hem and redo the lining to match the outer sleeve seam, then resew the lining to the sleeve.

WAISTLINES

A casing and elastic are one solution to a too big waistline and it's the easiest if it works. The problem is that most old dresses have closings, either zippers on the side or buttons down the front or side, and the elastic will pull on these closings and cause them to gap. Better is to run two lines of gathering stitches around and pull up to fit, then stitch down with a regular stitch. Better yet is to belt it in.

For a fitted waistline in a dress unpick the zipper (if it has one), remove the skirt from the bodice, and deepen darts in the lower bodice and skirt top, being careful to keep top and bottom the same size. Then stitch back together and replace the zipper. You can take in the side seams as well, but then you'll be getting awfully close to the armhole seam and may create some problems with the side closing.

Enlarging a waistline is rarely possible. Even when there is extra fabric in the side seams, most often the outer fabric has faded a bit and the fabric in the seams will be a darker shade. This is a major difficulty when enlarging the waistlines of those impossibly small boned bodices from the turn of the century. Often there is extra fabric in the seams and darts, and there are usually several seams and darts, which can add as much as two to four extra inches around. Unpick one seam first and steam it out to make sure the old seams won't show too badly and that there is not too much color difference between the inside seams and the outer jacket. It doesn't do any good to make something big enough to fit, if it's going to look tacky. If your experimental seam looks okay, unpick every seam and dart that has extra fabric, steam, resew, and then replace the boning. Another easier solution to enlarging these tops, assuming they fit in the shoulders and arms, is to make a front insert of a matching or contrasting color. Sew hooks and eyes along the edges to correspond to the hooks and eyes on the top front.

Often we find lovely white cotton blouses from the first two decades of the century that will fit around but are impossibly short waisted. Depending on how shortwaisted (if it barely covers your bust, you don't have much recourse), it's possible to lengthen the waist enough to allow for tucking in. Use a pattern (modern) for a skirt with a waistband. Cut the top 4 to 6 inches of the skirt pattern and *two* waistband pieces from a cotton that is consistent in weight with the blouse. Gather the bottom of the blouse to fit one side of the waistband piece and attach the "skirt" piece to the other side. Then use the second waistband piece as a facing. Press under the seam allowance all around and sew, wrong sides together, to the waistband. Put a hook and eye or button and button hole on the overlap and hem by hand. This works equally well with front or back closing blouses.

I won't say it's impossible to lengthen a too short waist. I will say it's a project the magnitude of which boggles the mind. If the bodice and skirt are gathered into a separate waistband, then you can replace the waistband with a wider strip without too much grief. However, do try to do right by the fabric in the dress. I once saw a very old white lace dress that someone had altered as above. Unfortunately, she had used a piece of modern $3.98 a yard eyelet for the new waistband. We're talking tacky! With an old white like this, there is no reason that the person couldn't have done some scrounging and come up with an old fabric or piece of lace that would have complemented the original fabric.

SHIRTS AND SLACKS

A much too enormous straight skirt can easily be made smaller by making an off center pleat down the front or back, or both, if necessary. Put on the skirt and pin the pleat, waistband and all. Then stitch it down, leaving enough room in the bottom of the pleat to walk comfortably. A skirt that only needs a little adjustment can be a project. Remove the waistband and zipper (if it's a side zipper), put on the skirt, and have someone else pin it to fit. Turn it inside out and mark where the pins are with chalk. Then unpin and sew up new seams and darts along your chalk marks. Reinsert the zipper and attach the waistband, altering the length if necessary. A totally meatball approach is to make little pleats in the waistband at four evenly spaced places around the waistband without removing it. This can look all right under a jacket but will show with a tucked-in blouse. Do this rather than make one wadded up tuck on the side of the skirt, which I know some are prone to make do with. It's not much more trouble and will look one hundred times better.

Men's pants are fairly easy to take in or let out because it isn't necessary to remove the waistband. You can take four to six inches off (or add 2 plus inches of width) with minimal effort. To take in: put on the pants and pin in a one inch deep pleat on each side, about two inches from the zipper. Work around the belt loops and remove suspender buttons if necessary. This will take off four inches immediately. Stitch down the pleats by hand or machine, sewing the loose edges to the waistband to keep them from flapping. If you still have too much room, move to the back seam and pin in a new seam. Unless the pants have been altered previously, it should be possible to take up another 2 to 3 inches without putting the pockets in too weird a position. The back seam of men's pants goes right through the waistband, so rub a piece of chalk on the inside where your pins are then unpick the facing and the old seam. Stitch along the chalk marks, press the seam open, sew the facing back down, and there you are!

To let out pants: unpick the back seam, pin to new width, and resew the new seam. A note: men's pants from the thirties through the fifties are cut differently—higher waisted and baggier—than most folks are used to. Changing the style is a complex and difficult alteration, which involves removing the waistband, zipper, and pockets, then literally recutting and reconstructing the pants. If you really can't live with this look, better to purchase the modern, updated version. Leave the authentic pants to those who can, because there are lots of them!

SUMMARY

Are you ready to cry "Uncle" yet? Well I am. All this stitching and fixing just makes me feel like another shopping trip. And this time I'm going to stick to things that don't need repair and fit perfectly. I am. I really am.

Maybe if all it needs is replacing the hooks and eyes, I can make an exception. I mean, that's practically unavoidable. If the hem can really be fixed up easily, I'd consider it. That's not such a big project. I'd think about it carefully if it only needs a little adjustment in the neckline; but only if there's no collar! I might weaken if there's just a little hole and I can sew a doily over it; but no underarms, absolutely not! Oh, nuts, that little flapper dress is so cute with all the appliqué and fringe . . . all it'd take is just a patch under the arms. I don't have to replace the whole underarm; and since it's black silk I should be able to match it. But I will not get involved with that beaded dress, it'll take the rest of my life to put those beads back on . . . but. . . .

Do you wonder why I have five shelves full of projects? Do you wonder why my family is threatening to have me committed? Do you wonder why I might go along with them? Happy mending!

CHAPTER EIGHT

HOW OLD IS IT? OR IF IT HAS A ZIPPER, IT'S NOT FROM THE 1890's

Most of us like to have some idea what period our clothes came from, just out of curiosity. It's part of the fun of vintage clothes; part of what makes wearing them special and individual. It's also nice to have an answer ready when you're wearing something vintage and someone asks what period it's from. We're going to take a look at some general guidelines for dating vintage clothing. Then we'll take each era and list some details common to that era, so you'll know what clues to look for when you find a garment that you're curious about.

For general interest purposes it isn't necessary to get too involved in being accurate to the exact year. Most of us find it's just fine to be able to place a dress in the twenties or thirties and not one bit necessary to have to narrow it down to 1925 or 1936. Certainly it's possible to become more expert, and some people can pinpoint clothes within very exact time limits. If you get interested in this aspect of vintage clothing, you might want to delve a little further and the research chapter has some suggestions for materials that will help.

GENERAL GUIDELINES

Learn to use phrases like "typical of," "approximately," or "circa" when talking about your vintage clothing. People simply refuse to be shoved into categories, and their clothes reflect this. Some women liked high-top, laced shoes (which were commonly worn 1900–1919) so much they wore them right through the 1920's. Brand new high top shoes were sold in mail order catalogs and stores all during that period, even though they were far from being a current style. There's no way to know for sure when your much prized vintage high tops were bought new, but you *can* say that they were "typical of the early part of the century."

Some styles of clothing were popular for so long that trying to date them, even within an era, is futile. For example, women's middy blouses (loose fitting overblouse with a sailor collar) were worn from the early 1900's through the 1940's. I've seen a 1903 high school class picture with one half the girls wearing middy blouses, and another snapshot of a group of girls wearing middies that was taken in the forties. A photograph with a date of 1921 on the back shows a young woman wearing a middy blouse. If you find a vintage middy blouse that you like, enjoy it, and say "I don't know" when asked how old it is. White cotton petticoats and camisoles are nearly as difficult to place as middies, and the majority of men's clothing styles remained the same for many years at a time.

Some styles were only in fashion for a year or two, more a fad than a fashion, and these can be pinpointed easily. In 1928–29 dresses with uneven hemlines, usually longer in the back than in the front, became very popular. They went out of style in 1930, so can be dated fairly accurately to the year.

Most clothes within an era are designed within a certain line. They are intended to make everyone look as though they have the same shape, whether they did or not. A dress from the twenties will rarely, if ever, have shoulder pads (unless some vintage clothing lover has added them at a later date) because part of the desirable line for women in the twenties was narrow shoulders. Getting in touch with the line of a specific era will help you immeasurably in dating clothing. The details in the clothing will usually add up to creating the overall desirable line.

A little knowledge about fabrics is also helpful in dating. No need to become a textile expert, just get a handle on when certain fabrics might have been used. When you know nylon was used for clothing after 1945, you won't try to date a nylon blouse in the thirties.

Always have fun with dating clothes. Unless you're a museum, dating clothes is just a pleasant part of the vintage fashion scene. Some folks I know get extremely uptight and dogmatic about the date of one vintage item or another. Usually they want the garment to be as old as possible, with little regard to what it is. Each era has an appeal and charm all its own and deserves to be appreciated for that. A vintage garment is not better because it's older. In fact, when you're actually wearing vintage clothes, the reverse is true.

I'm not attempting a comprehensive history of costume here, but instead focusing on the details of items that we most often find in vintage clothing. The styles described are typical of the era, and I'm aware that you'll sometimes find something that is atypical in style. Even so, it will usually bear some resemblance in general shape to the standard fashion of the time. When in doubt, always place the date later rather than earlier. Few people wore clothing years before it was in common style.

1900–1910

The line in women's clothing at the turn of the century was narrow shoulders, emphasized bosom, tiny waist, curved hips, floor length. Legs were ignored, and it was politely assumed that women glided along the ground without them. This continued until about 1909, give or take a year. Men's clothes were designed to emphasize broad shoulders and a muscular appearance. Paris designers had a major influence on everyday fashion. The House of Worth, which specialized in elaborate suits and evening gowns, had an important impact. Popular plays, such as *The Merry Widow,* also affected fashions of the period.

There's some confusion about what to call clothes from this era. The Victorian era officially ended with the death of Queen Victoria in 1901, and the Edwardian era began. The clothes, however, didn't obligingly make a serious change until a few years later, so it can be difficult to know whether a specific garment should be called "Victorian" or "Edwardian." Great debates rage over this issue among serious vintage clothing people. More confusion is added when we realize that Victoria reigned for seventy-four years, and clothing styles changed a few times during that period. When someone says Victorian it can mean any of a number of styles. For practical purposes when dealing with clothing that dates from around the turn of the century it's safer to use both terms, then you have a fifty-fifty chance of being accurate.

Most of the dresses of this period were in two or three pieces. The jackets were to the waist or slightly below. The jackets were fitted to the body with lots of seams and darts and frequently had strips of bone, occasionally metal, sewn into the seams. The skirts fit smoothly over the hips, flared at the bottom, and were very long. Some skirts had a pleat or gathers at the center back. A short blouse or guimpe was sometimes part of the outfit.

Cotton and silk blouses were popular, especially the Gibson Girl blouse, with high neck, pleats over the shoulders, and puffy upper sleeves. White cotton blouses with lace, tucking, pleating, or white on white embroidery are common finds from the period 1900–1919. A clue to placing them is that blouses from the first decade often are very full in the front, creating a puffed out look at the bosom. Higher necklines with collars covering the neck are also tip-offs. This, of course, is one of those cases when "typical of" is a useful phrase.

There were some one-piece dresses for day wear, but they weren't as common, although one-piece cotton house dresses were. And one piece sheer white cotton dresses with lace trim were worn by young women for dress up. One-piece evening dresses were in style, fitted tightly to the bust, waist, and hips.

Necklines on blouses and daytime wear were typically high with collars that came up on the neck and sleeves were long. Evening dress bodices were sometimes very low cut, but many women preferred high necklines even for evening. It's hard to find any 1900–1910 evening gowns intact, but don't decide that a high neck evening gown isn't from this time, everything else being equal. Evening gowns were extremely elaborate, heavily trimmed and beaded, with much use of lace. For daytime, necks and shoulders might be covered with a wide lace collar called a "Bertha." The most popular sleeves were slightly puffy at the top with fitted forearms, known as "leg o'mutton sleeves." Sleeves that were fitted from the armhole to the cuff were also common. If you find a top with very full sleeves tapering to a narrow forearm, it is likely a bit earlier than this period.

Cotton petticoats, corset covers, and drawers were common to this era. The petticoats were usually fitted at the hips and then flared to the hemline. Occasionally you'll find a silk petticoat, often with some ruffles at the bottom. Lots of the drawers we find are open in the middle for convenience sake. Undergarments that are combinations of a camisole and drawers, called combinations or all-in-ones, often date from this time.

Fashionable women's hats were very large, with lots of exotic trimming of birds, fruits, and flowers. There were also plenty of plainer hats throughout the time, however, and continuing on into the late teens. These are harder to place accurately within the time frame. As I mentioned earlier, a tip-off to the hats is that they were often very large inside the crown and frequently will have an extra piece of fabric attached to the inside of crown, gathered with a hole in the center. Straw hats with wide brims were fashionable, and they can often be dated because they may have the fabric piece inside. Hats from this time were often of velvet in the winter, cotton batiste in the summer. They were usually very stiff, even the smaller, more tailored versions, and some of them were stretched over a wire frame.

We often find long coats made of cotton or linen which were used to cover clothes when riding in open automobiles. Known as dusters, they were used by both men and women with appropriate differences in style.

The most stylish men's suit jackets were long, usually single-breasted with padded shoulders. Less fashionable men's suits hung straight down, had high lapels, and were called sack suits. Frock coats and morning coats were formal daytime wear. Vests are often cut low in front, and had small, curved collars. Some of the very old tuxedos and tailcoats that we find may date from this period. Shirts had long tails and fastened with shirt studs rather than buttons. Some of them buttoned up the back with a shaped yoke in front with small holes for shirt studs. Shirt collars were often rounded, and wing collars were worn for formal day and evening.

Men's hats had fairly high crowns and broad brims, and were made of felt or straw. Caps were common and a flat, small brimmed straw hat called a boater was stylish for both men and women.

Both men and women also wore high top shoes, either laced or buttoned. They were made of leather in the winter and occasionally of white canvas in the summer. I've known a few people who have found the canvas versions in good condition. Women's dressy shoes were low, pointed-toe pumps with bead decorations. Both men and women wore spats to protect their good shoes on the street.

Most women's clothes of this era were made at home or by dressmakers. Even those that have labels indicating they were ready-to-wear have some finishing work done on them by hand. Some people are under the impression that all embroidery and lace was handmade at this time, but that's incorrect. Machine-made eyelet, lace, and embroidery were common. However, there certainly were many garments, particularly undergarments, blouses, and nightgowns that had hand needlework on them. Lace was used on underwear, nightgowns, and some styles of blouses. The fashion for decorations of braid and beading was less prevalent than it had been but was still worn by a number of women. Wool was used extensively, even in summer clothing, and most fabrics were somewhat stiff. Women's clothes fastened with snaps, hooks and eyes, or tiny buttons.

1910–1920, WWI

Women's styles changed drastically about 1910. The shape was longer and fuller, almost shapeless. Waistlines were still in place, but the clothes hung loose and the waist was suggested, rather than hugged by the clothing. Shoulders were still narrow, but hips and bust were not emphasized. Many older and more conservative women did not adopt this style and continued to wear the clothing of the preceding period, but the majority of women did take to it fairly quickly. This style change was probably the most dramatic of our century, because it was so sudden. Most other changes eased in over a period of time. In men's clothes the padded, muscular look was replaced by a more natural line. By the end of the period a more casual daytime appearance was acceptable for men. Parisian designer Paul Poiret had a big influence on clothing of the teens. Dancer Irene Castle started many styles in clothes and hats and was most famous for popularizing the short haircut called the bob in 1918.

Dresses were usually one piece with a waistband that hung slightly away from the waist and a slender skirt. Often the dress waistline was situated a little above or below the natural waistline. For a short time in the early teens an empire waisted dress was in style. Tunic dresses were also popular with very long and slim skirts. Some of these skirts were so tight the woman could barely walk in them, and they were called "hobble skirts." Very often tunics are found minus their skirts and will appear to be very short dresses. They aren't! Skirts were at or above the ankle and an abortive attempt to shorten them all the way to the calf was made at one point. Public opinion wasn't ready for this however. Jumpers worn over lacey blouses were stylish, and some of these were cut as tunics or with empire waistlines.

Women's suits had long jackets, below hip level, and sometimes even to the knee or midcalf. They were often belted, but the belts were merely decorative and the jackets hung loosely on the body. Double breasted suits were also worn and can sometimes be found, and some of the more elegant winter suits had fur trim on the hems, collars, and cuffs. Skirts were slim, most often in an A-line shape. Lacey white "lingerie" blouses were popular, worn with a simple skirt. Tailored shirtmaker or shirtwaist blouses were often worn by women who were working in offices and factories. Short silk overblouses with beading and embroidery were in vogue in the late teens.

Necklines were to the base of the neck and sometimes slightly lower. Sleeves were a little shorter, although rarely above elbow length. The sleeve shape was usually simple and uncomplicated, no puffs or unusual shaping. Sometimes you'll find a dress with a kimono sleeve from this period. Evening clothes were styled in the soft outline of the day dresses, but were elaborately beaded or covered with lace.

Underwear didn't change much from the preceding era, although petticoats were shorter and slimmer. Corsets were cut straight with little or no indentation at the waist and bust-binding bras were often worn with them. It's sometimes possible to find silk underwear from this time, but cotton was more common.

Fashionable hats were still elaborate and large in the early teens, but became smaller and more tailored by the late teens. The large hats became completely outrageous in decoration, and at one point some types of birds had to be protected by law because they were being killed off for hat trims. The smaller hats had very small brims, turned up brims, or no brims. Velvet and silk were the main fabrics used for winter hats with straw most common in summer hats. The cloche appeared toward the end of the era. Large evening headbands with flowers or feathers were popular in the late teens, and these occasionally survive intact. It's unusual to find a hat from this era that is not lined. Nearly all of them were, including the straws. The bag for padding the hat was still used to the middle teens. If there's a maker's name, it will most often be printed in the lining of the hat.

Men's suits were straight and had little shaping with a high lapel. A tweed jacket with a low lapel, and a belt at the back was very popular in this period. After WWI shirt collars were often softer and lower than earlier. Some of them were still round, but the pointed collar was catching on. Shirts primarily were made with detachable collars, and sometimes detachable cuffs, although the attached collar was available. A fashion for men's silk shirts appeared for a while, and they can now be found occasionally. The fedora hat, just as worn by Humphrey Bogart thirty years later, became fashionable and continued through the fifties. The modern overcoat also became common wear.

Men wore lower shoes, and some wore spats on muddy streets. Most women still wore high top shoes regularly, but more fashionable women adopted the low, pointed toe pump with a strap. By the late teens only very conservative women (and their daughters!) continued to wear the high top shoe. Spats were sometimes still worn by women, although fashion eventually overtook practicality in this matter.

Most women still sewed their own clothes or, depending on income level, had them made to order, but ready-to-wear was making big strides. Ready-to-wear clothing, however, was not made like our modern equivalent. It often had hand embroidery or beading, was individually assembled, and finishing was still done by hand. Lace was used on daytime clothing during much of this period, and there were lots of white blouses with lace trim.

Trims were in style, and braid or bead designs on dresses, coats, blouses, and evening wear were very popular. A type of beading called tambour was used, which made it possible to do intricate designs directly on the clothes. Tambour beading is worked very quickly and was the method used by ready-to-wear manufacturers. You can tell it by looking on the inside. Tambour beading is done upside down, and the underneath stitch looks like a chain stitch. This stitch was used for beaded clothing for the next few decades.

Most teens' dresses were made of silk, which is unfortunate for us as this was a period when much of the silk was heavily weighted during manufacturing. So many of them have disappeared, that finding a silk dress in one piece from this period is a circumstance to celebrate. Suits were made of dark colored wool for winter, white or natural linen for summer.

The inside of the garment will have several seams and complex shaping. One of mine, although simple in shape from the outside, has ten pieces in the bodice, which is lined, and an inner bodice as well. Many of them have a wide piece of stiff banding around the inside of the waistline, which was used to stabilize it. Dresses from this period often have very complicated closings, which are murderous to figure out. There may be dozens of tiny hooks and eyes that proceed up the side, across the middle, and around the bodice. Many have an inner bodice for shaping that has its own system of snaps or hooks as well.

THE ROARING TWENTIES

In the twenties the unstructured line of the teens was carried to its extreme, and clothes became very loose with no suggestion of the body shape at all. Waistlines nestled around the hips. The line was straight up and down, and any hint of bosom or hips was most unfashionable. An important part of the overall line was the look of a small head, which was achieved by hats that hugged the head (cloches) and very short hair. Shoulders were narrow, and some young women adopted a slump called the debutante slouch. Elderly women frequently continued to wear clothing from the turn of the century. Toward the end of the twenties clothing began to be trimmer, and uneven hemlines appeared which were longer in back than in front.

It is popularly believed that the hemline was knee length from 1920 on, but in the interest of accuracy I have to correct that notion. The hemline continued the climb up the leg that had begun in the teens but was still below mid-calf in 1920. Some designers came out with knee-length dresses that year, but there was an enormous outcry and hemlines were actually at ankle length in 1922. In 1925, however, another try was made to popularize the knee-length hem, and this time it succeeded. From 1925 to 1929, all but the more conservative women adopted it. Older women usually wore slightly longer skirts.

You may find an authentic twenties dress in any length from ankle to knee.

The line in men's clothing became established in this period and remained pretty much the same throughout the next three decades. Shoulders were broader; the waist was defined but not nipped in. Some jackets were cut to hang straight. The overall affect was shorter and square.

Paul Poiret was still influential in setting trends, but Coco Chanel, Vionnet, and Jacques Fath were also making their marks with suits and dresses. The movies were also beginning to have an impact on clothing styles.

Dresses had lowered waistlines and were straight and simple in basic design. Absolutely plain, round necklines are common throughout the period, although occasionally these are relieved by beading, embroidery, or some other decorative touch. This very plain neckline is not easy for everyone to wear, so some women added scarves, collars, or long ties to help soften them. When design details were used, they were usually done on the skirt, and many skirts have flounces, pleats, drapes, or some sort of appliqué. One-piece dresses were the most common everyday and evening apparel, although hip length overblouses also appeared. A garment that we frequently find is the silk beaded blouse. They are usually cut very loose and often consist of only two pieces, a front and back sewn together at the sides and shoulders with a large beaded design on front and back. Skirts from the twenties have a top like a slip and hang straight from the shoulders. Few suits survive, although they were a style in regular use. The jackets are hip length or longer and either hang straight or have a suggestion of shaping slightly below the natural waistline. A suit with a cardigan jacket, designed to be worn open over a long loose vest and pleated skirt can sometimes be found.

Round necklines were usually just below the collar bone, or somewhat lower, and some V-necklines were used. Evening dresses and summer clothes were sleeveless, which was at least as revolutionary as the shorter skirts. Although far from décolleté, sleeveless dresses with scooped necklines, front and back, excited much comment and were thought daring. Long sleeves were tight to the arm and most often straight from cuff to armhole. Large embroidered, fringed shawls of silk or rayon were tossed on the shoulders for dressy occasions.

Underwear was another feature that caused uproar from the conservative during the twenties. Petticoats and camisoles were still worn by a number of women in the early twenties, although corsets were all but obsolete. When the short, sleeveless dress entered the scene something had to give. A one-piece, very short, very skimpy undergarment was adopted, which has come down to us as the teddy. It hung straight from the shoulder by narrow straps, was usually cut straight across the chest above the bust, and ended well above the knee. It was made of lightweight silk, rayon, or cotton, and was often decorated with embroidery or lace. Sometimes you'll find a teddy with a matching short sleeveless robe. The teddy was often the only undergarment worn, although occasionally a garter belt was used. At least as often, women rolled their stockings into a knot above the knees to hold them up. Oriental style kimonos were popular for dressing gowns, and silk pajamas appeared.

The major hat style of the twenties was the cloche, a hat with no brim that fits down over the head and hugs it tight, causing the head to look small. Most versions completely cover the hair. Early in the period the cloche is occasionally found with trimmings of lace or flowers and is sometimes made over a stiffened frame so it will stand slightly away from the head. The cloche of the middle twenties was very severe and plain, tightly fitted, and most often made of felt. At the very end of the twenties a small brim was a design feature. Broad brim cloches are occasionally found, although they tend to be scarce. Berets and tams were also worn during the twenties but much less often.

The double-breasted pinstripe suit became standard for men, although single breasted suits were also popular. The pants were cut to be very roomy, and the legs were often wide. Vests were an important part of the suit, and rarely was a suit bought without a matching vest. The rounded shirt collar almost completely disappeared, and the wing collar was worn only by older men for day and for evening by young and old. More and more shirts were made with attached collars, although the detachable collar continued to be common through the thirties. Shoes as we know them today were standard, although older men continued to wear high top laced shoes or spats. Straw panamas or felt fedoras were most men's choice in hats.

The majority of women wore shoes that had low (not flat) to medium heels with a pointy toe, although the degree of pointiness varied. These were either plain or detailed pumps, or strapped shoes. The vamp, or side of the shoe, was often quite high on the pumps.

Women's clothes were about half homemade and half store bought at this point. From the inside the clothes have very little structure and few seams. You sometimes see one with an attached full or partial slip. Almost all of them pull over the head, with no fastenings on the body of the dress. The tight long sleeves often fasten with a snap at the wrist. A fair number of the dresses we find are made of rayon, although there are still lots of silk dresses available. Weighted silk was still being made, but more of the twenties dresses appear to have been made of pure silk than those of the teens, so more silk dresses survive. Many twenties garments are beaded, including the ready-to-wear dresses. Cotton dresses, often print, or plain with embroidery, survive in some number. Lace was out of style for part of the twenties, but there are some beautiful examples of white cotton lace dresses in existence. Late in the era, lace evening dresses of silk or rayon were worn, and these turn up on occasion. Chiffon velvet, an extremely lightweight velvet that draped beautifully, was used for evening wear. (This is my favorite vintage fabric.) Occasionally you'll find a dress made of this fabric that has a design etched in it with acid. These are remarkably fine and lightweight, and . . . wonderful!

THE THIRTIES (1930–1938)

The line of the thirties was long, sleek, and slender. Clothes were close to the body but draped to it by means of cutting and shaping of the fabric, rather than rigid seaming. The natural body shape was emphasized with an exaggerated length of line in the lower body and leg. Busts, waists, and hips were acceptable, but the ideal look was slender. Some shoulder padding was used in the early thirties on some garments. By 1935 shoulder pads were common in most women's clothing. At the beginning of the era daytime skirts were almost ankle length. They began rising again toward the middle thirties and were knee length by 1938. Evening gowns were floor length. In Paris, designer Frances Vionnet was cutting her dress designs on the living model and shaping them by using the bias or cross-grain of the fabric. This cut was basic to the fit of much thirties clothing and occurs in many dresses. The movies had the most pronounced effect on everyday clothing with many of the most popular styles for both men and women copied from movie stars of the time.

Dresses had most of their detailing on the bodice, while skirts were straight and long. Until late in the thirties dress shoulders were not often padded or occasionally were padded lightly in a rounded shape. Sleeves were an important design feature of dresses, often with unusual detailing or shapes. At one period the leg o'mutton sleeve was revived, and the Bertha collar is also found in some thirties dresses. The shirtwaist dress with short or long sleeves, tailored collar, buttons down the front, and shoulder pads was worn from 1930 throughout the decade and into the next. Occasionally you'll find one with a bias cut skirt. The longer the skirt, the earlier the shirtwaist. Cotton house dresses were often made in this style. Occasionally two-piece rayon print crepe dresses, which safely date as thirties, can be found. The top is designed to be worn over the skirt and very often will have distinctive buttons. Oftentimes only the top remains. Two-piece dresses with ankle length skirts were stylish for afternoon entertaining, and they will sometimes surface with both pieces intact. Knit and crochet blouses usually waist length and fitted, sometimes with sleeve or bodice detail, were worn much, and some of them have survived.

Suits had padded shoulders. Jackets were long, to the lower hip, and belted or darted to fit the waist. They had lapels similar to modern jackets, and might have had a self-belt. Skirts were long and straight with a kick pleat. Some blouses were tailored and often resembled modern blouses. Others had short puffed sleeves, were fitted to the body, and had a small peplum. Evening dresses were long usually with a simple basic style and all had bias cutting in the skirt. Sometimes the entire gown was bias cut. Gowns often featured one elaborate detail, such as a cape collar, beading, or a dramatic back treatment. Fun women's styles that we occasionally come across from this period are jodhpurs, shorts and sunsuits, and culotte skirts.

Necklines were high and usually accented with a collar or some detail. Sleeves were long; many had cuffs and some sort of unusual shape or trim. Short sleeves were worn for summer. Sleeveless dresses were not fashionable in this era, which doesn't mean they weren't worn, they just weren't fashionable. Evening dresses often were cut low in the back, and if so, were high in the front. Some were similar in look to slips with a tiny top that covered the essentials for modesty and shoulder straps.

Underwear consisted of wide leg underpants called step-ins or tap pants, brassieres, and long bias-cut slips. Most underwear, including brassieres, which were soft and unstructured, was made of silk or rayon. Long bias-cut nightgowns and pajamas were also popular. Kimonos continued to be a standard style of robe, and bed jackets appeared.

Early thirties hats fit closely to the top of the head. They usually had small, turned down brims that stood away from the face. As the period progressed, a wide variety of hats, including broad brims of various materials, medium brim felts, and tiny hats that were sat on the front or side of the head, were worn. Hats were often plain or had simple trims or veils.

Men's clothing was little changed from the twenties, except that the padded shoulder, tweed, single breasted sports jacket, entered male fashion. Shirts with attached, soft collars continued to gain popularity. There was a fashion for bush jackets, and Tyrolean hats (not worn together). And today thirties bush jackets are treasured vintage finds.

The evening sandal was adopted, and saddle shoes for both men and women became popular in the thirties. Otherwise, early thirties shoes were identical to the twenties, and by mid-era the shorter, stubbier looking shoe that we think of as forties was worn. Of course this means this style is really thirties, since it was first worn then, but fashion usage doesn't always make sense. Women's sling back heels, open toes, wedge heels, and spectator shoes were all worn in the thirties.

Fabrics in the thirties tended to be soft and have good draping properties. Chiffon velvet was used in lots of evening clothes, as were satin and rayon and silk crepes. Rayon and silk crepes were also routinely used in daytime clothing. Distinctive buttons are often found on thirties clothing, and sometimes they may be very large. Trims were used on dresses and more commonly on suits at the end of the period. Late thirties suits and dresses may have beading on the bodices, even on daytime clothing. Prints were very popular and came in a wide variety of colors and patterns.

When you look inside a dress from the early to middle thirties, you may find seaming in a V-shape or X-shape on the skirt or in the waistline area. This indicates that some sort of bias shaping is present. Other than shirtwaists that buttoned down the front, dresses were fastened at the side seam with snaps or buttons. The zipper began to be used in women's clothing in 1935, and it was most often put in the side seam. Although sometimes a dress will have a large, obvious looking zipper right down the front with gatherings and ruchings emphasizing the zipper.

THE FORTIES STYLES (1938–1946)

The ideal body shape was the real body shape, bust, hips, and waist acknowledged, with nothing exaggerated or disguised. Proportions were also natural, although the padded shoulder line put more width on the top so the shape was somewhat tapered from top to bottom. Hats were important to the overall line, balancing the wide shoulders by enlarging the look of the head. Skirts were knee length for daytime, long or mid-calf for evening. The war in Europe made it possible for American designers to take over, and Hattie Carnegie in New York created many of the most important looks of the day. In California Adrian and Irene had both been trend setting designers for the movies during the thirties, and each of them opened commercial design studios in the forties. The movies continued to influence fashion.

All dresses had natural waistlines and shoulder pads, and some had draping at the bust and/or hip. The plain shirtwaist dress was ubiquitous. Occasionally we bump into a princess style dress from the period. Skirts were most often cut in a slight A-shape, sometimes straight. Peplums, a short over-skirt, were popular at various times during this period on both day and evening dresses and suits. Suits had padded shoulders, varying from enormous to almost natural. There was a bewildering variety of styles and lengths of suit jackets—lapels, no lapels, detailing, and no detailing—but almost all fitted at the waist. An exception is the swingback, a three-quarter length jacket that flared from the shoulders into a full bottom.

Blouses were most often worn with suits or cardigans and were simple in design. They might or might not have had shoulder pads. Some were similar to modern shirts, although forties versions usually had darts at the waist. A suit blouse with some detailing on the front, a plain round neck, and buttons up the back was popular, as were dickeys, which looked like the front and collar of a blouse but had no back or sleeves and were meant to be worn under a jacket. Sweater sets were standard for daytime, and beaded sweaters were often worn for evening. Sometimes you can find hand-knit sweaters with puffed sleeves and knitted shoulder pads. Tailored slacks were commonplace although they weren't used for the office or for social occasions. Many of the forties slacks we find have enormous crotches (goodness knows why) and pleats at the front. Evening gowns were long or mid-calf, of rayon crepe or velvet, often with draping on the bodice and hip, and beading.

Necklines were high. Simple round necklines on dresses usually had some detailing to relieve them, although others were plain so jewelry could be displayed. Evening dresses had modest necklines, often up to the neck. The sweetheart neckline was popular, particularly for teenage girls. Sleeves were all lengths. Short and three-quarter length sleeves were usually fitted, but long sleeves were often slightly full and gathered into a cuff. For summer most dresses had very short sleeves, sometimes just a ruffle around the armhole, but seldom do you find a dress with a completely unadorned sleeveless armhole.

Men's clothes remained essentially the same as earlier periods, although jackets were often cut somewhat longer. Vests were not as important to the look as they had been, but were still worn a good deal. The white dinner jacket turned up for evening wear. Blazers appeared, but finding one from this period is most unusual. The majority of the old reindeer and snowflake sweaters come from this period.

Women's lingerie was pretty much the same as thirties, although the slips were shorter. Many a thirties slip got shortened during the forties. Cotton slips and underpants were worn.

Hats from the forties are available in an enormous variety. Some were very elaborate in shape. Often they were made to fit to the head at the base, but some part of the hat stuck straight up or shot out to the side. Sometimes the hat itself was shaped to do this and on others a feather or flower trim accomplished the purpose. Broad brim hats were also worn, particularly in the summer, and usually tilted. Small hats, however, were legion as well. During the war a tiny cap called a calot that fit on the back of the head was very popular, and you'll sometimes come across one shaped like a Dutch cap. Small hats designed to tilt over one eye, often decorated with flowers or feathers and veiling were very popular, and they can be found frequently. Often there is a band that fits around the back of the head to help hold the hat on.

With all the styles and quantities of hats that come from the forties, it's hard to believe that this was the beginning of the end for the hat as regular wearing apparel. A number of women stopped wearing hats during the war, and to go bare headed or with just a scarf was not unusual. After the war women who had never liked hats refused to take up the habit again, and others followed suit.

Shoes were sturdy with thick heels, sometimes wedge-shaped, and a wide, stubby overall form. Within this shaping were worn ankle straps, sling backs, open toes, closed toes, pumps, lace-up oxfords, and sandals. About the only style that you never see in vintage shops is the pump with strap across the instep. Saddle shoes were popular items for school girls and boys, and adult women wore them for sportswear.

The inner structure and basic cut of forties clothing is very similar to our own. The vast majority of forties dresses fasten at the side with a zipper, buttons, or snaps. Dresses with a fitted, round neckline may have a short zipper at the neckline, but it's unusual to find a dress from this period with a long zipper down the back. A good deal of forties clothing is factory made without any of the hand finishing common in earlier ready-to-wear. You will often find homemade hats of felt, as many were made because of rationing.

Regulation L-85 was in effect from 1942 through part of 1946, and it dictated the amount of fabric in garments. You can sometimes place a dress that dates from the war because of this regulation. The plainest and least drapey or decorated dresses are most likely war years vintage. Look for hems and self belts two inches wide, fake pockets, and narrow or no collars on dresses. Suit jackets (men's and women's) were often unlined or partially lined, and short jackets, with no lapels or pockets, are very likely war time garments. Of course, some folks fudged on this regulation. Rayon crepe, print or plain, was a major fabric for women's clothing. Faille, a stiff, slightly ribbed fabric, nearly always black, turns up in lots of dresses and evening suits. Wool or rayon gabardine, a hard finished fabric that wears like iron, was used a good deal for dresses, suits, coats, and men's shirts. Summer dresses and house dresses were of print cotton. Evening dresses were primarily of rayon crepe, but chiffon velvets and acid-etched velvets that date from the forties were also common and can still be found. After this the chiffon velvets disappeared from the scene—to my everlasting sorrow.

Beading can be found on semi-formal and formal evening wear of all kinds and even on some daytime dresses and blouses. The beaded evening suit dates from this period. Lace is less usual but is sometimes found as trimming on dresses.

THE FIFTIES LOOK (1947–1955)

The New Look, as it was called when it appeared, exaggerated the female figure. Clothes hugged the body and emphasized the bust and hips with a very nipped-in waist. Shoulders were padded lightly, but the shape was more rounded. The initial design showed skirts long and very full, held out with stiffened petticoats. An important part of the New Look, as it was originally presented, was a hat shaped like an upside down soup bowl, which repeated the shape of the full, wide skirt. In practice, while clothes did hug the body and curves were emphasized and even enlarged upon, the look was modified. Suits with straight skirts were actually more common than full, and while dresses often had full skirts, they were worn without stiff petticoats in everyday life. Paris designer Christian Dior was responsible for this look, and he influenced most of the fashions of this period. The movies still had some influence on clothes, but much less than before.

Women's clothing in the fifties has such an enormous variety that I'm only going to touch on a few of the more common styles that we find, focusing in on those that are particularly popular as vintage fashions. This era was a time when more people had more clothes than ever before, and the period is recent enough that much of it survives. Clothes from this period are only beginning to be appreciated as wearable vintage clothing, although a few odds and ends have found a following with some aficionados.

Dress bodices were fitted to the body with either a very full skirt or a straight skirt that hugged the hips. Skirt lengths started very long, but gradually crept up to mid-calf. Dresses with straight skirts occasionally had draping on the hip. Shoulder pads were smaller than their forties ancestors and eventually disappeared altogether. There was a style for dresses with a bustle-style back for a while, and these turn up occasionally. The shirtwaist continued on, having acquired a full skirt that was pleated or gathered at the waistline. A sheath dress with princess seaming, fitted very close to the body and below mid-calf in length came in about halfway through the fifties. Bright cotton summer dresses with full skirts, no sleeves, with scooped necks, and occasionally strapless were popular for most of the era. Suits were exceptionally well tailored with lightly padded shoulders. The jackets were often hip length with high lapels and sometimes had a small detail like a contrasting collar or self fabric tabs on the lower front. Suit skirts were usually straight, although sometimes you're lucky enough to find one with accordian pleats. Skirts were worn as separates with blouses, vests, or sweaters. Long, straight wool skirts with a kick pleat were worn for years, sometimes with big patch pockets. Pleated skirts, often plaid, also date from the fifties. Sweater sets, beaded sweaters, sweaters with collars, cardigans; all sorts of sweaters come down to us from the fifties.

A "peasant" look came into style and remained for a few years. We find quantities of these clothes, and they are very popular in vintage circles. Most common are the Guatemalan skirts, usually dark, with a figural design woven at the hem; peasant blouses, with a drawstring scoop neck and short gathered sleeves; full Mexican circle skirts with handpainted designs or pictures; and the wool Mexican jacket with bright appliqués. Pedal pushers, halter tops, and beach jackets are some of the sportswear items that we encounter most often.

Semi-formal dresses and cocktail dresses were often similar in style to daytime wear but made in dressier fabrics. The black cocktail dress was a required belonging for most women. Formal gowns had very full skirts, either ballerina length or longer, tight bodices, and were often strapless. They were made of luxurious fabrics like satin, taffeta, and moiré. The prom dress for teenage girls came into style. These had fitted bodices and very full, long skirts and were made of satins, laces, chiffons, and taffetas, usually in pastel colors. While there had been some formal wear for teenagers previously, this was the first era that anything as elaborate as the prom dress was typical for a majority of them.

Teenagers began to develop a style of their own in the fifties, and, as we know so well, this habit has continued to modern times. Fifties teenagers didn't run to pink hair or leather and chains, but the girls went in for felt circle skirts, pony tails, and bobby socks. Boys wore short sleeved shirts, chinos, letter jackets, and sweaters with their crew cuts.

Men's clothing underwent some change with a Bold New Look of its own. The look was long and lean, with broad shoulders and narrow waist and hips. A single-breasted, padded shoulder jacket, cut long and closer to the body, appeared. Pants were wide-legged at first, but were cut narrower and more tapered from about 1952 on. You'll still find some double breasted suits from the fifties, but they began to disappear about then. Sports coats, V-neck sweaters, sports shirts, and Hawaiian shirts all date from the fifties. Can we ignore the white sports coat, famous in song, which was worn to many a prom during this period?

Underwear pieces that are currently of interest as vintage clothing are the merry widow (a strapless bra and waist cinching corset in one piece); the garter belt; frilly, full petticoats; seamed nylons; and stiff black bras.

The only distinctive hat of the period is the Dior dish-shaped hat. Identify it by its shape, and the small inner framework that holds it on the head. There were also some broad brim hats, occasionally elaborately trimmed. Other hats were very small, often just a little cap of flowers or feathers, with a veil. Hats were still worn by lots of women but were definitely not required in most situations. This was the last gasp for the hat.

Fifties shoes were still rounded in the beginning of the period but more graceful than the forties. High thin heels and very pointed toes became popular later, and the ballerina flat also dates from this time.

Rayon crepe, which had been a wardrobe staple for decades, was still used for daytime dresses at the beginning of the period but had virtually disappeared by the middle fifties. We find a fair number of black cocktail dresses made of it, but otherwise dresses were made more often of cotton or wool, occasionally of silk, and then nylon. These fibers were blended with the new synthetics as they appeared, and much of the clothing of the middle fifties is either made from a blend of synthetic and natural fiber or is completely synthetic. The new styles worked better in stiff fabrics, so black faille was used extensively for dressier clothes.

Lace was rarely used in fifties clothing, even as trim. Beading and braid had a brief period of popularity, and some of the dressy sheaths were decorated with one or both of them, but for the most part clothes tended to be comparatively plain.

CHAPTER NINE

VINTAGE FABRICS OR WHATEVER GAVE RAYON A BAD NAME?

The basic ingredient of any garment is the fabric it's made from. Everything, from how long the garment will last to how we clean it, is determined by the fabric. In modern clothes federal laws require that there be a label that gives not only the fiber content but information about how to take care of it. These laws are relatively recent (within the last twenty years) so they are no help with vintage clothing. Every so often we'll find an old garment with a label listing fiber content, but for the most part we're left pretty much to our own devices in these matters. This chapter is to give aid and assistance in determining fiber content and provide information about each fabric, so you can take care of your clothes more knowledgeably. However, bring along your heart as well as your head. Fabric is not just a practical matter. It's a very senuous and personal thing. Lots of folks are attracted to vintage clothing because of the feel and look of the old fabrics. When I talk about vintage fabrics, I'm talking about love not just thread.

The fabrics we find in vintage clothing, from 1900 to 1950 are cotton, silk, linen, wool, rayon (in American clothing from 1911), and nylon (in American clothing from 1945). Many times vintage garments are blends of two or more of these fabrics.

Identifying what sort of fabric you're dealing with is the beginning step and no piece of cake. I know a museum textile expert who states categorically that she will not identify any fabric in a vintage garment without running a chemical test on it. Why? Because so many blends were used and processes employed to make one fabric resemble another.

Few of us need to be as minutely accurate as a museum expert. What we need is a good operating idea of what we're working with, so that we don't wash something that would be better off dry cleaned or put a garment out in the sun that should be dried indoors. If we can tell the difference between cotton and linen, for example, and learn enough to suspect that both of these fibers are present, then we should be able to manage.

My best suggestion is to educate your fingers to know the feel of individual fabrics. You can quickly become fairly expert at identifying specific fabrics and with practice be able to distinguish fabric blends. Fingers are also pleasantly portable, so you have your fabric testing lab with you whenever you need it.

Start out by spending some time in a fabric store touching fabric. These fabrics are labeled as to content, so you can refer to the label as you handle the fabric. Old fabrics have the same basic characteristics to the touch as new ones of the same fiber. You'll begin to feel and see the differences between fabrics immediately. Make sure you handle fabrics that combine two or more fibers as well. For example, touch 100 percent linen, then 100 percent cotton, and then find a linen and cotton blend. Look for different types of cloth made from the same fiber, such as 100 percent cotton broadcloth, 100 percent pima cotton, and 100 percent cotton muslin. Notice what feels and looks the same, and what's different.

Silk has a slubby feel and your fingers will drag slightly as they move over it. Weighted silk feels extremely brittle and will often crumble when it's touched. Rayon, which is made to look like silk in most vintage clothing, is very smooth. Your fingers will glide over the fabric. While most people like to be able to distinguish between silk and rayon, for purposes of cleaning and pressing it makes no never mind. You'll be treating them the same anyway. When wet, however, rayon becomes extremely stiff, so if all else fails, you can distinguish between the two at that point. Cotton is woven in many ways, so can have either a rough or smooth feel, also known as "hand." Linen has a distinctive stiff feel, even when the cloth is very fine and smooth, as in a handkerchief linen. Nylon has a smooth surface, not unlike rayon.

When confronted with a blend, treat it as though it were made of the more delicate fabric. For example, in a silk and linen blend clean it like silk. Since silk and rayon are cleaned similarly, there's no problem when they are combined. Wool was often blended with other fabrics, particularly silk and cotton, but occasionally rayon and even linen. Always dry clean anything that you suspect has wool in it.

There is a burn test for fabric, which some people swear by. I'm not a promoter of this method because it seems more iffy than the good old touch method. I remember finding a fabric at a thrift store that I was pretty sure had some silk in it, but couldn't quite identify the other fabric. A friend who advocates the burn method took a sample, burned it, and said, "Well, there's some silk in it, but I can't tell what the other fiber is." You get my drift. However, if you want to try it out, the basics are that cotton, linen, and rayon will smell like burning paper and produce as light gray ash. Wool and silk will smell like burning hair, with a brittle, beaded ash. Nylon has very little odor, with ash like hard beads. Acetate smells like vinegar and has a hard black beaded ash. You might pick up some remnants at the fabric store that are labeled for fiber content, and experiment.

When you have got a handle on the difference in look and touch between new fabrics, move on to vintage fabrics. Spend some time in a vintage clothing store (an excellent excuse for a shopping trip!) and practice on old clothes with your newly educated fingertips and eyes. Soon you'll be able to distinguish more than just differences between fibers. You'll find yourself able to identify between high and low quality within fibers. Since high quality fabrics tend to outlast the lesser ones, you'll notice that most of the clothing that has survived is especially fine.

RAYON

Everyone loves silk, and no wonder, it's divine. However, rayon—or "artificial silk" as it was originally called—is a fabric with virtues worth appreciating. It is often preferable to silk in older clothing that we wear regularly because it is sturdier. Whether rayon is a synthetic fiber or not is a subject for much debate. It is made from a vegetable or cellulose base and has the same qualities as any natural fiber: it breathes, absorbs moisture (although acetate, a version of rayon, doesn't do this well), and is comfortable in warm weather. Whether accurately or not, rayon is usually considered the first synthetic fiber.

Early rayons—and some of the inexpensive imports we see even now—tended to be flimsy, shiny, and cheap looking. This gave rayon a bad name that it has never quite lived down. Actually, rayon was improved enough after its initial appearance to become hard to distinguish from silk. Many people can't tell the difference between silk and rayon in vintage garments, particularly lingerie.

The notion of an artificial silk was first proposed in 1745. Various scientists worked on the idea without much success until a French scientist, Hilaire de Chardonnet, successfully produced it in 1884. Basing his process on the silkworm and how it turns mulberry leaves into silk filament, he used mulberry leaves as the basis for his fiber. He eventually switched to wood pulp and cotton by-products, which are still used as the basic materials for rayon production. He began manufacturing artificial silk in 1889 at Tubize, France. It was in universal use throughout parts of Europe from that time on. Artificial silk didn't catch on the United States until 1910, when it began to be manufactured in quantity. The name "rayon" (French for ray of light) was thought up in 1924 as a marketing technique and as an attempt to give the fiber an identification of its own. By the 1920's rayon was a standard fabric in American clothing of all kinds.

There were four common processes for making rayon: De Chardonnet's original one, named after him but later abandoned; viscose, the most common method (it still is); cuprammonium, developed in Germany; and acetate rayon. All are made from cellulose, which is a combination of wood and cotton by-products, but each uses a different method. Acetate is considered a different fabric but lumped with rayon because it's made from the same cellulose base. Manufacture of acetate developed after WWI when the term "Celanese" was adopted. "Lustron" is another term you might find on an old garment label; it means your garment is of acetate. Cuprammonium rayon was largely used for braids and passementeries and other trims in the United States.

Initially, dyeing rayon was a problem as each variety of rayon took dye differently. Other dye problems were caused by attempts to dye rayon as though it were silk. But when it was dyed by cotton methods, the problem began to disappear. Some manufacturers took advantage of the way dye was absorbed differently in different fabrics and would weave a combination of fibers (silk, wool, and rayon, for example) together and dip the finished cloth in one dye bath. This produced an unusual cloth with many shades of color.

Rayon was continually being developed and improved throughout the teens, twenties, and thirties, but it was not the same fabric that we buy in the store today. Earlier it was stiff and didn't drape well, unless it was blended with some other fiber. It was less elastic, and its strength was reduced 33 to 50 percent when wet. Because of these characteristics, it is crucial to be extremely careful when washing rayon garments from the twenties. It's also best to avoid pulling or tugging on the clothes as you handle them. Put them on and take them off carefully. Despite these difficulties, rayon fabrics from the twenties were still more durable than silk and can be expected to last longer.

Some of the problems were eliminated, particularly the difficulties in dying and draping qualities, by the early 1930's. The tendency of rayon to weaken when wet was improved dramatically as well but was never completely eliminated. Rayon had been fully developed by the forties, when it was used in most women's clothing as a substitute for silk. During WWII, silk was needed for parachutes in the war effort and was unavailable for civilian use. Rayon from its beginning was regularly blended with other fibers: cotton, silk, wool, and occasionally linen.

If you have European vintage clothing, it's possible that there is some rayon fiber present, even as early as turn of the century. In U.S. clothing, garments made after 1910 may contain some rayon fiber. Not until 1937 was a law enacted requiring manufacturers to label clothing made of rayon and acetate (Celanese) as such, so many old garments will have no indication on the label.

You've likely noticed that some vintage rayon garments have faded or discolored areas. This is not correctible, even by dying, as the faded areas will take the dye differently than the rest of the garment. Vintage rayon did not survive interaction with perspiration very well. Dresses or blouses made of it are often found with damage or discoloration in the underarm areas. Wear dress shields with vintage rayon dresses for best protection from further damage. There is no way to remove old stains from rayon without damaging the fabric. Use appliqué cover-ups or cosmetic surgery, if possible.

Many of the very thin, drapey velvets from the twenties, thirties, and early forties that people call "silk velvet" are really made of rayon. They were called "chiffon velvet" in their day, a name I have resurrected in the interests of accuracy. Virtually the only way to distinguish silk from rayon velvet of this type is by chemical test. When someone claims to have a silk velvet, they're only guessing. Don't argue with them, because some folks get all insulted when they think their silk purse might really be a sawdust derivative.

NYLON

Nylon is either the first or second synthetic fiber, depending on who is doing the talking. Some consider rayon to be, but since rayon is made from a vegetable base, others consider it a natural fiber. Certainly nylon was the first fiber made from something other than vegetable or protein base. It is made from bituminous coal, air, and water, and was considered a miracle fiber when it first came out. It was much easier to take care of than the silks, cottons, linens, and rayons that preceded it. In later years nylon lost face, as other fibers were invented that were even more miraculous. It's easy to forget its good qualities and how much it meant to the people of that time. For purposes of vintage clothing however, we have to consider it the wonderful development that it was.

Nylon was first introduced to the world in 1938 as a fiber of amazing strength and stability. It was first used in stockings, the famous "nylons." It was much appreciated as the stockings were stronger, longer wearing, and easier to clean than silk stockings, while the appearance was as good. Since nylon could be manufactured in very small threads with no loss of strength, women loved the sheer look they were able to get with nylon stockings. During WWII nylon was manufactured almost exclusively for the war effort, and nylon stockings were highly prized and hoarded.

After the war nylon garments were manufactured, and it was generally accepted for use in blouses, dresses, men's shirts, and lingerie. In a world where ironing was a requirement for all other clothing, it was a joy to be able to wash a nylon garment, hang it to dry, and then put it on with no further fuss. Nylon washed easily, wasn't damaged by bleaches and various soaps, and could be dried quickly, indoors or out. Nylon loses some strength in the sunlight but much less than any of the other fibers. It could be ironed easily if necessary but seldom needed pressing. It was resistant to mold, mildew, and moths; and was not damaged by acids such as underarm perspiration or deodorants. It retained its shape well, but was elastic, which was especially important in stockings. Nylon dyes easily, best in a dye designed for cotton. In other words nylon was something pretty special in its day. In some old catalogs of the middle 1940's, you might find nylon blouses priced higher than silk ones, they were so desirable.

Nylon can be combined with other fibers, and even a very small amount of nylon will increase the total strength of the combined fibers several times. Socks that are 20 percent nylon, 80 percent wool will last many times longer than 100 percent wool socks, for example.

Vintage garments made of nylon are sturdy, safe to use, and easy to care for. White nylon garments should be washed separately, as they tend to absorb dyes rapidly. You can be sure that any garment made of nylon dates from post-WWII.

COTTON

Have you ever found a vintage garment made of cotton that was so elegant and smooth that it seemed almost like silk? I have and have been guilty of marching around saying, "Why can't they make cotton like that any more?"

In the 1920's the United States was the largest cotton growing country in the world and exported millions of bales of cotton yearly. The finest and most luxurious cotton, Sea Island cotton, was grown in the islands off the coast of Georgia, South Carolina, and Florida. That, it turns out, is the exceptionally fine cotton that we so rarely find anymore. Then came that old boll weevil, famous in song and story and devastating in its effect. For example in 1914, 90,000 bales (bales are about 500 pounds) of the beautiful Sea Island cotton was produced. But in 1923 only a couple of thousand bales were harvested and fewer still in 1950. In other words, it isn't that they can't make cotton like they used to, it's that they can't grow it like they used to.

The fineness and quality of cotton is determined by the length of the staple, or thread of the raw cotton. The longest staple was the Sea Island, followed by Egyptian, although the Egyptian cotton was usually a brownish color because of the color of the Nile. Upland cotton was the most common cotton grown in the United States and still is, with the staple varying from ¾ to 1 ¼ inches. By 1954 cotton from Egypt was a very different quality than it had been earlier. It had become coarser and shorter in staple. A variety of cotton called Egyptian/American cotton, later known as pima, was grown in Arizona and California and had taken its place as the second best quality.

Cotton was manufactured with a variety of different finishes or sizing, most of which washed out. Organdies and some crinolines retained their sizing, however, and it's possible to find garments made from these fabrics that are still stiff. Shopping tips from old reference books recommend holding the fabric up to the light or rubbing a corner to determine how much sizing was present and how easily it would come off. Usually the sizing was (and still is) made of some form of starch, gum, chalk, and even clay in heavy weight cottons. Every factory had its own formula, and it was impossible to say what any one was really made of, unless you had the formula for that manufacturer. Sizing, for those purists among us, has been used in production of cotton since before recorded history, so it's kosher!

The quality of raw cotton was extremely variable with little standardization in seeds or soil from one farm to the next. The first industry standards were established in 1923, which helped with pricing raw cotton but had little effect on the finished cloth purchased by the consumer. It really isn't possible to say that all old cottons were wonderful and better than modern ones as is so tempting to do. After all, we are dealing with the cottons that survived intact. Obviously, though, there was a lot more of the finest quality cotton available in bygone days than there is now.

Mercerized cotton is cotton that has been dipped, while stretched, in a strong solution of sodium hydroxide. This increases the luster, strength, and affinity to dyes. This process was invented in 1850 but was used very little until the 1880's when further developments made it more economical. Yes, odd as it may sound, your turn of the century petticoat might be made of mercerized cotton, just like modern day underwear. At one time patterns were created by mercerizing cotton goods in stripes or other patterns with a printing process. The unmercerized portions would crinkle because the adjoining mercerized parts would shrink. Crepes were sometimes made by mercerizing the entire piece without stretching it.

Combed cotton meant, and still does, that a combing step was added to the process before weaving. Usually only the finest, long staple cottons were given this treatment as it added to the cost of production. It made the cloth much softer and finer. Later improvements in the process made it possible to use on lesser types of cotton.

Sanforized cotton means the cotton cloth was preshrunk. Some of the better cottons were sanforized, but many vintage cottons were not treated. A seventy-five-year-old friend of mine told me that her mother would make her a dress without putting in the hem until after it had been washed. She had to wear it with the hem pinned up until the first washing, since it was wasteful to wash something that hadn't been worn! See how much you should appreciate your modern appliances? Don't talk about the good old days, unless you're prepared to do without all the nice things we have now!

There were many more different types of fabric made of cotton in the days of our vintage clothing. In a sewing book that dates from the mid-twenties (*Women's Institute Library of Dressmaking,* 1926) I found a list of sixty-eight varieties of cotton cloth commonly available at that time. We find far fewer available to us now. With the advent of the miracle fibers, which made ironing unnecessary, cotton seemed less desirable and was used less often in clothing and household items. Cotton has many good qualities, most prominent among them is that it is possible to get fairly tough with it in the wash process. It isn't hurt by boiling water, weak alkali, or soap, and the fiber is stronger wet than dry. This mattered a lot to our foremothers, who were working under very primitive conditions. When dealing with vintage cotton fabric, we can use stronger measures than with other fibers, but still allow for the deterioration that takes place with age. Cotton's less attractive qualities are that it is the least elastic fabric and the least resistant to the elements. It also absorbs soils and wrinkles easily.

Cotton's worst enemies are mildew and mold. They are tough enemies to have because the spores are present in the air all the time. The best defense is to keep the clothing dry and at moderate or cool temperatures at all times. Store them clean and don't wrap them in plastic.

SILK

Silk has always been considered the most elegant and luxurious of fabrics. At one time it was a fairly expensive fabric but was still used extensively in clothing until after WWII when the new synthetics became available. Silk is a difficult fabric to clean and press, and you can't blame folks for wanting to use something a little more on the wash and wear side. In vintage clothing silk is a very important fiber, and there were many different types of cloth made from it. The same 1920's sewing book listing sixty-eight varieties of cotton lists sixty-seven different varieties of silk fabric, although it's unusual to find more than a dozen in use in modern times.

Silk is a protein fiber spun by silkworms who munch away on mulberry leaves and then spin a cocoon. The process of making silk from these cocoons is unbelievably involved and labor intensive. Look at the raw edge of silk fabric and see the size of the threads; then realize that each thread is several strands spun together. It's mind boggling that silk fabric can be made at all, let alone that there was so much of it available.

We've all had the experience of finding a wonderful vintage silk garment that is crumbling. These garments will often feel stiff and brittle, and when you touch them the fiber breaks. We also find coats, bags, and hats where the lining consists of only a few silk threads. At the same time, we find old silk garments that appear to be soft and flexible and in good condition. What goes on here? The answer is weighting. Many vintage silks were made by adding metal salts to increase the weight and to get more mileage from the raw silk. This produced a fabric that could be manufactured for much less money. Dark colors, particularly black, had even more salts added in the dying process. In short a manufacturer could add as much as 40 percent (and many did) to the weight of the fabric. The resulting fabric was significantly weaker. Weighted silk was a problem even at the time the clothes were new, as some garments made of it deteriorated after only one or two wearings. Those that survived to become vintage garments, as weak as they seem now, were actually stronger than others when they were new.

At that time there were no labeling laws, such as we take for granted, and therefore no way for the shopper to tell whether her silk was pure or weighted. To make it more confusing, some silk was not weighted, some was only slightly, and some was heavily. Prices were no indicator, so a heavily weighted silk might cost a great deal, and a purer silk be less expensive. That's why we can now find a very elaborate dress that's made of weighted silk and therefore crumbling, and at the same time find a silk coat lining from the same period that's still in perfect condition.

In 1938 federal labeling laws were instituted for silk. The Trade Product Rules for the silk industry required that all products labeled "silk," "pure silk," "all silk," or "pure dye silk" must contain silk and no other ingredients, except necessary dyeing and finishing materials not to exceed 10 percent of finished weight (or 15 percent for black). The presence of metallic weighting was indicated as percentage, by weight, to total weight of finished silk, e.g., "Silk, Weighted 25%." 1938, however, is a few years after many of the garments we treasure were made. In general weighted silk disappeared from the market because it didn't wear well and was replaced by rayon, which gave almost the same appearance but longer wear for the same price.

The problem of weighted silk has caused many of us vintage lovers a lot of grief. I've found silk dresses and petticoats that are absolutely breathtaking and completely falling apart. It's enough to make a person cry, because there is no way to save a weighted silk garment when it starts to go and no way to predict when it will. Usually, if a garment is weighted silk, it has begun to fall apart by now. However, I have known women who have bought dresses that felt a little brittle but seemed in one piece, only to have them fall apart on their backs. If you find such a garment, and someone tries to tell you that you can fix it, don't under any circumstances believe them. It ain't so.

Living with vintage silk, wonderful as it is, is a tricky proposition. Silk is a relatively strong fiber (assuming no weighting) when dry but is slightly weakened when wet. That means it has to be handled very carefully and be well supported during the wash and dry process. Silk must be dried carefully and slowly away from direct sunlight. It loses 50 percent of its original strength after only a couple of hours in the sun, and weighted silk loses strength even faster. A mild soap will not harm silk but strong detergents will. Some flat silks are better off when washed than dry cleaned, but pressing is such a problem because heat is so hard on the silk that you may choose to have all silks dry cleaned. Chlorine bleach and enzyme presoaks will attack and destroy the fiber, so stain removal options are limited or nonexistent. Perspiration is deadly to silk garments, which is why we find so many of them that have ruined armpits and are weakened across the shoulders. Deodorants with aluminum chloride also weaken the fabric. Wear underarm shields with silk garments and wash both garments and hosiery immediately after wearing. All the foregoing applies to new silk garments as well as old ones, incidentally.

WOOL

Wool is far less sexy than other fabrics. It's a wonderful fabric, and we should honor it appropriately, but there isn't too much exciting to say about it. It is the oldest fabric manufactured by man and the sturdiest. It's possible to find very old wool vintage garments that are in unbelievably good condition, if they've been well protected from moths. Unlike clothing made of other fibers, many wool vintage garments can be worn with less worry about them falling apart, even if they're quite old. One reason that wool suits (both men's and women's) from the thirties and forties are so popular is that they will give more wearability in relation to their price than any vintage purchase that you make. Hard finished woolens, like gabardine, broadcloth, and worsteds, can last a very long time.

Vintage wools that we encounter were not only made from sheep. Camel's hair, vicuña, various types of goat, including the angora and cashmere, and llama wools were used for luxury items for the rich. Shawls made of cashmere are very desirable vintage items and a number have survived. Items made of vicuña, angora, and llama tend to have shorter lives, probably because a softer surface wool does not wear as well as the hard finished ones.

As the rangelands in the United States were taken over by farmers and cattle ranching became more profitable, the raising of sheep declined seriously in the United States and wool became a very expensive fabric. From the vantage point of the 1980's this change is often seen as interesting subject matter for western movies and television shows, but it had a serious impact on the people of the time. Wool fabrics were badly needed, as their properties of holding body heat in and absorbing moisture were very important in a world without temperature control and central heating. To meet the demand for low cost wool, it was often blended with other fibers. Cotton and wool, for example, made a very sturdy and comfortable fabric but it had less longevity than 100 percent wool. It was much in use for underwear and considered more hygenic than 100 percent wool undergarments. Silk and wool has a luxurious feel and was used for very expensive women's winter clothing. A common low-cost wool was called *shoddy* and consisted of new wool and recycled wool from old clothing. This wool was not well thought of, as you can tell from the name, but actually wore as well as fabric made of all new wool. There was a lively trade in old woolen clothing because of this, and the term *rag trade*, which eventually became slang for the clothing industry, originally referred to this activity.

Your options for dealing with wool are limited. Wool shrinks when wet and felts if rubbed or put in too hot water, so the only reasonable option for most wool garments is dry cleaning. Sweaters can be hand washed in Woolite or Ivory Snow in lukewarm water; however, very careful handling is required. Dry cleaning is a better option not only because of the problems of felting and shrinking but also because the dry cleaning fluid gives moth protection. Wool tends to release soils easily, and some very old stains may come out during the cleaning process. Chlorine bleach and enzyme presoaks attack and dissolve the protein fibers, and should be avoided.

If you think we have problems cleaning wool, think of the original owners of vintage clothing, who had less access to low cost dry cleaning and mild detergents than we do. The most common solution was not to clean it at all. Wool clothing was often hung outside to air rather than be cleaned. Sometimes a wool garment was never cleaned at all, and if it was cleaned, it wasn't often. If this sounds disgusting to you, realize that people in the early part of the century weren't quite so fanatic about cleanliness as we are now. The difficulty in obtaining plenty of hot water and lack of central heating made it not uncommon to bathe and wash hair every one or two weeks, rather than every day. A wool garment that was aired to smell fresh, then brushed and pressed, rather than thoroughly cleaned, seemed perfectly acceptable to most people at the time. One reason we find so much very old wool vintage clothing in good condition is directly attributable to how seldom it was cleaned. Cleaning contributes directly to deterioration, and wool clothing was cleaned so seldom that it suffered less damage than other fabrics.

The worst enemies of wool, besides home laundering, are moths and carpet beetles. It hurts to find beautiful old wool coats and suits that would still be usable if they weren't riddled with holes from these pests. Do take action to prevent bugs from ruining these clothes, either herbal moth repellents or standard mothballs or crystals.

LINEN

At one time linen was woven in most American homes as a regular part of homemaking. When factory production of cloth replaced home spinning and weaving, about 1830, cotton replaced linen as the most common household cloth. That's because the machine production of linen didn't develop as rapidly as that of other fabrics. Linen, while a much prized cloth, was very expensive because of the amount of hand labor required to produce it. Flax requires a certain combination of climate and soil to produce good quality linen fibers and this limits the amount of raw flax that can be produced.

During WWI a crisis in the production of linen occurred. Battles were fought on the flax producing fields of France and Belgium, and the Soviet Union, a major producer of flax and rough linen, was effectively cut off from the rest of world. The war was almost over before cotton could be manufactured to take the place of linen in making airplane wings. To compensate for this machine methods of growing flax and manufacturing linen cloth were developed. However, the best linen was still produced by a long, labor intensive process, and linen has remained an expensive cloth to this day. For example, chemical bleaching required six days, which is not negligible. But the highest quality linen was bleached by being moistened and laid out on the grass, then remoistened and laid out again, and then again, and even again, until the desired amount of whiteness was obtained. This often took weeks and loss from rodents was high. Irish and Belgian linens were the finest in the world (and still are) because the climate was ideal for the growing of flax and the slow hand manufacture of the cloth.

Linen is the strongest of the vegetable fibers. Moisture is absorbed without penetrating the fibers, so it evaporates very quickly. It releases soil easily, and bacteria grow slowly on it, so that it remains clean longer and is easy to get clean. It is a beautiful cloth that tends not to produce lint and will withstand very hard wear. It was much used for table linens, handkerchiefs, surgical dressings, and underwear, as well as hot weather suits for both men and women, and fine white dresses and blouses. Linen is heavier than cotton, but feels much cooler because it doesn't absorb water in the same way. Linen can be divided into the most minute threads without losing its strength, which makes it an invaluable fiber for fine lace making. It was used for many of the same types of cloth as cotton, including the familiar batistes and lawns. You can assume that a vintage white garment made of linen was originally far more expensive than one made of cotton and will likely last much longer.

Don't use boiling water on linen and experiment with the heat setting on your iron as too much heat is not good for linen. Iron linen while it's still damp. You can remove slight scorch marks with soap and warm water.

CHAPTER TEN

DOING RESEARCH OR DO YOU REALLY BELIEVE POLYESTER DOUBLE KNIT PANT SUITS DISAPPEARED IN THE LATE 1970's

Here's an exercise that will give you an important perspective as you learn about dating vintage clothing. Spend some time looking at current fashion magazines, then go to the fabric store and study some of the pattern books. See what these sources have to say about what's being worn right now. Watch television, paying special attention to how people are dressed. Then for the next day or so, keep your eyes open wherever you go and pay attention to what people are *really* wearing. It should be quite an eye opener.

Think of how many people one-hundred, or even sixty years from now might try to date the clothing we're wearing now and of what impressions they will get from the materials available to them. If they based their opinions on fashion magazines and television video tapes, they'd think that no one has worn polyester, especially double knits, since the 1970's. A walk around town will tell you that lots of men and women wear polyester double knit clothing on a regular basis. Another mistaken impression would be that most men and women are very slender, and only a very few are chubby, let alone fat. This when we see statistics indicating that at least one third of people in the United States are overweight and most of that group enough so to qualify as obese. Our future researcher is going to have to pour a few grains of salt on her data in order to be accurate. We encounter the same problem as we pour through old magazines and history of costume books.

Basically, while the clothing was different, people were just like you and me. Some liked to be in style; some didn't give a hoot; others went for comfort; while still others would suffer any extreme of physical pain and financial deprivation to look the way they thought they ought. They did this within the context of the clothing styles around at the time, just the way we do now.

When we look at the major sources of information it's good to keep in mind that most of the vintage clothing that follows us home was owned by ordinary, regular people like you and me. While some of us occasionally stumble on a Paris original, this is not the general run of vintage clothing that we find. Also, people tended to save their "best," so that we are going to find more dress-up clothing than everyday duds. Economic conditions are a big factor as well. Until the turn of the century and the beginnings of a large middle class in the United States, there were a few rich, a few more well-to-do, and a whole lot of poor people. Poor people rarely had clothing that they could afford to save for future generations, so we don't find very much clothing from that category. At the same time we seldom have much chance to get our hands on clothing that belonged to the very rich because it's snapped up by museums and collectors. Most of the vintage clothing that you and I bring home comes from that middle class sector. Where the people in that group got their clothes and how is important to accurate dating.

The three major places to get information on vintage clothing are contemporary magazines (including sewing patterns and mail order catalogs), history of costume books, and, for clothing of this century, movies and word of mouth from the people who wore the clothes. Other things like letters, diaries, and books are also helpful and can be used to supplement. To become a really savvy dater use all three together. This way you can cross-check references and supplement where one source might be inaccurate and this will help you keep an overall perspective.

MAGAZINES, SEWING PATTERNS, AND MAIL ORDER CATALOGS

It's hard to make a switch in thinking from now, when we can watch a television show, observe the clothes of the real or imaginary wealthy and pick up reasonable facsimiles in K-Mart within a couple of months, to a time when the major source of information about new styles was magazines. But that's the way it was during the 1800's and throughout the first twenty years of this century. Before that, especially here in America, fashion mannequin dolls were sent from Paris to local dressmakers. All the women who could afford to indulge in fashionable dressmakers rushed to see what styles they would choose for their new dresses and bonnets.

In America one of the first and most popular fashion magazines was *The World of Fashion and Continental Feuilltons*. It was published by a Mrs. Bell in England, beginning in 1824. Mr. Bell also contributed to the fashion world with his *Gentlemen's Magazine of Fashion*. Style conscious Americans read these magazines and took their lead as well as the English. Mrs. Bell, incidentally, was quite a character and wrote several different columns and articles for her magazines under various fictitious, but supposedly fashionable, lady's names. She ran a very high toned dressmaking establishment, had a speciality in corsets, many of which she invented herself, and served the royal family in this regard. She also invented a bonnet that folded up for indoor wear.

Later came the *Godey's Lady Book*, *Peterson's Magazine*, and *The Lady's Friend* published during the middle and late 1800's; these included fashion along with short stories and articles of interest. You couldn't step down to the local department store and pick up the newest dress or bonnet or top coat as pictured; you took the picture to your dressmaker to have it copied, or copied it yourself. Later, the magazines published pattern diagrams, which the enterprising women copied, enlarged, and then used to sew the very latest style.

Ready-to-wear clothing became common for American men following the Civil War, when the factories that were established to make uniforms simply continued on after the war. Of course, the wealthy, or even well-to-do middle class gentleman, had his clothing made by a "bespoke" tailor. Acceptance of women's ready-to-wear was much slower, gaining ground after the turn of the century and catching on seriously by the 1920's. Even at that, most women had at least some clothing that was either made at home or by a dressmaker. (Prices for ready to wear clothing were about the same as for clothing made by a local dressmaker. A fashionable dressmaker would charge much more, and homemade was much cheaper.) The Depression of the thirties made it financially difficult for the majority of women to buy all of their clothes ready made, but the return of prosperity with WWII pushed ready to wear over the brink and by the forties most women bought the majority of their clothes ready made from stores. And when I went to school in the fifties homemade clothing was something one preferred not to admit to.

Pictures of couturier clothing are fun and interesting, but the styles of the sewing patterns were what most women wore. *McCalls, The Ladies Home Journal, Priscilla, Needlework,* and *The Delineator* are magazines that you should look for. In them you'll see drawings of the-up-to-date fashions of the time as well as other fashion information about hats, gloves, fabrics in style, automobile and bicycling attire, and so forth. One danger of these magazines is you may get lost in them. I once spent an afternoon supposedly researching clothes but got hooked on a story called "Don Quixote in a Flivver" (*McCalls*, 1922), advice to the lovelorn, an article about "What Mothers Want for Their Children" (McCalls, 1917), and a 1938 *Woman's Home Companion* piece about "How to Improve Conferences." Are you wondering what mothers wanted for their children in 1917? The same things they want right now! And I sent a copy of the article on conferences to a person who was chairing a state convention. The ideas and complaints were identical to those I'd had after my last conference. I warn you, these magazines are addicting!

Some public libraries have back issues of magazines available to read on the premises in reference sections. If you live near a large university, particularly one that has a home economics department, check out the college library for old magazines. Flea markets, thrift stores, and antique shops often carry such items, and some of the mail order book dealers have vintage magazines in stock. One of the problems in acquiring old magazines is the current interest in collecting advertising memorabilia; this demand has increased the prices by a tremendous amount. These collectors will often cut up magazines and they usually take off the covers, which means the magazines are hard to find intact. On the other hand, since their interest is specifically for the ads, you can sometimes get your hands on the fashion segments.

Sewing patterns themselves are also helpful, but most don't have a date. McCalls patterns are an exception. You'll find a copyright date on the pattern envelope for the specific pattern in the small print, if you look carefully. Early Butterick and some Pictorial Review patterns will have a patent date—but this date is not necessarily the exact year of the individual pattern. The patent date, however, can put you within a few years of that particular garment. Vintage sewing patterns are becoming almost as desirable as vintage clothing at this point, so grab them up when you find them.

While more women were buying ready to wear from the 1940's on, sewing pattern fliers will still give fairly accurate examples of what current clothing styles were. Sewing patterns were made to be sold in large quantities and had to represent what was in at the moment. Never underestimate the power of the dollar and realize that any item that was intended to sell in quantity is more likely to be representative of the majority's taste than one that was meant for a small audience.

In the 1940's publications like *Glamour, The Magazine for the Woman Who Works* showed ready-to-wear. The prices in the ads are enough to make you want to rent a time machine. All those pretty clothes, with full page ads for dresses priced at $11.95! Alligator shoes and bags for $6.95. Let me at 'em. *Vogue* and *Harper's Bazaar* also showed ready to wear clothing as well as the couturier fashions from Paris, but this was the high rent district and the prices are a little less appealing.

Knit and crochet pattern books are also very helpful. They were first marketed in the middle 1800's. While few sweaters survive from earlier than the 1940's, the pictures are a tip off to general styles that were being copied at home. Gloves, hats, and other accessories are shown as well. Expect some surprises as you look through them. Most of us think of the roaring twenties as a time when women wore teddies and silk stockings under short dresses. Not all of them. Patterns for crocheted corset covers and nightgown yokes were very popular. Cute little boudoir caps were still something that many women made and wore. One of my crochet pattern books for 1931 has several patterns for the "new, fashionable" gauntlet gloves that were the rage, including a pattern to make detachable gauntlets for updating old gloves.

Mail order catalogs for ready-to-wear clothing are also great sources, particularly from the late 1800's through the early 1930's. Even well-to-do women purchased clothing from these catalogs, which makes sense when you think of how spread out the population was in the United States. A stylish woman who lived far away from a bit city might not be able to hit the fashionable stores more than once a year. She depended on mail order from her favorite stores to keep up to date and expected the catalogs to show the latest styles. These catalogs occasionally show up in antique stores and flea markets.

Home economics and sewing books offer a wealth of information. If you can learn construction techniques common to the different eras, you'll be way ahead in terms of identification. Information about fabrics, advice on choosing appropriate styles for age, height and weight, colors, even suggestions about hat choices, and budgeting are included. I have a 1916 home economics book that lists the items that should be included in a wardrobe and their approximate cost. It suggests planning a woman's wardrobe around spending *$150* per year, using a three year plan. Try that idea out on any teenager you know and see how far it gets! Old sewing and home economics books are still easy to find at used book stores, and mail order book dealers that specialize in old textile books often feature them.

HISTORY OF COSTUME BOOKS

History of costume books have good information, and a whole lot of limitations when using that information for specific garments. But for an overview of costume and seeing styles in transition, these books are invaluable. Anyone with an interest in vintage clothing owes it to him or herself to spend a few hours reading a selection of these books. Most local libraries have them available under "costume." A list of history of costume books that I especially recommend is included in the Appendix.

Some books will focus on a specific period; others cover the range of clothing from prehistoric to modern. The major difficulty with the latter is that all the information about modern clothing is often tucked into a couple of chapters at the end. The objective of most of these books is *not* to provide anyone with information for dating clothing but to provide an overview of costume over time. Lack of space can lead to statements that are so sweeping that, while they may be accurate in the long view, are actually inaccurate when applied to specific garments.

For example, many history of costume books will say that skirts were knee length in the 1920's. Period. Now this is one of those things that is true but not quite. Skirt lengths actually varied from ankle length to knee length, and many older or more conservative women never wore the shorter skirts.

Most history of costume books use designer clothing as the basis for their discussions of historic clothing. Few of the clothes we encounter are from this category. More importantly, while Paris set the tone and the style, many Parisian styles were far too avant garde to be accepted in Indianapolis or Seattle. If you see that Poiret (a famous fashion designer of the first three decades of this century) shows pants suits in 1915, don't you believe that they were seen anywhere outside the most exclusive and bohemian circles. Not all history of costume books use designer clothing exclusively, and those that mention contemporary magazines, diaries, and letters will often have a more realistic touch.

WORD OF MOUTH, OLD PHOTOGRAPHS, AND DIARIES

It sometimes happens that you find yourself buying a garment or some accessory from its orginal owner. Certainly this is a time when you'll be able to obtain an accurate date, of origin, right? Well, I'd be a bit cautious about accepting the date given unless it checks out with information that you have from other sources. I recently spent a few hours with a charming seventy-five-year-old woman, from whom I bought some great vintage clothing. We had a nice chat, and she was obviously getting a kick out of talking about the clothes. However, she showed me a pink polyester double knit mini-dress and swore that she'd worn it in the 1930's. Since polyester wasn't used for clothing until the early 1960's and certainly wasn't invented in the 30's and since clothing in the 1930's was mid-calf to ankle for most of the decade, rising to just below the knee in 1938, I knew I had a case of overenthusiasm.

This can and does happen, so do keep some perspective. Usually if the person in question is tying the garment into a specific event ("I bought this on a trip to San Diego in 1950," or "I wore this the first year I taught school") the information is more likely to be reliable. Incidentally, if you try going through your own closet remembering the dates you bought things, particularly the older ones, you'll quickly see the difficulty.

I wish people would put dates on their old photographs! I like to pick up old photographs at estate sales and antique stores and enjoy looking at the clothes as they were worn originally, but more often than not there is no date. When there is one you get a good idea of what was being worn when—and how. But dates or not, don't ignore this source of information. There's nothing like seeing a well rounded woman stuffed into a boned top, obviously dressed in her best to have her picture taken, to get a hint of what it must have been like to be a real person wearing those clothes. A much more realistic way to see it than in a drawing from a fashion magazine.

When you have a minute, get out all your own family photographs and write the dates and names on the back. Do it while you're having your coffee tomorrow morning—or why wait? Do it as soon as you finish reading this chapter. Then sixty years from now the people looking at them will not be trying to figure out who was doing what, when.

It's possible to find photographs that date well back into the 1800's, usually studio portraits or pictures taken by traveling photographers. Informal snapshots can be found that date from the early teens, and by the late teens and early twenties they are fairly common. Incidentally, looking at old photographs is a truly fun occupation. If this is research, and it is, more of it! I can never figure out how people can bear to sell or throw out their old family pictures. I'm not complaining, mind you, but I don't understand it.

Occasionally diaries, family letters, and so forth can be found that refer to specific garments. I know a woman who inherited trunks full of clothing from relatives. By some miracle, she also found photographs and diary documentation for many of them. This is the kind of windfall that happens rarely, but it is wonderful when it does.

FILM AND FICTION

The movies had—and have—an enormous influence on clothing. Beginning in the 1920's and particularly in the thirties and forties many style trends were born because of movie stars' wardrobes. Clark Gable, a man's man as well as a lady's man, precipitated a crisis in the underwear industry by appearing without an undershirt in *It Happened One Night* in 1934. On the other hand, he also helped establish the style for the sports jacket, which created a whole new line in menswear. In 1922 Wallace Reid appeared in a soft unstarched shirt with an attached collar. Men demanded them from stores, but there were hardly any available. When shirt manufacturers complained bitterly to Hollywood moguls, they suggested that the manufacturers start making them. They did, and the man's shirt as we know it today arrived. George Raft, William Powell, Fred Astaire, Humphrey Bogart, and Cary Grant are among the male stars that influenced important trends in men's clothing.

The spectacular padded shoulder suits and dramatic hats worn by Joan Crawford set the tone for two decades of women's clothing in the 1930's and forties. The mannish style slacks, jackets, and trenchcoats worn with elegance by Marlene Dietrich and Greta Garbo paved the way for many of the clothes we take for granted today. The female Hollywood stars were absolutely idolized by millions, and their clothing, hairstyles, makeup, even their ways of walking and talking were copied slavishly. Whether or not Hollywood designers can be credited with originating the styles is open for some debate, but certainly they promoted them and made them popular.

Keep in mind that the clothes were designed to flatter the individual star and minimize flaws. However, this is a step beyond Paris, where clothes were (and still are) often designed with no regard to the human body whatsoever. Joan Crawford, for example, had broad shoulders and hips, and the gorgeous clothes designed for her were specifically made to turn these into assets rather than liabilities. Jean Harlow's perfect body was shown off to advantage by a dress that clung to all her curves. Of course, this caused some trouble when women whose figures weren't quite so perfect copied the style, but copy it they did! Another factor when viewing the original movies is that there was a certain amount of symbolism in the clothing. Pay attention to whether the character is supposed to be very rich or very poor, and notice that the clothes tended to be somewhat exaggerated along these lines.

Now that we can rent old movies on video tape, it's possible to take a look at the original trendsetting movies whenever we feel like it. These old movies set the clothes in a context, and we can see not only the actual clothing but also the makeup, hairstyles, and general ambience that went along with. Another bonus is that most movies have a date, and this will place the specific clothing within a couple of years (allowing for the amount of time taken to make the movie and release it over the country).

Recently movie and television costumers have made great efforts to research the periods that the films are set in and to provide clothing that is painstakingly accurate. This is a real boon to us vintage clothing types. However, do pay attention to the economic level of the characters. For instance, *Out of Africa* shows clothing from the teens and twenties, and has spectacular costumes but is, after all, about a baroness. This is no reason to avoid it or not to enjoy the clothes to the fullest, but it is a reason to keep perspective. Great Aunt Minnie might have sold her soul for all these gorgeous hats (I certainly would!), but she probably couldn't afford to look at them, let alone buy them.

Some recent movies that are very accurate to period clothing are *Kitty and the Bagman*, an Australian film set in the 1920's; *Places in the Heart*, not for pretty clothes but for a good representation of clothes as worn by many people in the 1930's; *The Cotton Club*, glamorous clothing of the 1920's and early 30's; and *A Room With a View*, for teens clothing.

The most impeccable period costuming shown on television is in public broadcasting programs and in many of the series produced in England. You'll seldom have a better opportunity to see vintage clothing so perfectly matched to period and shown in such a variety of social and economic conditions. The English have always taken the matter of costume seriously. Period television programs produced in the United States in the last few years are usually accurate reproductions and sometimes authentic. At times, the clothing is the best part!

Often novels from a period will give descriptions of the clothing worn by characters in them. This varies, of course, but if you find a really good descriptive writer, pay attention. A good example is Raymond Chandler, who wrote short stories and novels in the 1930's and forties. He used descriptions of clothing to help set the stage for whether a character was wealthy, sleazy, "normal," or down and out. He has some wonderful descriptions of women's hats, men's shirts and suits, and so forth. Biographies are also worth browsing through (or even reading!) to look for clothing descriptions and photographs. If you don't want to spend time looking through antique stores or junk shops for snapshots of people in period clothing, biographies are a good alternative and have the added virtue of including dates. Books about the history of movies often will show photographs of the movie stars in costume as well as in their own clothing.

You don't have to do all this research in order to enjoy vintage clothes. Certainly just wearing and treasuring them is enough for lots of folks. But it can add a lot to see pictures of how they were originally worn and what people were doing in them. Clothing is such a personal thing. Think about it. You're sharing something that belonged to another person who liked it, wore it, and enjoyed it just like you. Maybe the guy who originally owned your favorite vintage pinstripe suit proposed to his wife while he was wearing it. Was he wearing it when he got called to serve in WWII? At least you know he wasn't buried in it! When you get the background and general flavor of the times and see pictures of people wearing garments similar to those you have, you begin to feel more in touch with the clothes. And if that's part of what attracts you, then it's worth pursuing.

CHAPTER ELEVEN

IF YOU LIKE IT, COPY IT

A good reproduction can be a wonderful investment of time and money. Think of it. Those spectacular vintage styles available in your size, in a color that suits you, and when you want them. Okay, so it's not playing the game, and it's not quite so much fun. After all stalking the elusive vintage hat, stumbling into the lair of the lace petticoats, pushing through racks of polyester to find the perfect pinstripe suit—in other words the hunt—is a big part of vintage appeal. However, having access to unusual styling and unique clothing is another part and not to be ignored. To put together a reproduction requires a pattern, fabric, and some sewing ability. I can't do much about the latter, but I can give you some tips for the first two.

Only you know how authentic you want to be. If you're working toward an historical pageant or are determined to come up with the real thing, then you've got some research to do. If all you want is the look, then you've got more scope. Even so, I would spend some time looking over clothing from the period you want to copy. Pay attention to some of the internal detailing, and decide what part of that detail contributes to the final look. Here's an example: looking at a Victorian wool skirt, I see that it has a heavy polished cotton lining, has all the seam edges encased in seam binding, has a separate inner waistband, and has a hem faced with heavy velveteen. The hem facing of velveteen contributes to the way the skirt hangs and is what makes it flair out at the bottom. The facing is important to the way the finished skirt will move and should be copied whether you're after authenticity or not. The inner waistband and encased seams don't add to the look, so they are authentic details, but are not pertinent to appearance. The heavy lining gives the skirt weight and will influence the drape and appearance, so is a better choice than a lightweight lining. Pick and choose the details that will contribute to the outcome you're aiming for, and don't lose sleep over those that don't. Making reproductions can be fun if you don't get all tangled up in whether or not they're perfect. If you like what you end up with, then it's plenty perfect!

There are three sources of patterns: vintage sewing patterns, reproduction sewing patterns, and making your own from a garment of the period. A note for those who don't sew: people who don't sew often think that patterns are only for making clothes. Not so (yuk!yuk!). Most dedicated sewers buy masses more patterns than they will ever use. I've sewn for over twenty-five years and feel good if I use 10 percent of the patterns I buy. Patterns are for looking at and pretending you've made them. There is no need to feel obligated to put one together. This is a secret that most sewers have kept to themselves for years, and I hope I don't get drummed out of the corps for revealing it. If you don't sew, you can look at the patterns and dream, and remember, that's what most sewers are doing.

Recently there has been a serious demand for authentic vintage sewing patterns as more and more people of all shapes and sizes get hooked on vintage clothing. Paper patterns were sold all through the 1800's, but the Butterick company really established the sewing pattern as a product on a large scale in 1868. Butterick, incidentally, claims to have invented the paper pattern, but that's not really so. Various stores and dressmaking establishments had been making and marketing them in a haphazard way for some time. After Butterick, Simplicity and McCalls appeared, and most women's magazines produced and sold their own. The oldest pattern I've found is from 1899, but it is possible to locate even older ones if you're really lucky.

Vintage sewing patterns are similar in many ways to modern ones, and also different in enough ways to cause some consternation.

Vintage sewing patterns tend to run about four sizes *smaller* than modern sizes. So, if you are size 8, get a size 12 pattern, etc. It doesn't hurt to go even a bit larger. Still, measure carefully against a garment that you know fits, and be prepared to lengthen the waist. Patterns as late as the 1950's may have much shorter waists than modern clothing. Also pay attention to the waistline width, particularly in patterns up to 1915 and from 1946 to 1960. During those periods you were expected to be pulling any excess flesh in with a corset and patterns were cut accordingly.

McCormick's Idiot Fitting Technique: every sewing book ever written goes on at great length about how to make clothes that fit. I've tried all the methods and found that most are complex and few actually work. What does work is to put the pattern pieces on a garment that you *know* fits, then cut it that size. It'll fit. A lot of people think this method is too simple, but what works works.

Let's go on to pattern instructions, which can be a touch daunting. Very old patterns have what instructions there are on the pattern envelope. Sometimes there's nothing but a drawing of the pattern pieces and a list of what they are. After all, before the paper pattern was available, you had to draft a pattern from a diagram in a magazine, so the pattern companies figured they were already doing you a favor. Study the envelope carefully, because some patterns will put the pieces in the order they are supposed to be sewn and they are numbered on the envelope in that order. Others will give more detailed instructions, but there's a limit to how much will fit on an envelope.

From the 1920's on, many of the pattern companies included a deltor, or instruction sheet. McCalls patterns often printed instructions on the pattern pieces. Even at that, considering that modern patterns will give four pages of instructions for a simple blouse, old pattern instructions can seem a trifle sketchy. Don't worry. Take a deep breath and plunge in and you may be surprised at how much you can figure out just from the information provided. Locate sewing books from the appropriate era and use them to supplement the pattern instructions. If you get stuck, call up a friend who sews and consult; two good heads can sometimes put together one good blouse. No matter how complex a garment seems to be, garments are logical.

Every blouse has a place for the neck, a place for the sleeves, a bottom, and some way to fasten it. There are design variations, but if you've got a picture of the end result, and a basic understanding of where everything is, then you should be able to put almost anything together.

When you open up the envelope, you'll find sheets of blank pattern paper cut into shapes with perforations on them. Don't panic. Carefully lay out the pattern pieces and look at the instructions. This will show a drawing of the shapes and a letter or number for each that matches the perforations. For instance, you'll find a drawing of the sleeve piece, labeled sleeve, with maybe an "M" or a "2" on it. The pieces have letters or numbers perforated on them that correspond, so find the piece shaped like the sleeve drawing and check that it has the right number or letter on it. Take out all the pieces, one at a time, and make sure you've got one to match each piece in the drawing. Once you've got the pieces pinned on the fabric and cut out, keep them pinned to the material until you are ready to sew, or else you'll be tearing out your hair. You'll find other perforations that indicate pleats, darts, and so forth. Again, the drawing will show the markings and say what they're for. The instructions will also give you the seam allowances. McCalls patterns can be found with printed pattern pieces from the 1920's on, but other pattern companies didn't print the pieces until the early 1950's.

If a piece is missing, you may decide to abandon ship, which is reasonable behavior under the circumstances, or you can try to construct a replacement. It's going to be easier to come up with a substitute sleeve than a whole front piece, so whether you proceed should be based on what's missing. Fit the pieces you do have together, and see what kind of shape you've got to come up with. Look through other patterns, both vintage and modern, and maybe you can find something similar enough to convert.

Sewing terms haven't changed much, but sometimes you'll come across an unfamiliar one. "Plait" for "pleat," "slide fastener" for "zipper," "revers" for "lapels," are some examples. Work with your old sewing book in one hand and your common sense in the other, and you'll do just fine.

When you're lucky enough to have vintage sewing patterns, it's a good idea to take a little trouble about storing them. My friendly neighborhood museum director suggests that when you are using a pattern regularly, you should store the pieces flat, sandwiched between sheets of acid-free tissue. You can make a Xerox of the pattern envelope and instruction sheet (if any), and tuck the originals away in inert plastic. If you're working with certain vintage patterns frequently, you might want to install a thick piece of doweling or a long towel rack on the wall and lay the tissue pattern sandwich over the top. When not in use, store patterns in inert plastic envelopes, which you can get from stores that sell old comic books. Another reasonable course of action is to trace the vintage pattern on to tissue paper. You will probably feel easier about cutting up the pattern and altering it when you aren't working on an original, particularly if it's a very old pattern.

There are now several companies that make patterns for vintage clothing. These companies are a boon to people who want to make their own vintage, assuming that you are looking for patterns for older clothing. A list follows in the Appendix, and where I have information about degree of difficulty and cost of individual patterns, I've included that. The cost and difficulty vary wildly, so my best suggestion is to send for the catalogs and give them a try.

CHAPTER TWELVE

SELLING VINTAGE CLOTHING FROM ONE PIECE TO RUNNING A SHOP

Vintage clothing tends to circulate, with one piece found in a closet in Indiana, next moving to Oregon, then New Jersey, and goodness knows where it'll end its days! Once you get involved in vintage, you'll find youself adding and subracting to the general flow, in a small way at least. It's part of the fun and general ambience. In fact, many a vintage clothing shop started from these humble beginnings. Most vintage clothing shops are run by vintage lovers who got carried away and turned pro. People who buy vintage clothing almost inevitably do some selling, and people who sell it are always buying. So it's important to look at how to sell wisely, as well as buy wisely.

SELLING YOUR MISTAKES

Always get rid of your mistakes. There is nothing as depressing as having a miserable dress or suit that you never wear staring you

in the face every time you look in the closet. For some reason getting rid of things is like pulling teeth for vintage clothing lovers. The same person who will mortgage the house and sell the car to buy a beaded dress will hold on to stuff for years that makes her look like a tow barge in an advanced stage of deterioration. Goodness knows what we're waiting for, but I know this happens. I've kept hats for years that I wouldn't be buried in, because when it comes right down to parting with them, I can always see their basic charm. Then back in their boxes they go, to sit for another couple of years until I get down to weeding out again. Then I feel guilty when I bring home something new, because I've got two hundred hats already. From the beginning try to rise above such madness.

You'll be a happier vintage clothing lover if you tape a note on your wall that says "Get Rid of it!"

Go through your closet periodically, and get tough with yourself. See that darling dress that was too tight in the hips, but you were already on a diet and knew it'd fit in a month or two except that your hips remained the same, so you've owned it for three years without wearing it? Out! There's that marvelous suit with its outrageous button and peplum. What a deal it was! Perfect condition and only $15. Too bad that particular shade of fungus green makes you look like Lon Chaney on a bad day. Out! Uh-uh. Don't close that closet door yet. I saw the black silk dress that you've had in there for five years, intending to replace the rotten underarms. Aren't you ready to admit that you're never going to get around to it? Maybe there's someone else around who would just love to hang it in *her* closet for the next five years. At least you'll have room for something new. Out! Okay, I know that you'll never part with the wonderful white cotton and lace turn of the century nightgown. You may never wear it, you may never learn how to repair lace so you can fix it, but you really love it in your soul. That you can keep.

What's really depressing about all this weeding out is when you discover that out of one hundred items you only really use twenty-five. This might be a good time to assess your buying habits. It might also be a good time to congratulate yourself on how far you've come since you started. Most people get pickier and cannier at buying vintage as they go along. If the majority of your mistakes are from the beginning of your interest in vintage clothing, you deserve a good pat on the back. And after you've cleaned out all those mistakes, you owe yourself a good shopping trip to celebrate. Empty closet space is such a waste.

Once you've girded your loins and determined to do the deed, you have to decide where to sell your rejects, how to price them, and how much time and energy you intend to devote to the entire project. All these considerations are interrelated: to get the maximum amount of money, you'll have to *spend* a fair amount of time, energy, and money. Ask yourself what that's worth to you, and you may find that the quickest and easiest way is actually the best.

The first rule of pricing vintage clothing is to be realistic. Many people have an extremely exalted notion of what their clothing is worth and are sadly disappointed when they find out no one else is willing to pay that price. Ask yourself what you'd be willing to pay for the garment, and don't put on rose colored glasses to do it. For example, just because you don't sew, don't assume that someone who does would be willing to put a lot of money into something that "would be perfect but it just needs a little mending." It isn't worth any more to the person who has to do the work on it than it is to you. You don't want the darned thing yourself, and there's a reason for that. While you are hoping to find someone who will like it enough to take it off your hands, consider what you'll do with it if no one does.

People tend to get vintage clothing confused with antiques when they want to sell it. Antiques often appreciate over time, and because people have bought, for example, a round oak table for $100 and resold it five years later for $400, many assume that vintage clothing works the same way. Sometimes yes, but most times no. An oak table can be used for years without wear and tear or substantial damage, but the same cannot be said for clothing. Clothing deteriorates constantly, even if it's just shoved in a box in a closet. As fashions change, what is considered a desirable vintage style changes too. If you bought a white Edwardian dress at the peak of its popularity, you may have paid a premium price for it. But now you'll probably find that, while you can still sell it, you may have to settle for substantially less than you paid.

Keep your expectations low, and don't expect to make lots of money. That way if you do, it'll be a pleasant surprise, and if you don't, you'll be satisfied with what you have done. You've gotten rid of some things you don't have any use for and made room for some things you do. If you picked up most of the clothes you're eliminating at garage sales for a couple of dollars each, and they are in good condition, reasonable sizes, attractive colors, and desirable styles, you will probably make some money. Although why the heck you'd get rid of clothing like that is beyond me!

The quickest and easiest way to sell vintage clothing is through a vintage clothing shop. Most shops pay by a formula: they pay one quarter to one third of their resale price when buying outright; one half if you sell on consignment. This varies certainly but is common enough to use for calculating. If you're willing to trade, known as "exchange credit," you can plan on getting credit equal to about 30 to 35 percent. Shops have to cover their own expenses in the mark up. They will be more generous if they know your items will sell quickly, and definitely less generous if you bring them things that need cleaning and repair.

Vintage car clubs often hold swap meets that include vintage clothing. Check around to determine the standard of pricing common in these meets. Usually there is more interest in clothing that is in perfect condition, clean, mended, and so forth, all of which takes some work and time on your part. You will also have to devote the time to pricing and sitting around in a booth, not to mention hauling the clothes back and forth. Usually you pay a fee or a percentage of total sales. On the other hand, you can sometimes get a higher price here than in other local outlets. If not, you have to haul the stuff back home and come up with some other way to dispose of it.

Another option is to have a vintage clothing sale. This option takes a lot more work, as you have to advertise, provide racks for hanging and a place to try on, set up mirrors, mark the clothes, and clean up your house. The last may be worst of all! Then you have to sit around all day selling things, clean up afterward, and do something about the things that didn't sell. The advantage is that you get to keep all the money, after you subtract expenses, and that you'll get it all in one lump. The disadvantage is that it's a lot of work, and people expect bargains in this sort of setting. If you're going to be successful getting rid of stuff, you'll have to provide same. Price below standard shop prices in your area for best results.

It's possible to join forces with some other vintage people and work together on a project like this. This has potential for being fun and can provide opportunities for trading back and forth as well. To keep it fun, and to prevent potential bad feelings, get organized. Figure out how much time and money the whole project will involve, and make it clear up front how much time and/or money will be required from each person. With any luck this will sort itself out. However, don't leave this to chance. If it starts getting too complicated, just charge everyone a percentage and be done with it. Maybe 25 percent if you do nothing but drop off your clothes, 15 percent if you work a shift, or put out thirty posters, and so forth.

Use a simple but careful accounting system so there will be no confusion about the money. I've seen two people spend hours trying to find out what happened to $5 at the end of an all day group sale. You'd think they would have enough sense just to say, "The heck with it, let's all split the difference" and go home (which was what happened in the end anyway). But people get weird about money. A good method is to have everyone mark his clothing with a distinctive tag, then have a separate manila envelope for each person. Remove the tags as things are sold and put them in the envelopes immediately. With any luck the total of the tags will equal the total of the money taken in, less the starting change. If not, everyone splits the difference, whether it's under or over, no arguments. Prepare to keep emotions (your own included) on an even keel. It really is not worth anyone having fits over, after all. If you can encourage that line of thought, you'll have a nicer time. It's not impossible to have some shoplifting, so make it very clear that no one who's working is responsible. This has to be an "at your own risk" proposition, or it will become overwhelmingly miserable for those who work at the sale. You will save masses of time and hand wringing if you get hold of a printing calculator.

A new wrinkle in selling your own clothing is by mail by list. This takes some organizing and work but not too much money, and it will give you wider exposure. It's a good method if you have a lot of garments to get rid of and don't want to have to fuss with a sale in your house. Make up a list describing each item, with approximate era, color, size, and condition. If you're not sure about the size, provide measurements (28 inch waist, 36 inch bust, etc.). It's reasonable to charge enough to recover the cost of your list and postage, but don't make it so expensive that people hesitate to send for it. Some folks offer to provide photos, for an extra charge, usually $1. Some charge a dollar for the list, which covers postage; others request an LSASE (Long Stamped Self Addressed Envelope); others request both. Advertise in a vintage clothing newsletter, car club newsletter or antique buy-and-sell periodical.

No one will buy sight unseen without the option of returning, so do allow for that. Three to seven days from the date it's received is a reasonable amount of time for a decision. Require payment in advance, preferably with a certified check. If you take personal checks, let people know that you'll wait until they clear before sending the merchandise. I recommend using UPS, as it is much more reliable than the mail. Get a UPS price chart, and either add the individual shipping price to each order or set a standard shipping charge. Don't forget to figure in the cost of boxes, wrapping paper, etc.

People who charge low to medium prices for their items tend to do very well. I've seen some who did one list just to clear out the closets continue on and make a business out of it. Those who charge premium prices, I've noticed, usually end up with most of their merchandise left over.

If you want to sell an entire collection intact and don't want to bother with a list, you will have to settle for less than if you sell individually. Most collectors can't or won't buy in large quantities, particularly when they may only want a few of the pieces. Because then *they* would have to worry about how to dispose of the rest of it. Shops will buy large collections, but require that most of the pieces be in good condition, standard sizes, and sellable without extensive cleaning or mending. Expect to get a price based on the standard wholesale percentage given above.

If you are getting rid of a large number of choice pieces, you might consider hiring an auctioneer and putting on an auction or contacting a company that holds auctions of its own. This method will bring in the largest prices, gross, but will have the highest costs to you. Professional auctioneers charge a percentage of the total and will run the sale themselves. You will have to prepare the clothing and provide the location. Auctioneers who hold their own auctions charge a larger percentage. They usually will only take very special clothing, often only in mint condition. However, they frequently get the highest prices for the clothing. If you hold your own auction, advertise well and make sure to send notices to the shops in and around your area, as well as vintage car clubs and other groups that might be interested.

A HARD DOSE OF REALITY

I've done as much as I can to keep your feet on the ground about the millions you can expect to make selling your vintage mistakes and extras. However, this is where I hit you with the real cold water. Let me tell you a story about Jacquie, a lady who collected and wore appliqué circle skirts and beaded sweaters for years. One day she decided to change her whole image, so put together a list to sell her vintage rejects. Her garments were in good condition, desirable, and she charged reasonable prices. She found lots of interested buyers. More important, she had lots of interested traders. In fact, she was able to pick up an alligator bag she'd been wanting, and a fur topper she'd been looking for, and then a suit that fit her new look . . . and so on and so forth. At the end she had acquired at least as many garments as she'd gotten rid of and was only slightly poorer than when she started.

I tell this story because I feel you should be warned but can't bear to relate my own excesses along these lines. A person can't write and clutch her breast at the same time. Vintage clothing is a world unto itself. Facing facts, if we were all that hard nosed and practical, we'd be buying up stock options instead of old clothes. Keep your expectations in line with who you are and prepare to end up in the hole. If you come out slightly ahead, throw a party. Better yet, go shopping. You deserve it!

PICKERS

The entire vintage clothing business rests on the shoulders of pickers. In a small way, you may already be a picker yourself. A picker is a person who scrounges through garage, estate, and rummage sales, picking out the best items and reselling them to shops and large scale wholesalers. Most people who are regular garage salers do some picking, but there are those who do it for a business.

A good picker is much in demand, and shops will guard the names of their pickers with their lives. Actually to make money at picking, you need good doses of luck (being in the right places at the right times), front money (for gasoline, car expenses, and to make purchases), enormous patience, a love of scrounging, and some reliable retail outlets. All but the last are more or less by chance, but you can and should control your outlets.

A wise picker will have more than one outlet, depending on where he or she is located. For example, one shop may do a good business in men's clothing, another in funky stuff, another in Victorian. Since pickers will run into a variety of clothing, it's wise to cover as many resale options as possible.

Remember that a vintage clothing shop needs you as much as you need it. Be as choosy about the shops you sell to as the merchandise you pick. The most important criterion is that the shop have a quick turnover in stock. You need to get your money regularly, so aim for a shop that prices to sell. At the same time, set your prices so that the shops can function with them. You have to make a profit over and above what you pay out, including your travel expenses and time. If the prices you're paying have risen, let the shops know that and prepare them for it. (And we wonder why the prices on vintage clothing have gone up so much!)

Some pickers work strictly on consignment, others sell outright, and most combine the two. Usually outright sales on run of the mill stuff save enough time and effort in record keeping to be worthwhile. Often pickers will have different arrangements with different outlets. Just make sure the arrangement is to your benefit as well as to the shops.

Pickers have been helped and hurt by the popularity of vintage clothing. Their markets have increased, but the sources they buy from have begun raising prices as well. Many a person who would have tossed old clothes out before has gotten the idea that he can charge the moon for them. This has made picking harder, more expensive, and riskier. A good knowledge of your outlets and a variety of outlets are the best lines of defense at this point. When you are confident that you can sell certain things and know for sure that a shop wants specific items enough to pay a little more, then you can play the game more confidently.

Most pickers know they are going to pick, whether they make money or not; this is one of those born, not made occupations. Unfortunately, the qualities that make a great picker don't necessarily add up to great record keeping as well. Most pickers start casually, with an occasional resale item, then find themselves in a full fledged business by chance rather than design.

Get in touch with an accountant as soon as you realize that your picking has begun to be a serious occupation. She will tell you what records you need to keep for tax purposes. You should be able to deduct a percentage of your expenditures for transportation, any out of town trips that include picking, outlay for stock, and other related costs. You should also keep some records so you know whether you are actually making money, and if not, why not.

I know a picker who sold mostly through one shop for years. She had other minor outlets, but took most of her stuff, particularly the good items, to that shop. For taxes she kept overall records of cash in and out and expenses, but she had never worked costs and income out on a shop by shop basis. When she sat down and figured it out, she realized that she was barely recovering her real expenses in that shop. Once she got the whole picture, she began to explore other buyers. Since she is a darned good picker within a short time she was making a reasonable profit.

It can be difficult to keep absolute track of individual items, particularly when you deal in volume. Add consignment sales, which can spread out over months, and no one can blame you for refusing to deal with any of this. However, a relatively easy way is to keep a notebook with sections for each shop you sell to. Every time you make a delivery, write down how many items and how much you paid for them. In another column enter the amount you receive when you get a check. Every few months add the columns and compare them. Figure out your mileage and other expenses for that period and divide them in proportion to business you do with each shop: 50 percent to one shop, 10 percent to another, and so forth. This will give you a good idea of how much return on your investment you're getting from each place and will tip you off when you need to shift your business around. You may be born to pick, but why not make some money at it?

While most pickers operate on the local level, some work on a large scale. They purchase entire estates, make buying trips, and have several outlets in different parts of the country. They work with both collectors and retailers and do a lot of shipping. Because some types of vintage clothing sell better in certain areas, while in other places no one will look at them—and vice versa—a picker can cover the scope of vintage clothing. Usually a picker on this scale will cultivate a number of regular customers, search for specific items on request, and be assured of sales on these garments.

A wise picker will sell with advance payment. You don't know who you're dealing with, and it's hard to collect from halfway across the country if someone defaults. But once you've established relationships, it will pay to send approval boxes to regulars who can be trusted. The customer buys what he or she wants, then returns the rest. Other pickers sell by box lots only, and the buyer must take everything, like it or not. Most collectors or private people won't buy on this basis, and a shop will only agree to this if the majority of the contents are really good.

This level of picking takes more up-front money than local picking and requires considerably more time, but usually the income is larger and more reliable. It also requires a certain amount of storage room, supplies for shipping, and more extensive record keeping. Picking is an art and if you're good, you'll find all the markets you want or need fairly easily.

WHOLESALERS

Since a picker is essentially a wholesaler, why am I putting wholesale in a separate category? Because, while the dividing line is fuzzy and an ambitious picker may slip over the line, a large wholesaler is something else again. Usually a wholesaler works on a countrywide scale. A wholesaler sells individual vintage clothing but often depends on finding and buying new/old stock for bread and butter. This often means the wholesaler—or agent—hopes to stumble across factory or warehouse lots of clothing and accessories that didn't sell originally and have since been stored away. These lots can be anything from 1940's shoes to 1930's buttons to 1970's army surplus. Reproductions of things like feather boas, jewelry, cigarette holders, and other vintage-related accessories are also frequently found. Most wholesalers publish some sort of catalog or flier and are constantly looking for new markets as well as new sources for merchandise.

FLEA MARKETS

Some people take a booth at a flea market occasionally, and others have regular booths at several monthly or weekly flea markets. The person picks, buys up estates, and scrounges through thrift stores, then brings the pickings to her booth. This is one of the hardest ways to go about selling vintage clothing, as it involves hauling the clothes around, which is about the most miserable chore on earth. It also requires sitting at a booth all day. However, the flea market world is a social system in and of itself, and those who sell there regularly become part of it and can't seem to manage without it.

People who shop at flea markets are bargain hunters and are more than a little resentful if prices are high. On the other hand, flea market prices have risen considerably in the last few years. The objective is to sell as much as you can so you don't have to pack the stuff up and take it back home afterward. How lucrative this whole thing is depends on how much you sell compared to how much you've spent for the stock and your cost for the time put in. People who sell at flea markets tend to buy there as well, so know in advance that you may spend a day of selling and come home with less money than you left with in the morning! I never said any of this makes sense.

Often someone will use a booth at a flea market as an interim step between picking and opening a full-fledged shop. It's a good training ground for learning pricing, dealing with customers, and discovering what will and won't sell.

RUNNING A "HIDDEN" VINTAGE CLOTHING SHOP

It's amazing how many hidden vintage clothing shops there are. By hidden I mean that someone has a small vintage clothing shop in her or his home and either sells by appointment or is open a few hours a week. Assuming you've got the room, it's a good alternative to opening a shop. It certainly involves much less money and often less time. One such shop I know is located in a townhouse apartment. Vintage clothing is all over the living room, the bedrooms, and even in the closets. Two nights a week, from seven to ten o'clock, and on Saturday, you can go shopping there for vintage clothing. The hours are geared, obviously, for working vintage clothing lovers and a working vintage clothing seller. This is only one method, and there seem to be as many systems as there are hidden shops.

Word of mouth is the usual mode of advertisement and use of business cards and posters is standard. Some develop a mailing list and host invitational house parties periodically. Others will put on parties, much like the parties that some national makeup or plastic kitchen goods companies provide: They ask someone to hold the party, then display vintage clothing and accessories, often with a small fashion show or chatty presentation, and the host or hostess gets a percentage of the income to spend on merchandise.

The hidden shop method works very well for people who aren't ready to take the major financial plunge that a shop requires. It allows for a full-time job, small children, or other commitments—none of which work well with a more traditional vintage clothing shop.

Similar to the hidden shop concept is keeping a booth in an antique mall. Antique malls are a relatively new development in American life, but have become pervasive in a short time. Their size and complexity vary—sometimes the mall is owned and operated by a firm that hires a manager and rents space to the dealers. Occasionally a group of dealers will get together and form a co-op, taking turns working and sharing costs. This is a good way to sell vintage clothing on a part-time basis.

OPERATING A VINTAGE CLOTHING STORE

People who love vintage clothing often dream of opening a vintage clothing shop. What could be closer to heaven than being surrounded by vintage clothing every day and finally having as much as you want? Just think—you can buy as many clothes as you desire and it's all legitimate! Unfortunately, like so many visions of heaven, this one is fairly far off the mark. The objective of operating a shop is to *sell* vintage clothing, not to buy it or have it. That means the rules of the game change, and, unless you can afford an expensive and time consuming hobby, you have to play by them.

I meet and chat with dozens of vintage clothing store entrepreneurs all over the country and have found that the most successful shop owners, the ones who make money (real money, not pin money), have a good deal in common. (1) They are extremely businesslike about their shops and about vintage clothing in general. They all appreciate vintage clothing and most have some for personal use, but when it comes to their business, it's merchandise. They put the best items they find in their shops, not in their closets, and they are interested in volume, not individual pieces. (2) They all have some background—even self taught—in fashion retailing. For example, Ray Cantrell, proprietor of Rick's Fashions Americain, in Springfield, Ohio, the largest men's vintage clothing store in the midwest, had twenty-five years of fashion retail experience before he began selling vintage. He operates his vintage clothing store by exactly the same principles as he did his new clothing stores. (3) They all commit enormous quantities of time and energy to their businesses. Harriet Love, owner of Harriet Love, New York, one of the oldest and most successful vintage clothing stores in the country, often works in her shop all day, brings paper work home at night, and spends weekends on buying trips. (4) They are always exploring ways to expand and add to their merchandise and meet customer wants, even if it means stocking new items along with vintage. When Zeke Waranch, a large national wholesaler, realized his market for vintage linens and lace was outstripping his supply, he found an import source for good quality, handmade, new linens. Purists might cavil, but customers were pleased. (5) They are excited about what they do and have fun with it, even after years in the business. Not incidentally, nearly every one has a good sense of humor.

HOW TO RUN A VINTAGE CLOTHING SHOP

I saw a sign in a small business that read, "Why work 8 hours a day, 5 days a week for someone else, when I can work 12 hours a day, 7 days a week for myself?" A small business of any sort takes unbelievable amounts of time, energy, and money, with the compensation that it is a high risk and may not produce enough income to live on for the first few years. With vintage clothing you get all the above, plus merchandise that has to be sought out with difficulty and requires special handling to boot. In other words we're talking about a major commitment.

It's possible, of course, just to rent a store, stroll in with a few armloads of clothes, and be in business. There are even people who've done that with some degree of success. However, if they were successful, it's because they quickly learned some basic business practices. One thing that becomes very clear is that it takes almost as much effort to operate a shop that just gets by as it does to run one that makes money. A successful vintage clothing store owner is a juggler who keeps a number of balls in the air at one time.

The business ball: A vintage clothing store is a small business, and shopkeepers who start with business experience, or acquire training in small business management through classes, avoid a number of expensive pitfalls. Statistics show that 75 percent of all small businesses fold within two years, and most experts say that knowledge of basic business practices could have made a difference.

Before opening the doors, it's wise to spend time with an accountant to become familiar with what records are necessary for taxes and for business information. One shopkeeper I know opened up with a record keeping system that met his needs, he thought. Then at the end of the year he had to redesign and then redo his books completely for the entire year, because they weren't what the IRS wanted. Details are the name of the game in modern business. There's a local ordinance, state statute, or federal regulation to trip over with every step, and good, solid information about capitalization, advertising, cash flow, and other basics can put a small business person ahead of the game.

Starting with enough money makes a big difference. A vintage clothing store is an expensive sort of small business to operate and needs a substantial amount of cash on hand at all times. Most of the stock has to be bought outright from individuals who want money in hand and it's impossible to predict when merchandise will surface. Lack of money to make improvements, hire help when necessary, purchase labor saving equipment, and to buy enough sellable stock, is the major factor that has held back many vintage clothing shops and the major cause of failure in the vintage clothing business.

The Selling Ball. There may be a successful vintage clothing store that's run like an antique shop, but I've yet to encounter it. Successful vintage clothing stores are run by the principles of fashion retailing, even those that are located inside antique shops and malls. Fashion retailing is an area that has been explored and written about at great length. There are good courses in it, often easily available through community colleges or other local sources. If there are none available in your area, there are some excellent books at the public library on the subject.

In order to make real money, a vintage shop has to display and manage merchandise in a way that attracts a wide variety of customers, not just people who already are interested in vintage clothing. Facing facts, vintage clothing is not a basic human need, contrary to the belief of many addicts. On the other hand there are enough people making a success of vintage clothing businesses to know that there's a market if you can reach it. The trick is convincing enough people they want to spend their money on it.

A good location is critical. You may have heard the joke, "What are the three most important things about being in business? Answer: location, location, and location." For a vintage clothing shop this isn't a joke. Spend every penny you can afford, manage without enough space, live with cockroaches if necessary, just get that window on Main Street. If you've had to settle for a less than ideal location when you open, move into a better one as soon as you can possibly afford it. You're after visibility and accessibility, and without them you're going to have to come up with some serious advertising money. But even good advertising won't make up for the loss of business when a shop is off the beaten path.

Speaking of beaten paths and windows on Main Street, the design of the shop window is probably the single most important form of advertising for a vintage clothing store. It has to draw attention to itself. It deserves careful thought and planning, and should be changed frequently. Vintage clothing is so charming that it's appealing by itself, but if not handled carefully, the window can look like you're running a museum. You want people to come in thinking buying, rather than viewing. Most important, though, you want people to come in.

The front window is critical, but advertising shouldn't end there. One man started a vintage clothing shop in a small town where no one thought he could make a go of it. He took this as a challenge and advertised heavily, not only in the town but also in every possible publication for miles around. He held promotions, distributed posters, gave out coupons, and promised he could find anything anyone was looking for. By the time he was through, the shop was a big draw and customers would drive for miles to his shop. He made lots of money, and of course, to do that he had to spend lots of money.

Advertising is one of the most important items to budget for, both the money to buy it and the time to plan it. It takes experimentation to learn where to advertise, what types of ads work best, and it takes careful assessment of the results and carefully thought-out new ideas to keep advertising fresh and appealing. You'll reach a certain number of people just by using the words "vintage clothing" in an ad. Other people may have no interest in vintage clothing, but when they see that you have "beautiful, one of a kind evening dresses and men's formal clothes at reasonable prices"—just before the holiday season—they'll think twice when they see your ad. Fashion retailing courses or books give lots of good ideas for attracting customers and are worth the time for this alone.

The telephone book is a critical place to be listed. It's a good idea to be in as many places as possible, such as "Clothing Bought and Sold," "Used Clothing," "Antiques," and "Vintage Clothing," if there is such a listing. Put a carefully planned, attractive box ad in at least one of those categories. It's mind boggling how many vintage clothing shops have no phone at all, let alone a yellow pages listing.

Some shops are beautifully arranged and decorated, but I've been in others that were masterpieces of disorderliness but still did a brisk business. In some cases this may have been despite the mess, but other times I've gotten a strong sense of a guiding intelligence. The shopkeeper is taking advantage of her customers' assumption that rummaging means bargains. Neat or messy, the point is some planning has to go into where things are placed, how they're displayed, and even if some items should be put on the floor. For instance, putting out prom dresses one at a time as they come in will never sell prom dresses like bringing out a rackful right before formal dances in the local high school.

Stock that isn't selling needs to be weeded out regularly. Some dealers routinely get rid of slow moving stock by putting it on sale after a certain period of time. But when an item is very special it may be worth storing away and bringing out at another time. There are always vintage clothing stores that cling to garments for months at a time, and regular customers begin to assume that those things are part of the decoration not the merchandise. If so, no problem. But if you need the money for new stock more than you need a decorative wall hanging, best to find a way to get it moving, even if it means selling it to another dealer in another state.

Pricing and stock selection is also part of this ball. If you live in a community where $10 dress shops and discount chain stores flourish, while expensive boutiques drop like flies, it's not reasonable to expect that a stock of $300 vintage designer originals will sell well. Luckily there is plenty of variety within the vintage world, and a focus on middle of the road vintage fashion can often go well in such a setting—boosted, of course, with good advertising and fashion merchandising. Some shops, for example, located in large metropolitan areas can focus directly on one population, upscale professional people or funky punky fashions, but in most situations shops do best with a range of styles and prices.

I get so many requests from beginners in vintage clothing sales asking how much they should charge and wanting a pricing book that I once wrote an article for my newsletter blasting the notion of national standardized pricing, which I'm opposed to. I expected some heated responses, but instead I got letters and phone calls from dealers all over the country agreeing with me. "I've been selling vintage clothing for seven years, and I've always priced to sell here, not by any book" was a typical response. There really is no simple, magic way to set prices. Veteran vintage dealers have a firm finger on the pulse of their customer population and keep prices at a level to maintain volume sales. This may mean $100 for a rayon forties dress in one shop, $25 for a similar dress in another. The important point is that it sells.

Pricing to sell takes time, attention, and experience. Your prices are too high if people come in, try things on, but don't buy. They're too low if you sell plenty of merchandise, but don't cover your costs plus a profit. They're just right if you sell a lot of items, cover expenses, and take enough money home to justify your time.

The Buying Ball. Whenever someone tells me she's thinking of opening a vintage clothing shop but wonders where to get enough stock, I think she'd better consider another business. If you don't already have some good ideas on this subject, starting a shop is pointless. Worse is the shopkeeper who's already in business but prices things so they won't sell, because he's afraid he won't be able to replace them. If you're not in business to sell things, you'd best reconsider the entire project! I'm not belittling the difficulty. I understand that vintage clothing is not the sort of merchandise you can order just by picking up a phone and saying you want a dozen Edwardian petticoats with thirty days after delivery to pay for them.

Here's how one very successful vintage retailer takes care of getting merchandise. He maintains a warehouse where he keeps ten garments for every one on the floor and has a goal of being six months ahead of his sales. He has pickers sending him garments from all over the country, standing orders for particular items with vintage wholesalers, and gets out and looks for things himself. He takes the time to educate his pickers about what he wants and buys only those things he knows he's got a market for. He is very clear about how much he'll pay for what, but pays promptly and, because his sales volume is large, buys a lot of garments. More than one picker who could make more on individual items by doing consignment in other shops, opts to sell outright to him, because he makes it easy for them. He lets as many people as possible know that he's looking and never misses an opportunity to follow up on a lead. There's no magic in finding enough stock; it takes hard work, aggressive searching, a serious cash commitment, knowledge of what will sell, and the understanding that the work never ends.

A certain amount of clothing will come through the door once a shop is open and people know it's there, but it's chancy to rely on this for the bulk of your stock. It can also be a lot more work than it appears, because you often have to educate every person who walks in with one silk nightgown that you can't pay $100 for it and why. It's better use of your time to educate a picker about the prices that you can pay and what you need, and then rely on that picker for a number of items.

Some shopkeepers seem to think they're entirely at the mercy of people who sell to them. Actually, most people who have vintage clothing to sell *want* to get rid of it. Even though they might start out asking more than you can afford, if you can explain in a pleasant, straightforward way why you pay what you do, you'd be amazed at how often they will accept that.

There is a fear among some vintage clothing shopkeepers that the supply of vintage clothing will dry up, and that someday there won't be any, or at least not enough to go around. Oddly enough, the retailers who are the least worried about that are the ones who do a fair-sized business. They believe that there is a lot of vintage clothing out there still undiscovered, but when, where, and in what condition it will surface is the issue. Edwardian whites still appear from trunks and attics, but in many places there isn't anywhere near the market for it that there was three or four years ago. Now the demand for alligator accessories, Hawaiian shirts, and men's clothing has put many a high volume dealer on the road in search of these items. However, demand for certain types of vintage varies from one state to another, so that allows for some serious trading around between dealers in various locations.

Fear of scarcity may prompt a new shopkeeper to buy up everything that's vintage, no matter how ugly, stained, or weirdly sized. These things don't sell, except maybe as Halloween costumes, and only tie up capital. This lesson gets learned over time but take a tip from experienced shopkeepers who will always recommend spending excess capital on advertising for clothes or a good buying trip. Plan in advance that you'll make some mistakes. Most veteran shopkeepers expect that a certain amount of their merchandise won't sell, no matter what they do. That's another reason for having enough financial backup; so a mistake is just that, not a tragedy. The objective is to buy as selectively as possible, and time and experience are the best educators for your individual operation.

Current fashion trends often have an effect on vintage clothing shops. Frilly fifties petticoats that sat on racks for years, suddenly took off when major magazines began to feature them. The degree of fashion influence varies from one location to another, but it's hard to avoid in some degree. Read popular fashion publications for ideas about what to buy and feature, and if you're in a location which is very fashion conscious, a subscription to a fashion trade publication may be a wise investment in planning purchases.

Vintage retailers who sell to a moderate or low price market fear that other dealers, who can pay higher prices, will come around and scoop up everything worthwhile. What often happens is that the dealer who can sell for more, can pay moderate retail prices as her wholesale, so she may regularly buy from other shops. The shop that reaches the high paying clientele has much less choice in what kind of merchandise it stocks, even though it may be able to pay higher wholesale prices. A customer who pays $150 for a rayon day dress is not prepared to put up a loose hem, drape a lace collar over a stain, or settle for less than fashionably wearable. The $25 customer figures that's part of the deal, so the shop she buys from has more scope, if less money, to buy stock in variable condition. The trick is convincing the people who sell to you that there is a difference.

A number of vintage shops deal with scarcity of stock by including new but related merchandise with the old. They can fill in many holes this way and have found that this works extremely well. Other shops combine vintage clothing with standard used clothing, tea rooms, lace and linen, or antiques.

The Time Management Ball: At this point it's obvious that running a shop takes an enormous amount of time. Even if you're thinking you won't try to sell on a big scale but will just run a modest little shop, all the things that go into a very successful shop still are present to some degree.

Learning to manage time so that everything gets done often occurs out of necessity. More important is managing time so you're spending it on what you like to do, rather than always doing stuff that you hate. Unless you take care of having some fun, you'll burn out quickly. More than one otherwise successful shop has closed because the owner got bored or overworked. It pays off to hire a bookkeeping service, if you loathe accounting, so you can concentrate on the buying that you love. Some small operations hesitate to invest money this way, but experience shows that it may well pay off with higher income as well as lower burn out rate. People tend to be better at what they like to do, and concentrating your energy and money on your strengths just makes more sense.

It's unusual for one person to be able to do everything it takes to run a shop by himself—he needs help. Whether it's a partner or employees depends very much on individual taste. Some folks absolutely cannot deal with a partner, and certainly business partnerships are complex arrangements. The most workable partnerships are between people with complementary skills. If you both like to sell, and no one wants to buy, then someone has to give, and this can cause friction. Some of the most successful vintage clothing store partnerships are husband and wife teams, because they've already worked out some of the bugs that a partnership tends to develop.

If you're going to spend money hiring people to work for you, spend that money as carefully as you do on stock. Hire the best possible people you can, and take the time to train them so they are a help, rather than a hindrance, especially if they're working in the shop. If you can pay only minimum wage, you may think you're limited to high school students, and you may be. But some high school students have an interest in retailing as a career and are eager to get work experience. You won't pay any more for someone like this than you will a teenager who just sits at the counter reading magazines. No sense in freeing up your time to buy stock, if the person selling it is busily turning off customers. Train your shop employees to work with the clothes so they are occupied all the time, even during slow periods.

Some shops keep a number of seamstresses, cleaners, pressers, and repair specialists on call. Others depend heavily on pickers and mail order for buying, so the owner can spend his time in the store. The important things are to choose carefully whom you hire, train them to be a real help, constantly supervise what's going on, and delegate the work that you don't want to do yourself.

At this point you know most of what it takes to run a vintage clothing shop successfully. More important, you should have a better idea of whether or not you still want to run one. As crazy as it seems, there are plenty of people who do, and lots of them are enthusiastic about the whole thing to boot. Maybe you're one of them. If so, don't forget—have fun!

FASHION FROM THE 1870's TO THE 1950's

1900–1919
1930's

1940's
1950's

APPENDIX

RESOURCES

(Note: LSASE means Large Self Addressed Stamped Envelope. Where specified, you'll get no response without one.)

Book Dealers

Many times fashion and costume books are out of print. These are bookdealers who specialize in finding and stocking books related to costume and fashion.

The Book Detective, 2607 Terrace Drive #12, Cedar Falls, IA 50613. LSASE for list, will search.

Bette S. Feinstein, 96 Roundwood Road, Newton, MA 02164. $1 per year for subscription to catalog. Carries out of print books and some new books on textile and costume related subjects. Will search.

Jo Bryant Books, 630 Graceland S.E., Albuquerque, NM 87108. $1 to be on mailing list. Specializes in new and out of print books about lace.

Joslin Hall Rare Books, P.O. Box 516, Concord, MA 01742. Write for occasional lists, specify costume. Will search.

John Ives Antiquarian Books, 5 Normanhurst Drive, Twickenham, Middlesex, TW1 1NA, England. Free catalogs with large costume section. Many books hard or impossible to find through U.S. sources.

R.L. Shep, Box C-20, Lopez Island, WA 98261. $2 to receive biyearly catalogs. Specializes in costume and textiles. No search service.

Wooden Porch Books, Rt. 1, Box 262, Middlebourne, WV 26149. $1 for year of periodic catalogs. Specializes in textile and costume. Will search.

Conservation Supplies

Full Circle Herb, 39582 Mohawk Loop, Marcola, OR 97454. Catalog $1. Herbal moth repellent in bulk or sachet.

Helene Von Rosenfield, 382 11th Street, Brooklyn, NY 11215. 718-788-7909. LSASE brochure. Sells acid-free tissue and other supplies in small quantities to individuals. Also will do restoration for individuals and institutions.

Mini-Magic, 3675 Reed Road, Columbus, OH 43220. $3 for catalog. Focus is fabrics and supplies for doll people, but supplies acid-free tissue and other conservation supplies in either large or small quantities.

Quintessence '84, P.O. Box 723544, Atlanta, GA 30339. Cotton garment bags that hold up to 25 garments. LSASE for price, shipping info.

Talas, 213 West 35 Street, New York, NY 10001. 212-736-7744. Supplier of all types of conservation supplies for museums. Will sell to individuals. Acid-free tissue, boxes, silk crepeline, and so forth. Has minimum order requirement, but not unreasonable for individuals. Free catalog.

University Products, P.O. Box 101, Holyoke, MA 01041. Supplier of all types of conversation supplies to museums, will sell to individuals. Acid-free tissue, boxes, silk crepeline, and so forth. No minimum order. Free catalog.

Vermont Country Store, P.O. Box 3000, Manchester Center, VT 05255. Free catalog. Herbal moth repellant in sachets.

Fur Repair Supplies

Samuel Bauer & Sons, 135 West 29th Street, New York, NY 10001. Phone 212-868-4190. $1 for catalog.

Ted Roden Company, 635 S. Hill Street, Room 403, Los Angeles, CA 90014. Phone 213-622-3131. Call or write for specific prices and information.

Fabrics, Patterns, Other Resources for Reproductions

Amazon Vinegar and Pickling Works Drygoods, 2218 E. 11th Street, Davenport, IA 52803. Carries over 400 period patterns, fabrics, notions, some accessories and hats, current Dover Books on costume. $4 for pattern catalog, $2 for general catalog. A number of the period patterns listed individually below are available in this pattern catalog.

Anello & Davide, 30-35 Drury Lane, London, WC2, B5 RW, England. Send $2 for catalog. Reproduction shoes and boots from 1940's back to Roman times, includes men's and women's. Made to order, with a selection of ready-to-wear available.

Cerulean Blue, P.O. Box 21168, Seattle, WA 98111. $3 for catalog. Hard to find cotton and silk fabrics.

"Copy Creations," P.O. Box 172 Whitewater, WI 53190. Workbook for copying clothing without taking apart. $11.95 plus shipping. LSASE for brochure.

Dazians, 2014 Commerce Street, Dallas, TX 75201. Phone 214-748-3450. Supplier to theatrical costumers, carries variety of unusual fabrics and findings, including hat forms, trims, and fabrics.

"Decorative Dressmaking," Sue Thompson, Rodale Press, 1985. Book showing methods used to decorate vintage clothing, pin-tucking, flounces, piping, and so forth. $12.95.

Eagle's View Publishing, 706 W. Riverdale Road, Ogden, UT 84403. Eighteenth and nineteenth century patterns. Catalog $1.

Folkwear, P.O. Box 3789, San Rafael, CA 94902. Victorian to 1950's. Catalog $1.00. Also available in some local fabric stores.

"From the Neck Up," Denise Dreher, Mad-Hatter Press, 3101 12th Ave. South, #5, Minneapolis, MN 55407. Book with instructions for making hats. $20. Brochure available for LSASE.

Garden Fairies Trading Company, 685 Clover Drive, Santa Rosa, CA 95401. $3 for catalog. Fine cottons, lace trims, some patterns.

Gohn Brothers, Box 111, Middleburg, IN, 46540. Free catalog. 100 percent cottons in catalog for Amish clothing.

Green River Forge, Box 257 Fulton, CA 95439. Catalog $4. Men's and women's patterns from 1800's, many with frontier focus. Catalog has interesting historical facts about frontier costume of 1800's.

Greenburg & Hammer, 24 West 57th Street, New York, NY 10019. Fabrics and notions suitable for reproductions. Has corset making supplies. Also professional size steamers.

Harriet Engler Patterns, 1930 W. Marne Ave., Glendale, WI 53209. Civil War era, men's, women's, childrens. Men's catalog $2. Women's catalog $2.

Heidi Marsh Patterns, 810 El Caminito, Livermore, CA 94550. Catalog $1. Men's, women's, and children's patterns from Civil War era. Many taken from Godey's Lady Book diagrams and patterns. Some accessories.

Heirloom Baby Bonnet Patterns, P.O. Box 6746, Dept T, Kennewick, WA 99336. LSASE for flier.

Heirloom Sewing Catalog, Margaret Pierce, 1816 Penbroke Road, Greensboro, NC 27408. Fine cottons, lace trims, some patterns.

Lacis, 2982 Adeline Street, Berkeley, CA 94703. Catalog $1.00. Lace, antique and new, silk crepeline, lace making supplies, some patterns. Also in and out-of-print books related to textiles and some conservation supplies. Will attempt to match antique lace.

"Making Patterns from Finished Clothes," Rusty Bensussen, Sterling Publishing Co., 1985. Method for copying clothes without taking apart. $9.95.

Mediaeval Miscellanea, 7006 Raleigh Road, Annondale, VA 22003. Catalog $1. Patterns and accessories for medieval garments.

Mini Magic, 3675 Reed Road, Columbus, OH 43220. Hard to find silk fabrics like velvets, brocades, satins, lace trims, buttons.

Natural Fiber Fabric Club, 521 Fifth Ave., New York, NY 10175. Membership $10 per year. Cotton and silk fabrics.

Old Fort Hill Mercantile, 102 East Somonauk, Yorkville, Il 60560. Catalog $2. Reproductions of colonial era clothing, some accessories (hats, bonnets) for that era.

Old World Sewing Pattern Company, Route 2, Box 103, Cold Spring, MN 56320. Brochure $1. Nine patterns 1805–1890.

Ornamental Resources, Box 3010 Idaho Springs, CO 80456. Phone 303-567-4987 or 303-595-4367. $12.50 for catalog. Wholesales beads, antique and modern. Minimum order $50.

Patterns of History, State Historical Society of Wisconsin, 816 State Street, Madison, WI 53706. Brochure LSASE. Nine patterns from 1800's.

Past Patterns, 2017 Eastern S.E., Grand Rapids, MI 49507. Catalogs: $5.50 for original pattern catalog, $3.00 each for catalogs of copies of authentic teens and twenties sewing patterns. Patterns for men's and women's clothing, primarily 1800's, including corsets. Some sewing supplies for period reproductions.

Pegee of Williamsburg, P.O. Box 127, Williamsburg, VA 23187. Brochure LSASE. Colonial patterns.

Quintessence '84, P.O. Box 723544, Atlanta, GA 30339. Catalog, updates $4.00. Unusual fabrics and trims.

Sutler of Mount Misery, G. Gedney Godwin, Inc, P.O. Box 100, Valley Forge, PA 1948l. Catalog $4.85. Large selection of authentically reproduced accessories (shoe buckles to flintlocks), hats, shoes and boots, clothing, some patterns, from Colonial–Civil War eras.

Testfabrics, P.O. Drawer O, Middlesex, NJ 08846. Free catalog, swatch books available for $7.50 each. Silk, cotton, rayon fabrics in variety of textures. Also special test fabrics for textile conservation, care, and cleaning. Special services, sometimes will search for specific fabrics.

Vermont Country Store, P.O. Box 3000, Manchester Center, VT 05255. Cotton fabrics.

Washington Millinery Supplies, 8501 Atlas Drive, Gaithersburg, MD 20760. $5 for catalog of hat making supplies and trim.

Newsletters and Pertinent Publications

B & R Creations, P.O. Box 4201, Mountain View, CA 94040. Newsletter for corset lovers. $15 year, bimonthly.

Biasline, 115 South Manhattan, Tampa, FL 33609, Bobbi Ann Loper, Costume Tech puts out this newsletter for theatrical costumers, amateur and professional. $10 year, 6 issues year.

Collectible Plastics, P.O. Box 199, Guerneville, CA 95446. Cat Yronwode. Newsletter for Society for Decorative Plastics. $10 year, bimonthly.

Collectrix, 146 Front Street, Hempstead, NY 11550. 3 times yearly listing of books and publications for collectors of various things, including costume items. $5 year.

Points, Lillian Baker, 15237 Chanera Ave., Gardena, CA 90249. Newsletter for International Club for Collectors of Hatpins and Hatpin Holders. Quarterly. LSASE for information.

Textures, 301 North Pomona Ave., Fullerton, CA. 92632. Newsletter of the Textile and Costume Guild of the Fullerton Museum. Write for subscription, membership information.

Vintage Clothing Newsletter, P.O. Box 1422, Corvallis, OR 97339. Terry McCormick. Newsletter for vintage clothing lovers. $12.00 year or $15.00 first class mail, 6 issues year.

VINTAGE CLOTHING BY MAIL

This list includes people who sell vintage clothing by mail, both wholesalers and retailers. Wholesalers will sell in quantity or minimum orders only, retailers will sell individual pieces to private people or shops. Some of the dealers listed will sell both wholesale and retail. I've noted these distinctions after each one. "New/old stock" means authentic vintage items that were factory or store leftovers at the time and never sold or used. Some wholesalers specialize in job lots of new/old stock. Repros are reproductions of vintage accessories or clothing. Always check to be sure the dealer has a return policy, and don't order unless she or he does. All the dealers listed have told me that they do, but do check for your own protection.

Ages Past, 2803 Ute Drive, Colorado Springs, CO 80907. Phone 303-635-5928. LSASE Call with wants. Will search. Retail/wholesale.

The Antiquarian, 18989 Sunny Lane, Culver, IN 46511. Phone 219-842-3727. LSASE or call, state wants, search service. VISA/MC. Retail/Wholesale. Mary Ann McClelland.

Beth Littlejohn, 1420 Whittaker Drive, Columbia, SC 29206. LSASE plus 39¢ in stamps for list. Write with wants. Will search. Retail/wholesale.

Bulla Antiques, Box 282, Rt. 5, Asheboro, NC 97203. Phone 919-381-3554. LSASE or call, state wants. Retail/Wholesale. Barbara Bulla.

Carol Ratz, Box 867, Rt. 44 South, Logan, WV 25601. Phone 304-752-5212. LSASE or call with wants. Wholesale only.

Carrie's Vintage Clothing, 503 E. University, Champaign, IL 61820. Phone 217-328-2022. LSASE or call, state wants, search service. Retail/Wholesale. Carrie Jo Homann.

Chris Jenn, 109 1st Ave South, Seattle, WA 98104. Phone 206-624-0853. Wholesale only.

Cinderella Unlimited, P.O. Box 1272, Kailua-Kona, HI 96745. Phone 808-329-4253. Catalog for dealers. Wholesale. Specializes in linens and lace. Cindy Peck.

Ella McArthur, P.O. Box 261, San Pedro, CA 90731. LSASE three 22¢ stamps for list. Wholesale/retail.

Emperor's Old Clothes, P.O. Box 727, South Wellfleet, MA 02663. Phone 617-349-9016 or 617-349-7554. Kimonos. Hank or Gail. Retail/Wholesale.

Estate Clothing, 5225 Jackson, Omaha, NE 68106. Phone 402-551-0427. LSASE Call or write state wants. Diane McGee. Retail/Wholesale.

Fashions of Yesteryear, 1780 Newmans-Cardington Road E, Waldo, Ohio 43356. Phone 614-726-2425. LSASE plus 39¢ in stamps for list. Call or write with wants. Wholesale/Retail. Caralee Biery Smith.

Gerry's Antiques, 4016 Boulder Drive, Dallas, TX 75233. Phone 214-330-7438. VISA/MC. LSASE. Call or write, state wants. Reproduction accessories. Wholesale only. Gerry Isaacs.

Greta's Vintage Clothier, Rt. 1, Box 25 A, Baker, OR 97814, Phone 503-523-2602. LSASE. Call or write with wants. Wholesale/Retail. Gretchen Martin.

The Haberdashery, 822 Lafayette, St. Louis, MO 63104. Phone 314-421-0110. Wholesale/retail. Will search. Joile Mackney.

Hullabaloo, 1908 Washington Ave., St. Louis, MO 63103. Phone 314-241-1969. Catalog. Wholesale only. New/old stock. UPS, COD, or cash.

Jennie Morgan, Sheep Street Antique Arcade, Stratford-Upon-Avon, Warwickshire, England. Phone 0789-294489. Linens and laces. LSASE list. Minimum $100 order.

Jill Ross Vintage Clothing, 1590 Philadelphia Street, Indiana, PA 15701. Phone 412-465-0044. LSASE Call or write state wants. Wholesale/retail.

Junk for Joy, P.O. Box 93039, Los Angeles, CA 90093. Phone 213-856-9560 Catalog $1 plus 39¢ in stamps. New/old stock. Repros. Wholesale only. UPS, COD, cash. Ron Ede.

Oldies but Goodies, 16806 Lorain Ave, Cleveland, OH 44111. Phone 216-476-3344. LSASE. Call or write with wants. Retail/wholesale. Reg and Jean Rattray.

Pahaka September, 19 Fox Hill, Upper Saddle River, NJ 07458. Phone 201-327-1464. Retail/wholesale. LSASE. Call or write with wants.

Rebecca Lowe, 804 W. Nash, Terroll, TX 75160. Phone 214-563-5069. Wholesale. Call or write, state wants.

Rebecca's Vintage Clothing, 806 Brethour Court, Sterling, VA 22170. Phone 703-444-3562. LSASE state wants. Rebecca Leimert. Retail/wholesale.

Sharon Bramlett, Box 535, Clyde, NC 28721. LSASE for list. Retail/wholesale.

Stelle's Stuff, 1596 Nut Tree Lane, Anderson, CA 96007. Phone 916-365-1740. Wholesale/retail. LSASE plus $1.00 for list. State wants. Carolyn Stelle.

Somewhere in Time, 103 Newcastle Drive, Lafayette, LA 70503. Phone 318-235-1081 or 318-233-5077. LSASE call or write state wants. Wholesale/retail. Sarah Fox.

Vintage Vanities, 218 West Avenue, #44, Jerome, ID 83338. Phone 208-324-3067. LSASE. Call or write with wants. Retail/wholesale. Carries larger sizes and maternity in addition to regular vintage clothing. Marian Posey Ploss.

The Vintage Vanity, 158 Imperial, Kalamazoo, MI 49001. Phone 616-344-3690. LSASE. Retail/wholesale. Write or call state wants. Nancy Lomske.

Zeke Waranch, 111 Parkway, Cleveland, MS 38732. Phone 601-846-1343. LSASE for list. Call or write with wants. Search. Linens/laces. Wholesale/retail.

BOOKS
A COMBINED BIBLIOGRAPHY AND RESOURCE LIST

I'm a booky sort of person. I love books in general, and even more, I love books about fashions (old and new), fabrics, and costume. Most of the books listed here reside on my own shelf, well thumbed, and well used. Others come highly recommended by other vintage clothing enthusiasts. Unfortunately a number of them are out of print. That means you can't just stroll into a bookstore and pick one up. However, they can often be located in public or university libraries, and, should you want a copy of your own, one of the bookdealers listed on the resource list may be able to help you. The copyright date is often a clue, as the older it is the less likely to be still in print. You can always check with a local bookstore for ordering information. In some cases certain books are available from the author or another source, and I've included addresses wherever possible.

An Introduction to Lace, Gabrielle Pond, Scribners, 1973.

And All Was Revealed, Doreen Caldwell, St. Martin's Press, 1981.

Antique and Twentieth Century Jewelry, Vivienne Becker, N.A.G. Press, 1980.

Antique Jewelry, Rose Goldenberg, Crown, 1975.

Antique Purses, Richard Holliner, Collectors Books, P.O. Box 3009, Paducah, KY 42001. $19.95 plus $1.00 shipping.

Art Deco of 20's and 30's, Beirs Hillier, E. P. Dutton, 1968.

Art Nouveau & Art Deco Jewelry, Lillian Baker, Collector Books, 1981. P.O. Box 3009, Paducah, KY 42001. $9.95 plus $1.00 shipping.

Arts of Costume and Personal Appearance, The, Grace Morton, John Wiley & Sons, Inc. Various editions from 1943 through 1962.

Bead Embroidery, Joan Edwards, Taplinger Park Co., 1966.

Bobbin and Needle Laces: Identification and Care, Pat Earnshaw, Robin and Russ Handweavers, 533 North Adams Street, McMinnville, OR 97128. $22.95 plus $2.50 shipping.

Book of Costume, The, Vol. I and II, Millia Davenport, Crown, 1948.

The Book of Costume; or Annals of Fashion, Countess of Wilton, 1846. Reprinted by R.L. Shep, Box C-20, Lopez Island, WA 98261, $47.50 ppd.

Chats on Costume, G. Woolliscroft Rhead, T. Fisher Unwin, 1906, England.

Clothing for Women, Laura I. Baldt, Lippincott's Home Manuals, Lippincott Company, 1909, 1916, 1928 (each edition substantially updated).

Collector's Book of Fashion, Frances Kennett, Crown, 1983.

Color and Line in Dress, Laurene Hempstead, Prentice-Hall. Various editions from 1920's through 1930's.

Complete Book of Sewing, Constance Talbot, Book Presentations, 1943 and other editions through early fifties.

Concise History of Costume and Fashion, The, James Laver, Harry Abrams, Inc., 1969. Updated 1982.

Costume Reference Number 9, 1939–1950, Marion Sichel, Batsford, 1979.

Costume Through the Ages, James Laver, Simon & Schuster, 1963.

Dressmaker, The, Butterick Publishing Company, 1911 and 1916.

Facades, Bill Cunningham, Penguin Books, 1978.

Fashion Bead Embroidery, Natalie G. Itsoff, 1971.

Fashion Dictionary, The, Mary Brooks Picken, Funk & Wagnalls, 1973.

Fashion Encyclopedia, Catherine Houck, St. Martin's, 1982.

Fashion Fundamentals, Bernice Chambers, Prentice-Hall, 1947.

Fashion in the Forties, Julian Robinson, St. Martins, 1976.

Fashion Sketchbook, 1920–1940, John Peacock, Thames and Hudson, 1976.

Fashion the Mirror of History, Michael and Ariane Batterberry, Crown, 1977.

Fundamentals of Dress Construction, Manning and Donaldson, Macmillan, 1926.

Godey's Lady's Book Style Guide, Dover Press, 1986.

Golden Age of Style, The, Julian Robinson, Gallery Books, 1980.

Grand Emporiums, The, Robert Hendrickson, Stein and Day, 1976.

Harriet Love's Guide to Vintage Chic, Harriet Love, Holt, Rinehart and Winston, 1981.

Hat Lovers Dictionary, Jessie Rasmussen, Wonderful World of Hats, 209 N.E. Harney Street, Newport, OR 97365. $12.50 plus $2 postage.

Hats, Fiona Clark, Costume Accessory Series, Batsford, 1982, England.

Hats, A History of Fashion in Headwear, Hilda Amphlett, Richard Sadler Ltd., 1974, England.

Hats in Vogue, Christine Probert, Condé Nast, 1981.

Hawaiian Shirt, The, Its Art and History, H. Thomas Steele, Abbeyville Press.

History of American Costume, 1607–1870, Elisabeth McClellan, Tudor, 1968. Originally titled *Historic American Costume,* 1899.

History of Costume, A, Carl Kohler, Dover Publications, 1963, reprint of 1928 edition.

History of Fashion Photography, Nancy Hall Duncan, Chanticleer Press, 1978.

Historic Costume, Lester and Netzorg, Chas. A. Bennette, Co., various editions 1925–1977.

How to Clean Everything, Alma Chestnut Moore, Simon & Schuster, 1977.

Identification of Lace, Pat Earnshaw, Shire, 1980.

Ladies' Garment Cutting and Making, F. R. Morris, New Era Publishing, 1940's, England.

Making Smart Clothes, Grace Dimelow, Butterick Publishing Co., 1930.

Mend-It, Maureen Goldsworthy, Stein & Day, 1979.

Mode in Costume, The, R. Turner Wilcox, Scribners, 1958.

Mode in Hats and Headdress, The, R. Turner Wilcox, Scribners, 1959.

New Butterick Dressmaker, The, Butterick Publishing Co., 1927.

Mr. Godey's Ladies, edited by Robert Kuncior, Pyne Press, 1971.

On Human Finery, Quentin Bell, Hogarth Press, 1947, England.

One Hundred Years of Collectible Jewelry, Lillian Baker, Collector Books, P.O. Box 3009, Paducah, KY 42002. $9.95 plus $1 postage.

One Hundred Years of the American Female, Harper's Bazaar, edited by Jane Trahey, Random House, 1967.

Recurring Cycles of Fashion, Agnes Brooks Young, Harper, 1937.

Secrets of Distinctive Dress, The, Mary Brooks Picken, Woman's Institute of Domestic Arts and Sciences, 1918.

Shoes in Vogue, Christine Probert, Condé Nast, 1981.

Shops and Shopping, 1800–1914, Alison Adburgham, Allen and Unwin, 1964.

Singer Sewing Book, Mary Brooks Picken, Singer Sewing Company, 1949.

Swimwear in Vogue, Christine Probert, Condé Nast, 1981.

Textile Fibers and Their Use, Katharine Paddock Hess, Lippincott, 1954.

Textiles, Woolman and McGowan, 1938.

Two Centuries of American Costume, Dover Press, 1970, reprint of 1903 edition by Alice Morse Earle.

Victorian Jewelry, Deidre O'Day, Charles Letts, 1982.

Victorian Lady Travelers, Dorothy Middleton, Academy Chicago, 1982.

Western World Costume, Carolyn Bradley, Appleton-Century-Crofts, 1954.

What to Wear? Elizabeth Stuart Phelps, James R. Osgood Publishing, 1873.

Women's Institute Library of Dressmaking, Series of books with sewing instructions, fabric information, and other pertinent information about dressmaking. Various editions, teens through 1930's.

Yestermorrow Clothes Book, Diana Funaro, Chilton, 1976.

VINTAGE CLOTHING SHOPS AROUND AND ABOUT

There are hundreds of vintage clothing stores around the country. It isn't possible to list them all—but here's a start.

ALASKA

Anchorage

The Rage,
423 G Street, Anchorage, AK 99501
Hours: Mon–Wed 11–6, Thurs–Fri 11–9, Sat–Sun 12–5
Phone: 907-274-7243
Owner: Elizabeth Pizzola

ARIZONA

Phoenix

Honey Buns,
5801 N. 7th Street, Phoenix, AZ 85014
Hours: Mon, Wed, Fri 12–5, Tues, Thurs 12–7
Phone: 602-266-4353
Owners: Adele Cobb and Miss Elli

CALIFORNIA

Bakersfield

Miss Charlotte's,
At Timeless Treasures, 168 H. Street, Bakersfield, CA 93304
Hours: Tues–Sat 12–5:30
Phone: 805-831-7669
Owner: Char Madruga

Berkeley

Lacis,
2982 Adeline Street, Berkeley, CA 94703
Hours: Mon–Sat 1–5:30
Phone: 415-843-7178
Owners: Kaethe and Jules Kliot

Chico

Dreamweavers,
300 Broadway, Chico, CA 95926
Hours: Mon–Sat 10–5:30
Phone: 916-345-9220
Owner: Elena Eisenlauer

Hollywood

Ragtime Cowboy,
1644 North Wilcox Ave., Hollywood, CA 90028
Hours: Mon–Thurs 11–6, Fri–Sat 11–7, Sun 12–5
Phone: 213-463-7811
Owner: Joe Yanello

Laguna Hills

Gypsy Moth Boutique,
25260 La Paz Rd., #F, Laguna Hills, CA 92653
Hours: Tues–Sat 10–5:30
Phone: 714-458-8899
Owners: Arlis Schillen and Sandra Carpentero

Long Beach

Meow Modes for Moderns,
2210 E. 4th St, Long Beach, CA 90814

Hours: Tues–Sat 12–6
Phone: 213-438-8990
Owner: Kathleen Schaaf

Los Angeles

The American Rag Cie,
150 S. La Brea, Los Angeles, CA 90038
Hours: Mon–Sat 11–10, Sun 12–6
Phone: 213-935-3154
Owners: Mark and Margo Werts

Ms. Sellaneous,
1048 South Fairfax, Ave., Los Angeles, CA 90035
Hours: Mon–Sat 11:30–5:00
Phone: 213-935-2282
Owner: Bernetta Jones

North Hollywood

Ragtime Cowboy,
5332 Lankershim Blvd, North Hollywood, CA 91601
Hours: Mon–Sat 11–6, Sun 12–5 (closed Sun in the summer)
Phone: 818-769-6552
Owner: Patrick O'Hara

Oakland

Lydia the Purple Merchant,
2368 High Street, Oakland, CA 94601
Hours: Tues–Sat. 12–6
Phone: 415-532-9149
Owner: Lydia

Sacramento

Cheap Thrills,
1217 21st Street, Sacramento, CA 95816
Hours: Mon–Sat 11–6
Phone: 916-446-1366
Owner: Linda McNally

San Francisco

Aardvark's Odd Ark,
1501 Haight, San Francisco, CA 94117
Hours: Mon–Thurs 11–7, Fri 11–8, Sat 11–7, Sun 12–6
Phone: 415-621-3141
Owner: Joe Main

American Rag Cie,
1355 Bush Street, San Francisco, CA 94109
Hours: Mon–Sat 10–8, Sun 12–7
Phone: 415-474-5200/474-5214
Owners: Mark and Margot Werts

The Way We Wore,
2238 Fillmore Street, San Francisco, CA 94115
Hours: Mon–Sat 11–7, Sun 12–5
Phone: 415-346-1386
Owner: Doris Raymond

San Jose

The Antiquary,
1310 Lincoln Ave, San Jose, CA 95125
Hours: Mon–Sat 12–5:30
Phone: 408-286-6739
Owner: Summer Read

Santa Barbara

Rare Finds,
P.O. Box 6431, Santa Barbara, CA 93111
Hours: By appointment
Phone: 805-962-7741
Owner: Teri Ascolese

Santa Rosa

Hot Couture,
101 Third Street, Santa Rosa, CA 95401

Hours: Mon–Fri 11–7, Sat 11–6, Sun 1–5
Phone: 707-528-7247
Owner: Marta Mathis

Tustin

Ginny's Antiques Et Ct,
190 Camino Real, Tustin, CA 92680
Hours: Mon–Fri 10:30–4:30
Phone: 714-832-7655
Owner: Ginny Flaherty

COLORADO

Colorado Springs

Repeat Performance,
829 N. Union, Colorado Springs, CO 80909
Hours: Tues–Sat 10–5
Phone: 303-633-1325
Owner: June Sullivan

Denver

Roots on Broadway,
1400 South Broadway, Denver, CO 80210
Hours: Mon–Sat 11–6, Sun 12–5
Phone: 303-744-0541
Owner: Jeri Schultz

Fort Collins

Repeat Boutique,
239 Linden, "Old Town" Fort Collins, CO 80524
Hours: Mon–Fri 11–5, Sat 11–4
Phone: 303-493-1039
Owners: Judy and Carrie Keiss

Victoria's Vintage,
210 Laporte Ave, inside Laporte Avenue Antiques, Fort Collins, CO 80521
Hours: Wed–Fri 10–2, Sat 10–4
Phone: 303-493-3447
Owner: Victoria Peer

Manitou Springs

Manitou Springs Vintage Clothing & Company,
725 Manitou Ave., Manitou Springs, CO 80829
Hours: Winter 11–5:30, except Tues; summer 9–7 daily
Phone: 303-685-9077
Owner: Lana Munsell

CONNECTICUT

Branford

Yesterday's Threads,
564 Main Street, Branford, CT 06405
Hours: Mon, Wed, Fri 11–6, Sat 11–3
Phone: 203-481-6452
Owner: Judith Young

DELAWARE

Wilmington

The Tree House Boutique,
414 Delaware Street, New Castle, DE 19808
Hours: Mon, Thurs, Fri 10–4, Sat 12–6
Phone: 302-328-6292
Owner: Nancy Baker

FLORIDA

Ft. Lauderdale

Stock Exchange,
2440 Wilton Drive, Ft. Lauderdale, FL 33305
Hours: Mon–Sat 10–5
Phone: 305-564-3090
Owners: Carol Levin, Mary Ptok

Miami

Dream On,
12181 SW 131 Ave., Miami, FL 33186

Hours: Mon–Fri 12–6, weekends by appointment
Phone: 305-233-9909
Owner: Mae Greenburg

Sarasota

The Glass Slipper,
28 S. Lemon Ave., Sarasota, FL 33577
Hours: Mon–Sat 10–5
Phone: 813-951-1547
Owner: Nancy Wilke

HAWAII

Kailua, Oahu

Treasured Memories,
326-3 Kuilei Road, Kailua, Oahu, HI 96734
Hours: Mon–Fri 9:30–5:30, Sat 9:30–4:30
Phone: 808-261-1989
Owner: Helen Walker

IDAHO

Jerome

Vintage Vanities,
218 West Ave., #44, Jerome, ID 83338
Hours: By appointment or by chance
Phone: 208-324-3067
Owner: Marian Posey-Ploss

ILLINOIS

Chicago

Flashy Trash,
3521 N. Halsted, Chicago, IL 60657
Hours: Mon–Sat 12–7, Sun 12–6
Phone: 312-327-690
Owner: Harold Mandel

Franny's,
2937 N. Clark Street, Chicago, IL 60657
Hours: Mon–Fri 12–7, Sat 11–6, Sun 1–5
Phone: 312-935-7448
Owner: Francis Serna

Champaign

Carrie's Vintage Clothing,
503 E. University, Champaign, IL 61820
Hours: Tues–Sat 11–5
Phone: 217-328-2022
Owners: Carrie Jo and JoAnn Homann

Normal

Babbitt's Closet,
121½ North Street, #203, Normal, IL 61761
Hours: Mon–Sat 12–6
Phone: 309-454-7393
Owner: Brian Simpson

INDIANA

Crawfordsville

The Marc Antiques,
124 W. Main Street, Crawfordsville, IN 47933
Hours: Mon–Sat 8–5:30
Phone: 317-362-1707
Owner: Marcheta Dixon

Indianapolis

Red Rose Vintage Clothing,
834 E. 64 at Guilford, Indianapolis, IN 46220
Hours: Mon–Sat 10–6
Phone: 317-257-5016
Owner: Daphne Harris

Modern Times,
5371 N. College, Indianapolis, IN 46220
Hours: Mon–Fri 12–9, Sat 10–9
Phone: 317-253-8108
Owner: July Mahern

Richmond

Zelda's Vintage Clothing,
805 Promenade, Suite 205, Richmond, IN 47374
Hours: Mon, Wed, Fri, Sat 10–5
Phone: 317-966-4425
Owner: Diane Lebo

KANSAS

Lawrence

Barb's Vintage Rose,
927 Massachusetts Street, Lawrence, KS 66044
Hours: Mon–Sat 10–5:30
Phone: 913-841-2451
Owner: Charlotte Dart

Topeka

Pastense,
418 West Sixth, Topeka, KS 66603
Hours: Mon and Thur 11–8, Tues, Wed, Sat 11–5, Fri 11–5:30
Phone: 913-233-7107
Owner: Susan Henry

Wichita

Allusions,
1422 E. Douglas, Wichita, KS 67214
Hours: 12–5:30
Phone: 316-263-7662
Owner: Margaret Saums

LOUISIANA

New Orleans

Glad Rags,
3117 Magazine, New Orleans, LA 70115
Hours: Mon–Sat 11–6
Phone: 504-895-7833
Owners: Ken Arata and Georgia Kavanaugh

Jazzrags,
1223 Decatur Street, New Orleans, LA 70130
Hours: By appointment
Phone: 504-887-4965/504-566-7835
Owner: M. B. Klotz

MARYLAND

Baltimore

Belle's Antique & Apparel Shop,
7399 Liberty Road, Baltimore, MD 21207
Hours: Tues–Sat 11–6, Sun 1–6
Phone: 301-944-9686
Owner: Belle Kline

Silver Spring

Back in Style,
14316 Sturtevant, Silver Spring, MD 20904
Hours: By appointment
Phone: 301-384-9316
Owner: Jennifer Ukstins

MASSACHUSETTS

Boston

Vintage Etc.,
1796 Massachusetts Ave, Cambridge, MA 02140
Hours: Mon, Tues, Wed, Fri 10:30–6:30, Thurs 10:30–7, Sat 10:30–6

Phone: 617-497-1516
Owner: Debbie Earl

Grand Trousseau,
88 Charles Street, Boston, MA 02115
Hours: Tues–Sat 11–7, Sun 12–5
Phone: 617-367-3163
Owner: Candace Savage

West Upton

Linda White Antique Clothing,
100 Main Street, West Upton, MA 01587
Hours: By appointment
Phone: 617-529-3358
Owner: Linda White

MICHIGAN

Battle Creek

The Way We Were,
151 Stafford, Battle Creek MI 49015
Hours: By appointment
Phone: 619-968-8795
Owner: Suzette Bradley

Detroit

Vintage Clothing & Cards,
4639 Second Ave., Detroit, MI 48201
Hours: Mon–Sat 11–6
Phone: 313-832-1230
Owner: Daniel Tatarian

Kalamazoo

The Vintage Vanity,
158 Imperial, Kalamazoo, MI 49001
Hours: By appointment
Phone: 616-344-3690
Owner: Nancy Lomske

Royal Oak

Passementerie,
115 South Main, Royal Oak, MI
Hours: Mon–Sat 10–6
Phone: 313-545-4663
Owner: Frances McCatty

Minneapolis

Lois's Attic,
2710 Lyndale Ave South, Minneapolis, MN
Hours: Tues–Sat 1–7:30
Phone: 612-872-1070
Owner: Lois Rovick

The Corner Store,
900 W. Lake Street, Minneapolis, MN 55408
Hours: Mon–Fri 11–7, Sat 11–6, Sun 12–5
Phone: 612-823-1270
Owner: Pat and Linda McHale

St. Paul

Grand Addictions,
1460 Grand Ave., St. Paul, MN 55105
Hours: Mon–Sat 11–5
Phone: 612-690-3165
Owner: Linda Nesset

Grand Nouveau,
236 Snelling Ave. South, St. Paul, MN
Winter Hours: Tues–Sun 12–6; Summer Hours: Tues–Thurs 12–8, Fri–Sat 12–6
Phone: None

MISSISSIPPI

Vicksburg

David & Lisa,
801 Clay Street, Vicksburg, MS 39180
Hours: Mon–Fri 10–6, Sat 10–4
Phone: 601-636-6791
Owners: David and Lisa Hughes

MISSOURI
Kansas City
Material Possessions,
4039 Broadway, Kansas City, MO 64111
Hours: Tues–Sat 10–6
Phone: 816-931-5932
Owner: Linda Flake
St. Louis
The Haberdashery,
322 Lafayette Ave, St. Louis, MO 63104
Hours: Mon–Wed 11–6, Thur–Sat 10–6
Phone: 314-421-0110
Owner: Joile Mackney

MONTANA
Helena
Karma's Vintage Clothing,
109 Lawrence (Behind Grand Street Theatre), Helena, MT 59601
Hours: 1:30–5:30
Phone: 406-442-1159
Owner: Karma Alfredson
Livingston
Grandma's Attic,
211 South Main, Livingston, MT 59047
Hours: Wed, Thur, Sat 11–4
Phone: none
Owner: Jennifer Lahren

NEBRASKA
Omaha
Old Gold,
5805 Florence Blvd, Omaha, NE 68110
Hours: By appointment
Phone: 402-455-0835
Owner: Mary Mather

NEW JERSEY
Burlington
Days Gone By,
Antique Row, 307-309 High Street, Burlington, NJ
Hours: Wed–Sat 11–5
Phone: 609-387-3050
Owners: Cindy and Kim
Upper Saddle Valley
Pahaka September,
19 Fox Hill, Upper Saddle River, NJ 07458
Hours: By appointment
Phone: 201-327-1464

NEW YORK
Binghampton
Especially for You,
177 Clinton Street, Binghampton, NY 13905
Hours: Mon–Sat 11–5
Phone: 607-723-9063
Owner: Audrey Orr
Buffalo
Red Balloons,
42 Allen Street, Buffalo, NY 14202
Hours: Mon–Sat 12–5
Phone: 716-881-2727
Owner: Mallory Merrill
Geneva
The White Peacock,
495 Exchange Street, Geneva, NY 14456
Hours: Mon–Sat 10–5, closed Wed
Phone: 315-731-0374/315-789-6316

New York

Antique Boutique,
712 Broadway and 227 E. 59th Street, New York, NY
Broadway store hours: Mon–Thurs 10:30–10, Fri–Sat 10:30–midnight, Sun 12–8. 59th Street store hours: Mon–Fri 11–10:30, Sat 10:30–10:30, Sun 12–8
Phone: 212-460-8830
Owner: Halsey and Gary Scheflen

Harriet Love,
412 West Broadway, New York, NY 10012
Hours: Daily 12–7
Phone: 212-966-2280
Owner: Harriet Love

Screaming Mimi's,
495 Columbus Ave., New York, NY 10024
Hours: Mon–Fri 11–8, Sat 11–7, Sun 1–7
Phone: 212-362-3158
Owner: Biff Chandler and Laura Wills

Trouvaille Française,
New York, NY
Hours: By appointment
Phone: 212-737-6015
Owner: Muriel Clarke

Schenectady

Time Warp,
179 Jay Street, Schenectady, NY 12308
Hours: Mon–Sat 10–5, Thurs 10–9
Phone: 518-370-3257
Owner: John Frascatori

OHIO

Cleveland

Oldies But Goodies,
16806 Lorain Ave., Cleveland, OH 44111
Hours: By appointment
Phone: 216-476-3344
Owners: Reg and Jean Rattray

Columbus

Kathryns,
1247 N. High Street, Columbus, OH 43201
Hours: Mon–Fri 1–5, Sat 12–5, or call for appointment
Phone: 614-299-7923
Owner: Catherine Conklin

Vintage Vogue,
245 W Fifth Ave., Columbus, OH 43201
Hours: Mon–Sat 11:30–6
Phone: 614-294-7319
Owner: Rita Case

Dayton

Dorothy's Vintage Boutique,
In the Oregon Emporium, 400 E. Fifth St. Dayton, OH 45402
Hours: Fri–Sun 11–6
Owner: Dorothy Morse

Springfield

Deborah's Attic,
23 W. High Street, Springfield, OH 45502
Hours: Tues–Sat 11–6
Phone: 513-322-8842
Owner: Deborah Stallard

Rick's Fashions Americain,
719 South Limestone Street, Springfield, OH 45505

Hours: Tues–Sat 11–6
Phone: 513-322-9303
Owner: Ray Cantrell

OREGON

Astoria

Persona Vintage Clothing,
1249 Commercial, Astor Bldg Suite 205, Astoria, OR 97103
Hours: Tues–Sat 11–5
Phone: 503-325-3837
Owner: Rosetta Hurley

Eugene

Old Friends,
1022 Willamette, Eugene, OR
Hours: Mon–Sat 11–5:30
Phone: 503-345-1414
Owners: Sheila Showalter and Linda Collins

Portland

Avalon Antiques,
318 SW 9th Ave., Portland, OR 97205
Hours: Mon–Sat 12–5:30
Phone: 503-224-7156

Keep 'Em Flying,
510 NW 21st Ave, Portland, OR 97205
Hours: Wed–Sat 12–7
Phone: 503-287-4381
Owner: Sandi Lang

Salem

. . . And Old Lace,
320 Court Street, Salem, OR 97301
Hours: Mon–Sat 10:30–5:30
Phone: 503-585-6010
Owner: Elizabeth Southwell

Seaside

Victoriana,
606 12th Ave., Seaside, OR 97138
Hours: By appointment
Phone: 503-738-8449
Owner: Ronda Johnson

PENNSYLVANIA

Ardmore

M. Klein,
126 Coulter Ave., Ardmore, PA 19003
Hours: Tues–Sat 11–6, Wed 11–8
Phone: 215-896-7171
Owner: M. Klein

Lewisburg

Linen and Lace,
337 St. Mary Street, Lewisburg, PA 17837
Hours: Thurs–Sat 11–5
Phone: 717-523-3999
Owner: Linda Doebler

Philadelphia

M. Klein,
203 South 17th Street, Philadelphia, PA 19103
Hours: Mon–Fri 10:30–5:30, Sat 11–4
Phone: 215-732-7171
Owner: M. Klein

Rigattieri,
322 South Street, Philadelphia, PA 19147
Hours: Mon–Tues by appointment, Wed, Thurs, Sun 12–6, Fri–Sat 12–9
Phone: 215-574-9704
Owner: Ivana Tyler

TENNESSEE

Kingsport

The Heirloom Collection,
Broad Street Antiques, 211 Broad Street, Kingsport, TN 37660
Hours: Mon–Sat 10–5:30, Sun 1–5:30
Phone: 615-323-4993
Owner: Judy Murray

Memphis

Frederica's Studio Collection,
990 June Road, Memphis, TN 38119
Hours: By appointment
Phone: 901-767-1034/901-785-6442
Owner: Fredricka Hodges

TEXAS

Austin

The Passionate Collector,
1011 West Lynn, Austin, TX 78703
Hours: Mon–Fri 11–7, Sat 10–6
Phone: 512-477-1232
Owner: Jayme Hatfield

Beaumont

Ideas, Inc,
2450 Calder Ave, Beaumont, TX 77702
Winter hours: Tues–Sat 11–4:30, Summer hours: 11–5:30
Phone: 409-832-9704/409-833-7179
Owner: Mary Douglas Stephens

Bertram

Jo's Jabots
(across from the post office), Flea Market, Bertram, TX 78605
Hours: Fri–Mon 11–5
Phone: 512-355-2141
Owner: Jo Izard

Dallas

Flaunt,
4230 Main, Dallas, TX 75226
Hours: Mon–Sat 11–7
Phone: 214-826-4154
Owner: Nick Hamblen

Factor,
2801 Main, Dallas, TX 75226
Hours: Wed–Sun 9 P.M.–2 A.M. (Hours correct, it's by a nightclub)
Phone: 214-744-3845
Owner: Nick Hamblen

Puttin' On The Ritz,
3113 Knox Street, Dallas, TX 75205
Hours: Mon–Sat 12–5:30
Phone: 214-522-8030
Owners: Patrick and Siri Ahearne

Denton

Secondhand Rose,
108 Fry Street, Denton, TX 76201
Hours: Mon–Sat 10–5:30
Phone: 817-566-1917
Owner: Judy Smith

El Paso

Deja Vu,
6201 Escondido 19E, El Paso, TX 79912
Hours: Wed 10–5, Sun 12–5
Phone: 915-584-8711
Owner: Margie Newell

Houston

Iszadora,
1500 W. Alabama, Houston, TX 77006

Hours: Mon–Sat 10:30–6:30, Sun 12–5
Phone: 713-520-1408
Owner: Mary Van Osdell

Lubbock

Deja Vu,
2705-A 26th Street, Lubbock, TX 79410
Hours: Mon–Tues 12–6, Wed–Sat 10–6
Phone: 806-799-6845
Owner: Carole Daniel

Webster

Elaine's Emporium and Tea Room,
17490 Hwy 3, Webster, TX 77598 (12 miles south of Houston)
Hours: Mon–Fri 10–5:30, Sat 10–3:30
Phone: 713-338-2690
Owner: Elaine Van Horn

VERMONT

N. Westminster

Dust and Glitter,
31 Gage Street, N. Westminster VT 05101
Hours: By appointment
Phone: 802-463-4958
Owner: Karen Augusta

VIRGINIA

Leesburg

Rebecca's Vintage Clothing,
132 Davis Ave. S.E., Leesburg, VA 22075 (all inquiries to 806 Brethour Court, Sterling, VA 22170)
Hours: Tues–Sun 10–5
Phone: 703-777-5358/703-444-3562
Owner: Rebecca Leimert

Richmond

Bygones,
2916 West Cary Street, Richmond, VA 23221 (Georgetown)
Hours: Mon–Sat 10–6, Sun 10–3:00
Phone: 804-353-1919
Owners: Maynee Cayton and Barbara Church

WASHINGTON

Bothell

The Glamour Years,
23929 Bothell Hwy S.E., Bothell, WA 98021 (above Red Barn)
Hours: Tues–Sat 11–5
Phone: 206-486-3418
Owner: Lou Trebitz

Richland

Time Was . . .,
226 Williams, Richland, WA 99352
Hours: Mon–Fri 11–6, Sat 10:30–5:30, Sun by chance
Phone: 509-943-2470
Owners: Elaine Davis and Debbie DeMeyer

Seattle

Deluxe Junk,
3518 Fremont Place N., Seattle, WA 98188
Hours: Mon–Sat 11–6
Phone: 206-634-2733

Jasmine Room,
109 First Ave. South, Seattle, WA 98188

Hours: Mon–Sat 12–6
Phone: 206-624-0853
Owners: Chris and Elaine

Madame & Company,
117 Yesler Way, Seattle, WA 98104
Hours: Mon–Sat 12–5:30
Phone: 206-621-1728
Owner: Carol Winship

Spokane

Zoolie's,
1401 W. First, Spokane, WA 99201
Hours: Tues–Sat 11–5:30
Phone: 509-747-9777
Owner: Keary Judd

Walla Walla

The Attic,
207 Wildwood, Walla Walla, WA 99362
Hours: Tues–Sat 10–4
Phone: 509-529-5891
Owner: Valerie Dague

WASHINGTON, D.C.

Mercedes Bien Vintage,
3061 ½ "M" Street NW, Washington D.C. 20007
Hours: Tues–Sat 11–7, Sun 1–6
Phone: 202-337-6969
Owner: Mercedes Bien

WEST VIRGINIA

Logan

Carol Ratz Vintage Clothes,
Box 867 Route 44 South, Logan, WV 25601
Hours: By appointment
Phone: 304-752-5212
Owner: Carol Ratz

WISCONSIN

Eau Claire

The Exchange,
426 Water Street, Eau Claire, WI 54701
Hours: Mon–Sat 10–5:30
Phone: 715-834-5060
Owner: Susan Stal

Milwaukee

Flapper Alley Ltd.,
1518 North Farwell Ave., Milwaukee, WI 53202
Hours: Thurs–Sat 12–5, or by appointment
Phone: 414-276-6252
Owners: Pat Stephens and Pat O'Brien

INDEX